Understanding Interceptions

A Key to Unlocking the Door

I.I. Chris McRae, PMAFA, CA. NCGR

Copyright 2000 by I.I. Chris McRae
All rights reserved.

No part of this book may be reproduced or transmitted in any form or by any means, electronic or mechanical, including photocopying or recording, or by any information storage and retrieval system, without written permission from the author and publisher. Requests and inquiries may be mailed to: American Federation of Astrologers, Inc., 6535 S. Rural Road, Tempe, AZ 85283.

ISBN-10: 0-86690-503-0
ISBN-13: 978-0-86690-503-9

First Printing: 2000
Current Printing: 2015

Published by:
American Federation of Astrologers, Inc.
6535 S. Rural Road
Tempe, AZ 85283

www.astrologers.com

Acknowledgments

THERE HAVE BEEN SO MANY special students over my thirty years of teaching astrology that have inspired and encouraged my path that there is not sufficient space to mention them all and I would not wish to leave out a single one. It is through their inquiring minds and intelligent questions that I was often forced to think more deeply. They have allowed me to try out my ideas and filled in details from their lives that gave me additional insight, particularly in the area of intercepted signs and planets. I thank everyone.

I thank each and every member of the Edmonton Astrological Society for their support and interest in my work and who also helped me test my ideas and theories.

A special thank you goes to Prudence Nuesink who, after having heard me lecture on this topic more than once, has repeatedly insisted I write this book.

I thank Jodeen Litwin, BSc., MJ, who read this manuscript, made corrections and offered suggestions. Jodeen was also an astrology student of mine several years ago.

I thank my husband, Don R. McRae, who has been my encouragement and love for the past forty-six years. He has supported my every endeavor, as I have his. It has allowed both of us to flourish with our individuality. What more can life give!

Lois M. Rodden deserves a special thank you for her diligent and conscientious effort over many years in clarifying birth data and cleaning up what she has called "dirty data." This has enabled astrologers to present accurate example charts to support their ideas and theories and to use a standard data rating. Lois voluntarily offered to check all the data used in this book. What I did not send her personally, I checked through her bi-monthly publications of *Data News*. In every case, the source of data is given.

Chart Examples and Illustrations

Figure 1, Hartwell Plane Crash
Figure 2, Prince Charles in 3 House Systems
Figure 3, Intercepted Pair of Signs
Figure 4, Single Progressed Chart for Wayne Gretzky
Figure 5, Wayne Gretzky, Three-Wheel
Figure 6, Aries/Libra Intercepted Diagram
Figure 7, Student 1
Figure 8, Rex Harrison
Figure 9, Liza Minnelli
Figure 10, Taurus/Scorpio Intercepted Diagram
Figure 11, Student 2
Figure 12, Merv Griffin
Figure 13, Shah of Iran
Figure 14, Gemini/Sagittarius Intercepted Diagram
Figure 15, Bill
Figure 16, Woody Allen
Figure 17, Agatha Christie
Figure 18, Cancer/Capricorn Intercepted Diagram
Figure 19, Student 3
Figure 20, Client
Figure 21, Student 4
Figure 22, Hermann Hesse
Figure 23, John Logie Baird
Figure 24, Jimmy Swaggart
Figure 25, Leo/Aquarius Intercepted Diagram
Figure 26, Lady Diana
Figure 27, Student 5
Figure 28, Student 6
Figure 29, Toulous Lautrec
Figure 30, Hal Holbrook
Figure 31, Virgo/Pisces Intercepted Diagram
Figure 32, Registered Nurse
Figure 33, Mario Lanza
Figure 34, Dr. Tom Dooley
Figure 35, Billy Graham
Figure 36, Blank Wheel
Figure 37, Patty Hearst
Figure 38, Bill Cosby

Figure 39, Erik von Daniken
Figure 40, Dorothy Hamill
Figure 41, F. Scott Fitzgerald
Figure 42, Ted Turner
Figure 43, Jay Leno
Figure 44, Lee Iacocco
Figure 45, Margaret Trudeau
Figure 46, Connie Francis
Figure 47, Bill Gates
Figure 48, Helen Gurley Grown
Figure 49, Emmaline Pankhurst
Figure 50, Montgomery Clift
Figure 51, Helen Keller
Figure 52, Carol Burnett
Figure 53, Mia Farrow
Figure 54, Lee Harvey Oswald
Figure 55, Tonya Harding
Figure 56, Vincent Price
Figure 57, John Paul II
Figure 58, Ray Bradbury
Figure 59, Harry Houdini
Figure 60, Annie Besant
Figure 61, Doris Chase Doane
Figure 62, Sir David Frost
Figure 63, Dr. Glenn Perry
Figure 64, John Denver
Figure 65, Christine Jorgensen
Figure 66, Shirley Mac Laine
Figure 67, Student 2 Cusps Only
Figure 68, Cusps Only
Figure 69, Natural Wheel
Figure 70, Client: Cusps Only
Figure 71, Horary Question 1
Figure 72, Horary Question 2
Figure 73, Neighborhood Pet Store
Figure 71, Ben's Trip to Victoria
Figure 75, A Political Event

Abbreviations
A: *American Astrology* magazine
ABC: *American Book of Charts*, First Edition, by Lois M. Rodden

ADIV: *Astra Data IV* by Lois M. Rodden
AFA: *Today's Astrologer*, American Federation of Astrologers
AJA: *American Journal of Astrology*
BJA: *British Journal of Astrology*
CSH: *Contemporary Sidereal Horoscopes*
CL: Church of Light
DN: *Data News*, edited and published by Lois M. Rodden
FIN: *Famous Nativities* by Maurice Wemyss, London 1938
F & WE: Funk and Wagnalls Encyclopedia
Gauquelin: Data collected by Michel and Francois Gauquelin
LMR: Lois M. Rodden
M/H: *Mercury Hour*, published by Edith Custer
P/C: Penfield Collection
PW: *Profiles of Women*, First Edition, by Lois M. Rodden
SS: *Sabian Symbols*

Rodden Rating
(reproduced by permission from Lois M. Rodden)
AA: Birth certificate (BC) or birth record
A: Memory; accurate data as quoted by persons, kin, friend or associate
B: Biography or autobiography
C: Caution: no source
DD: Dirty data, two or more conflicting quotes that are unqualified

Contents

Chapter One, Value and Effect of Interceptions … 1
    Definition and Effect of House Systems
    How Much of the Chart is Affected
    Effect on Signs
    Strength of Ruler
    Repeated Signs
    Vastly Unequal Houses
    Effect on Quadruplicities and Elements Progressions
    Transits
    Intercepted Planets Ruling Non-Intercepted Houses

Chapter Two, Development of Interceptions … 15
    Development by Transits
    Development by Progressions

Chapter Three, Intercepted Signs … 25
    Aries/Libra
    Taurus/Scorpio
    Gemini/Sagittarius
    Cancer/Capricorn
    Leo/Aquarius
    Virgo/Pisces

Chapter Four, Repeated Signs … 77
    First/Second and Seventh/Eighth
    Second/Third and Eighth/Ninth

  Third/Fourth and Ninth/Tenth
  Fourth/Fifth and Tenth/Eleventh
  Fifth/Sixth and Eleventh/Twelfth
  Sixth/Seventh and Twelfth/First

Chapter Five, Intercepted Planets   103
  Sun
  Moon
  Mercury
  Venus
  Mars
  Jupiter
  Saturn
  Uranus
  Neptune
  Pluto

Chapter Six, Effect on Quadruplicities and Triplicities   143
  Quadruplicities
  Triplicities

Chapter Seven, Other Applications   155
  Horary
  Electional and Event Charts
  A Political Event

Bibliography   163

CHAPTER ONE

Value and Effect of Interceptions

"There is no bar to knowledge greater than contempt prior to examination."—Spencer

I HAVE LECTURED EXTENSIVELY OVER the past several years on the topic of interceptions. After repeatedly being told by many students, astrologers and clients that I must write a book on the subject, here is the whole story for you to judge its importance. Many astrologers who have followed the line of reasoning being submitted here have found it to be exceedingly helpful, and additional understanding has been revealed that was not previously realized.

Some astrologers have told me that they do not consider interceptions because they see little value in doing so. Perhaps they lack perception or experience in this area. What is not included does not make one wrong, but in my opinion an important part of chart delineation could be missing. Whenever a pair of intercepted signs appears in a chart, more of the chart is affected than many astrologers realize, even if planets are not contained within the interception.

Other astrologers have suggested that intercepted signs and planets are some form of karmic lesson impinging on this personality embodiment. Others feel that intercepted signs or planets are lessons previously learned in other lifetimes and are not now required for external expression. It would be difficult to prove either one of these ideas. The bottom line is whether they actually add to the interpretive quality of the chart. Many astrologers do place significant value on interceptions, but there seems to be little consensus of opinion as to what that is. I do feel interceptions create a particular type of psychological thrust that requires understanding and development in order to round out this lifetime, and they also provide talent and impetus in other ways.

Concepts will be presented in succeeding pages and sample charts will be used to support these concepts. This will give you the ability to apply the principles of interceptions to your own chart and in the charts of your loved ones.

Some astrologers feel that the only significance of an intercepted sign is the amount of time a progression or transit spends in a particular house due to its elongation or extra degrees. It certainly has a bearing, but my experience indicates that it is not the only significance. I have fifty-six degrees in each sign of an intercepted pair in my own chart, which means planets do stay in those houses much longer than usual. I have never looked at it as an impairment, but rather as an opportunity for greater depth of development and understanding in those areas. Some houses with intercepted signs have as few as forty degrees in total.

I have often felt that the twelve signs of the zodiac are twelve remarkably conceived keys to living life to the fullest. We may not work on all of the signs at the same time with the same diligence due to planetary placements and other chart priorities, but sooner or later the more that we begin to understand and develop them, the more rounded our psyche will be and hence our human experience. This thought will be developed more fully as we move along because it has a bearing on how interceptions affect our psychological thrust.

Joanne Wickenburg, an astrologer who is highly respected in the astrological community, projected the idea that one's environment does not provide opportunity for development in those areas where interceptions occur in the birth chart and that those qualities "are suppressed in early life, making it difficult to express them consciously in outer life activities."

I cannot dispute the wisdom of this idea and I can understand her reasoning. I was born and have lived most of my life in a latitude from fifty-one to fifty-three degrees and have seen many young people coming "down" to Edmonton, Alberta, Canada from the vast, isolated regions of the Northwest Territories, lured by tales from oil workers, hunters and other travelers, or seeking education at the university. Their birth charts contain not one set of intercepted signs but perhaps two or three in a single house. By relocation into lower latitudes, many of these interceptions are released and there is a long period of awkwardness, insecurity and adjustment to new surroundings, attitudes and feelings as the new learning begins. There is also no doubt that their early environment did not allow certain areas of development, but I am sure it also enriched others.

Figure 1 is a chart cast for an extreme northern latitude. Although it is an event chart rather than a natal chart, it is a good example of the complexity that can occur at an extreme latitude and still tell a dramatic story.

My own chart contains the Virgo/Pisces pair of signs intercepted across the sixth and twelfth houses respectively. I cannot relate specifically to these qualities being suppressed, but they certainly were highly significant by circumstance. I see this as the axis of logic/faith. I was brought up in a very logical, Saturnian environment where Mercury/Virgo principles were stressed. I went to church and Sunday School three times every Sunday. Our minister would insist that our religion was something to believe in, not to question. This created within me a very strong need to dig beyond the traditional church-going mind. In this case the environment stimulated a deep need to stretch my spirituality beyond the boundaries of organized religion. It also stimulated within me, in my growing years, a need to research and gather information on a variety of subjects rather than learn more feminine activities such as cooking and home care in an era when little girls were expected to learn such crafts. I see these areas as profoundly significant in terms of internal drives.

My approach to interceptions is that they can be very useful. We are not blighted or stamped with the word "reject" across our anatomy somewhere. People who have interceptions often develop greater depth of understanding in those areas due to a powerful internal need. It is also useful having signs and planets move in and out of interceptions by progression in order to stimulate introspection. Transits moving in and out of both natal and progressed interceptions are equally useful. I do not look upon any part of our charts as being disadvantaged. I like to think that every part is for the purpose of some form of development or quest. I like to think that all life is evolving upward in an uplifting spiral of growth, excitement and intrigue. This philosophy does not make some of our aspects or chart situations any easier to deal with on a day-to-day basis, but it may provide some justification.

Martin Hartwell Plane Crash

This is a sample of an extreme northern latitude chart with three sets of interceptions in the same house.

Note: The true latitude of this location is 69N03, but the computer could not print the chart successfully for that latitude. The latitude of 66N will suffice for this purpose.

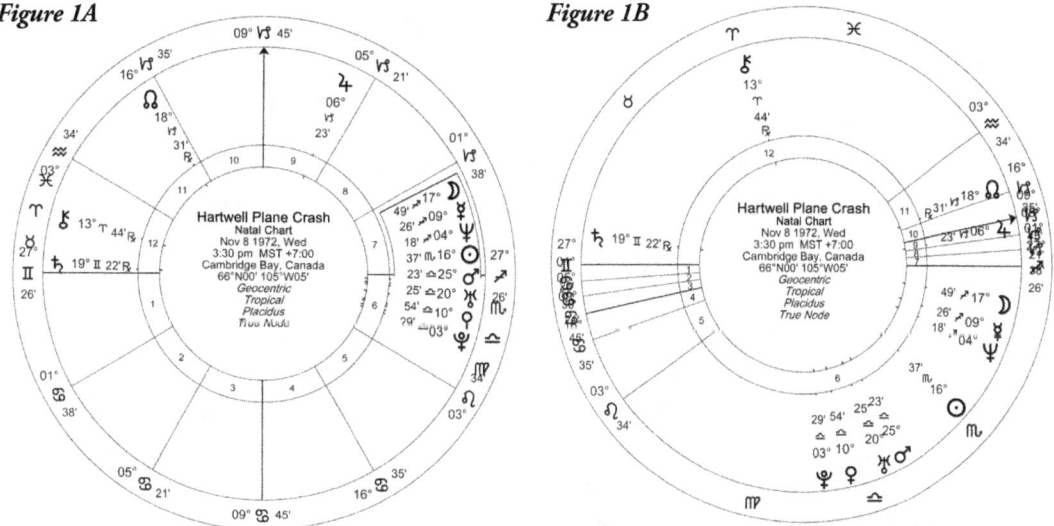

Figure 1A

Figure 1B

There are three sets of interceptions and the double signs cover four houses each. The same chart is printed in both proportional and nonproportional houses in order to give you a better view of the cusp distortion that occurs at extreme latitudes.

This was a mercy flight carrying a pregnant lady suffering from labor complications, a boy with acute appendicitis, a nurse and the pilot. This is implicated by the emphasis in the sixth house. The only survivor, after thirty-two days in sub-zero weather, was the pilot. He survived by eating human flesh. His injuries prevented him from foraging for food. Lengthy court battles ensued over this and other matters, but the pilot was eventually exonerated.

A concept of astrology that we must never forget is that for the purpose of study we may isolate one area of the chart, but when we apply those same concepts to a specific chart, it is necessary to synthesize them with the whole chart. One person might find his/her intercepted chart conditions easy to deal with and a true chart blessing, whereas someone else might find it more difficult to manifest positive action either societally or personally in the areas being influenced.

Therefore, all of the delineations contained in this book should be used as a study guide rather than a cookbook formula that would fit all charts. The fact that every chart is different is one of the intriguing and captivating charms of astrology. It is the study of human nature and response. Life is complex and it therefore follows that any system purporting to add insight into it is also complex. I have been working directly with my own chart for more than forty years and it still continues to unfold in surprising ways. Every time I reach a certain plateau of understanding, there is still another and another. It never ends and is never boring. Understanding interceptions, whether you have them natally or receive them by progression, can add to this unfoldment.

Another concept of chart synthesis is that if a trait or characteristic is truly prominent, it will be stated through at least three different major aspects, with additional supporting evidence through minor aspects. An intercepted condition in one chart might be less significant than in another except on an inner plane, whereas in still another chart it might be part of the main theme or thrust upon which most of the chart is played through. Much interpretation depends on house placement, as well as the sign. For instance, an intercepted Aries in the twelfth house will play out somewhat differently than if it was intercepted in the first house. A planet (or several planets) in an intercepted house is also highly significant. Conditions surrounding the rulers of the intercepted signs may relieve stress or contribute to it, particularly if the rulers of the pair of intercepted signs are in aspect to each other.

Definition and Effect of House Systems

An intercepted sign is when a sign is wholly contained within a house and does not appear on any cusp. Of course, the sequence of signs which begins with Aries and ends with Pisces is always maintained. When one sign is intercepted, the opposite sign is also intercepted. It is possible to have two or even three signs intercepted within one house and, of course, the opposite house (see Figure 1). It is also possible to have a separate set in a second pair of houses. This is dependent upon the house cusp structure being used and the latitude of the chart location. This phenomenon occurs frequently at extreme latitudes.

Using the Placidus cusp system at my latitude of 53N32, approximately eighty-two percent of all charts have one set of interceptions, about ten percent have two sets in one house and about ten percent have no interceptions at all. My son was born at noon in July and he has no interceptions in his chart. The further north one travels, days are longer in summer and shorter in winter. This indicates that some signs will remain longer on the Ascendant than others at various times of the day. In extreme latitudes, the sun does not rise above the horizon from mid-November to mid-January. It is perpetual night for this duration, which indicates that some signs do not rise or set at all during this period. This must have a bearing on interpretation, and will become more obvious when we discuss the delineation and see it operating in the charts of actual people.

There are various geometric processes that are designed to create astrological houses or spheres of influence. To attempt the creation of three-dimensional measurements in a two-dimensional media such as a flat piece of paper is a task for those with special mathematical and astronomical skills. Many of us can easily draw a scene showing a three-dimensional depth by employing a sense of perspective, but as soon as we attempt to include exact measurements the task becomes much more complex. There has been an evolutionary process over a period of many centuries to determine a system that can produce the most consistent and accurate results in our interpretation and prediction. Indeed, some astrologers feel that we should not consider the value of interceptions simply because we cannot agree upon which house cusp system to use, or even to use one at all. However, that is like saying certain surgical procedures should not be performed because of a variation in technique or that we should stop all total hip or knee replacements because the results are not always completely successful, nor are the prostheses durable. As Dane Rudhyar says in *The Astrological Houses*, "the method used in modern astrology to determine the cusps of the twelve houses is particularly chaotic." We continue to strive for improvement.

In the case of which house cusp system to use, I suggest that understanding interceptions can help you determine which system works best at the latitude you do most of your work. In other words, a carpenter does not carry only one tool, nor does he find that one tool works for all jobs. One can put a screw into a wall with a hammer, but a screwdriver works a great deal better.

Then again you may prefer to use cosmobiology and not use the traditional interpretation of the houses at all. In *The Combination of Stellar Influences*, Reinhold Ebertin states "an agreement on the correct one (house divisions) is not yet possible so (the) reader would be advised to give up the idea of interpretation of the chart on this basis." However, many astrologers feel that houses are important in order to apply the areas of life being affected by the planets and their aspects. Dane Rudhyar considered them essential in "interpreting the celestial instructions." Houses personalize our connection to the cosmos by helping us understand the way in which we express ourselves in acting out the various parts of our lives.

Figure 2A   *Figure 2B*

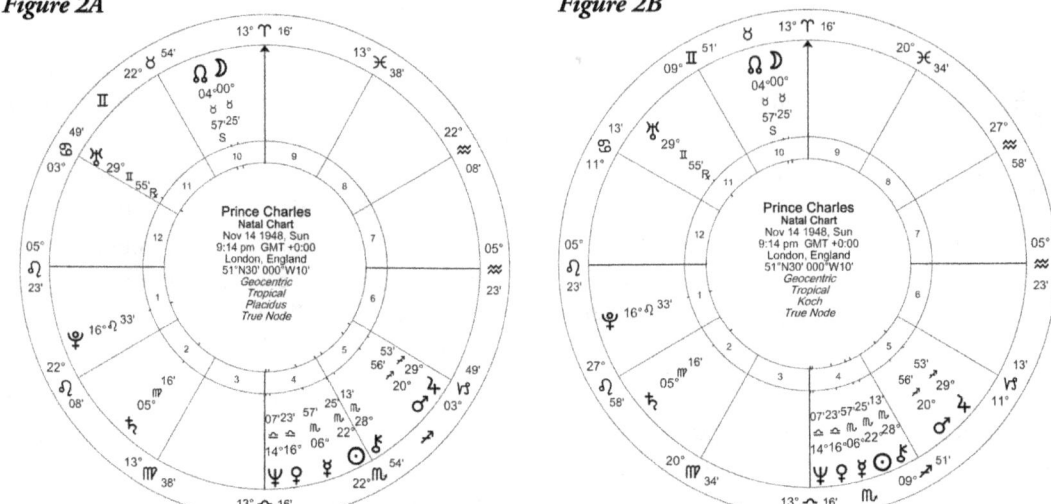

Most systems used today were developed within a range of geographic latitude in which the variations of intermediary cusps are somewhat minimal, these being the eleventh, twelfth, second and third houses and their opposites. We give a planet near a cusp a five-degree orb in influencing both houses, which would take up most of the potential variation. It is only when we move into extremes of latitude that a greater problem occurs. Some astrologers would then revert to an equal house system, thereby avoiding the complexity of interceptions. I would probably set up both charts.

However, it is not the purpose here to solve the age-old problem of which system is best or indeed if we should even attempt to create divisions or spheres of influence through which the planets play out their symphony. Any divisional process, except equal house, can create interceptions and much traditional astrology is based on the premise of house divisions and their interpretations.

The three systems most commonly used in North America at this time are Placidus, Koch and Campanus, in that order of popularity. The four angles of the chart remain the same for each system, but the intermediary cusps can change several degrees or very little, and the interceptions may also change. It is possible to have planets shift into an adjacent house and when this does occur it creates a dilemma of choice.

As far as the variation created by the intermediary cusps in different systems, this would undoubtedly create a greater concern for some astrologers than for others. If you only factor in the angles by progression, timing some developments will be overlooked. I believe it is important to use the progressed intermediary cusps and aspect progressed and transiting planets to them. Personally, I find it a significant year when the progressed twelfth cusp reaches the natal Ascendant. Memories that we may have "stuffed" in there at an earlier time may surface because we are now ready to deal with them. Action to and from the progressed second cusp can also be highly significant

Figure 2C

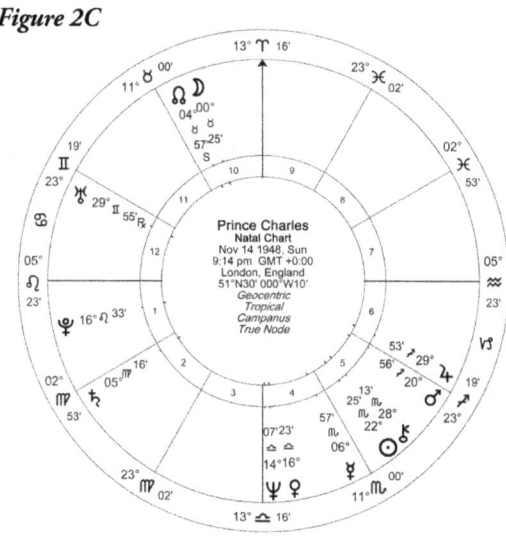

in dealing with financial matters. When the natal third cusp progresses to the fourth cusp, there is often a family matter that requires a deliberation or decision. These are only a couple of examples but any time we consider the minor cusps in the progressed chart, the choice of house cusp system becomes more critical. In fact, it may even help you to determine which system works most consistently at your latitude.

Figure 2 shows the chart of Prince Charles (A Data: AFA, April 1973) computed in three different house systems—Placidus (2A), Koch (2B) and Campanus (2C). Notice that the angles on all three charts remain the same but the intermediary cusps (i.e. eleventh, twelfth, second, third and their opposites) are different, and there is a different set of interceptions in each case.

Al H. Morrison often said that different house cusp systems can be used for different purposes. He felt that Placidus is good for vocational charts or people in context with society, while Alcabitius relates to man without considering his social interaction. Mr. Morrison felt that Koch is best for what happens on the streets because it deals with our inner psychology. He lived and practiced in Manhattan, New York City, where street events tend to be very dramatic. He further stated that Alcabitius is best for spiritual delineations and Porphyry is the desirable system for religious or metaphysical ceremonies. I do not believe this information is in print but he talked about it often in his lectures. I have noticed that several notable mundane astrologers of the past have used Campanus for stock market ventures and other financial dealings, and some may still think it is the best system for the study of such events.

I will not venture to verify any of Mr. Morrison's conclusions in this regard, but I did respect the work he did in many fields of astrology. However, we should note that many of these systems reach far back into the pages of astrological history and were developed because they were thought to be astrologically more sensible and accurate than the ones already in use. For instance, the Porphyry system was developed in the third century as the next step from the previously used equal houses and was a prelude to more elaborate systems. Campanus made the next significant improvements in cusp structures in the thirteenth century and Regiomontanus in the fifteenth century. When the old theories of the universe were being drastically altered through the Copernican Revolution, the inventive mind of Placidus de Tito, an Italian monk and mathematics professor in the seventeenth century once again altered the structure of the chart wheel. This system, which bears his name, is exceedingly popular.

On that note, without getting too tedious, perhaps it would be useful to give a very brief categorization of some of the best known systems. There are mainly two different types of measurement used to divide the intermediary houses between the angles, and they are divisions of either space or time within the celestial sphere.

The most noted space divisions, which basically divide the space between the horizon and meridian are:

- Campanus
- Regiomontanus
- Morinus

The most noted time divisions basically divide the time it takes for the Sun to go from the sunrise position to the noon position. The location of the house cusp is measured on the ecliptic. They are:

- Alcabitius
- Placidus
- Koch

Equal house could be categorized as an ecliptic system and is the most ancient way of looking at houses. According to Ralph William Holden in *The Elements of House Divisions*, "it is based upon the concept of reflecting the zodiac a second time upon the ecliptic. . . ." This concept divides the ecliptic into twelve equal divisions. The starting point is usually the degree on the Ascendant, but the degree on the Midheaven is also used. The Ascendant equal house concept allows for a more personal unfoldment of inner dynamics because it carries the significance of the Ascendant throughout the entire chart. The Midheaven equal house chart indicates one's interaction with the outer environment and it carries a more worldly significance throughout the entire chart. Rudhyar says "using only the horizon today . . . is the equivalent of lying down as the only significant position for man."

When using space divisions at northern latitudes, serious problems occur but they are by no means eliminated with the use of time divisions. The problems of Placidus at higher latitudes are less severe than those of Koch, according to Holden in *The Elements of House Divisions*.

The point of this discussion is to help you to understand that no system to date is infallible, particularly for extreme latitudes. It is often a matter of opinion, but choice may merely be a matter of the system into which one was first introduced. Beyond that you may wish to experiment with different systems to determine which produces the most consistent results. Using interception delineations could help you with this dilemma because if you are going to consider including them in your interpretation, your evaluation of any system undoubtedly will be greatly enhanced.

If you are intrigued by the actual geometric processes and problems of the various cuspal divisions, you might try to locate a copy of *The Elements of House Division* by Ralph William Holden (see Bibliography). I do not pretend to understand all that the book contains, but it did add to my understanding of the problems in ascertaining a workable system that satisfies at least most of the three-dimensional measurement problems.

In closing this section, it is important to realize that an interception is not a condition of the zodiac itself but of the geometric process used in defining the cusps or departments of life.

Novices learning to count degrees between planets to ascertain aspects should remember to count thirty degrees for each sign and not thirty degrees for each house. I find this a common error among beginners when there are interceptions. As already stated, some houses are made up of much more than thirty degrees and some much less.

Notice in Figure 1 that the two intercepted houses contain an astounding 143 degrees each!

How Much of the Chart Is Affected?

As previously indicated, more of the chart is affected when an intercepted condition exists than many astrologers realize or understand how to interpret. Perhaps my perception of this condition has been heightened due to the number of interceptions that are created at the latitude I was born and continue to live, which is between fifty-one and fifty-four degrees north. When you see them so frequently, you begin to pause, ponder and ask questions of clients and students who have them.

Effect on Signs

I believe that with one pair of intercepted signs there are actually six signs in those two houses that are affected. This affects the conditions in both of those two houses in some way by placing more emphasis on them due to the increased number of degrees and signs contained within them. There is the intercepted sign itself, the sign on the cusp of the house and the sign at the end even if the number of degrees is minimal or even fractional. Then, of course, the same situation occurs in the opposite house, which makes six signs in all, or fifty percent of the total number in the whole chart. This is further magnified when we consider that another sign somewhere around the wheel is extended over two houses, plus the opposite sign on the other side of the chart. If we are counting, that is now eight out of twelve signs, or about sixty-six and two-thirds percent, that is altered due to an interception of only one pair of signs. This is even more extreme and significant if more than one pair of signs is intercepted.

The demand on houses containing interceptions is considerably heightened because we are trying to fulfill additional psychological needs or urges through a narrower than usual field of operation. Perhaps here it would be helpful to interrupt the train of thought to give a brief keyword concept on the twelve magnificently conceived basic urges and needs for enjoyable and successful living as seen through the symbology of the signs.

Aries: The need to exercise initiative in order to develop a sense of selfhood.

Taurus: The need to consolidate or concentrate our efforts in order to create something of value and usefulness.

Gemini: The need to develop curiosity so we can learn, extend ourselves and interact with people and conditions around us.

Cancer: The need to gain emotional security through nurturing and then in turn to nurture others.

Leo: The need to be confidentially creative in order to project that creativity as an exploration and extension of ourselves.

Virgo: The need to analyze, categorize and discriminate so that information and resources have a practical application.

Libra: The need to integrate with others through the art of cooperation and compromise.

Scorpio: The need to transform individual ego thrust so it meshes more successfully with the ego thrust of others. This is a complex issue and involves the recognition and use of personal power.

Sagittarius: The need to conceptualize based upon knowledge and experience.

Capricorn: The need to be an integral part of society in a useful, participatory way.

Aquarius: The need to be an individual in the whole social fabric.

Pisces: The need to develop faith beyond tangible existence.

You may add other phrases to your own liking.

The sign on the cusp often seems to operate more stressfully due to the inner intensity of the intercepted sign. The sign urge at the end of the house often seems unfulfilled or frustrated, also due to inner intensity and focus. In other words, if Aries is intercepted that would put Pisces on that cusp (see Figure 3). In those house matters you would lack faith in the positive outcome of a situation (Pisces), would often submit, make needless sacrifices, even make excuses for a lack of decision; whereas, inside you would likely wish that you could be more forthright, initiatory, and even at times more aggressive (Aries). Due to the influence of some Taurus at the end of that same house, the situation may remain unresolved, unstructured and unsatisfactory resulting in you losing faith with yourself. There is often a feeling of helplessness and inadequacy. It is difficult to place substantial value on yourself when results are inadequate.

The words I use most frequently to describe a sign or planet in interception are *intensification due to internalization.* Any urge or need that is not an outer manifestation is under some kind of restraint. It is internalized for further study or experience before it is overtly developed or used in an outer manifestation of life experience. There is valuable "stuff" in there that eventually gets sorted out, examined, reevaluated and then cherished as the contents of a treasure chest. There is a developmental period and it usually takes until around age forty to forty-five, which is also considered the "power period" of life.

The opposite house in Figure 3 has Libra intercepted, which puts relationship fulfillment under tension requiring inner development and understanding in order to be fulfilled and become a satisfactory part of life. With Virgo on the cusp, you will likely be self-critical, feeling that other

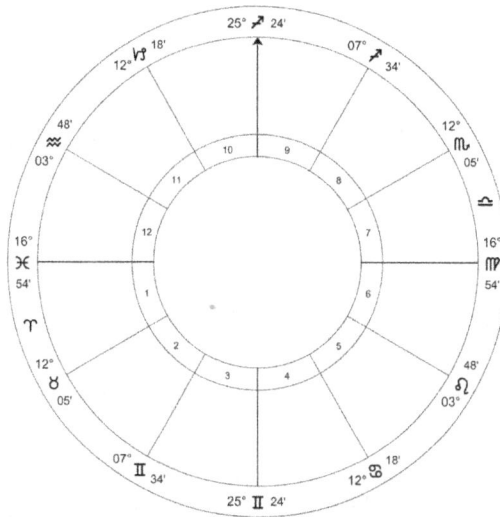

Figure 3. This figures shows an interception of Aries/Libra across the first and seventh houses. Gemini spans the third and fourth houses. Sagittarius spans the ninth and tenth houses. A blank wheel is used in order to retain focus on the cusps.

people will see little value in you because you see little value in yourself. Through Scorpio, it thus is difficult to transform your own ego thrust to mesh more successfully with the ego thrust of others because you see little value in your own ability to have a successful relationship. It takes a little longer to overtly exercise your own center of operation, which is your personal power base. By no means is it impossible to have a satisfactory relationship. It just means that it takes inner development, experimentation and forethought. It is an area of growth potential. Later on I will discuss how this development takes shape, but for now we will continue discussing the parts of the chart affected by the phenomena of interceptions.

Strength of Ruler

To judge the ease or difficulty of the sign urge development of the intercepted pair, observe the strength of each ruling planet by sign, house and aspect. It also is important to see if the rulers of intercepted signs are forming aspects with each other and, if so, can the aspects affect each sign's development in a meaningful way. If one of these planets is retrograde it further emphasizes the need for introspection and inner evaluation before one is comfortable with a more overt expression. One is not willing to risk taking action without careful consideration. This should not be considered an impairment. It just "is." It is the way one functions or operates. We should not try to become someone we are not. It creates more anxiety than if we try to understand who we are and grow into what we can be. In this way astrology is a valuable tool of self-awareness.

Repeated Signs

In Figure 3 you will observe that Gemini spans the third and fourth houses, whereas Sagittarius spans the ninth and tenth. This links each of the two houses or departments of life together in working through the dynamic urges that the sign signifies, giving the sign more significance than if it appeared on only one house. It also gives it a greater scope of influence.

Likewise, planets ruling these double positions also will influence a greater area of life than they would otherwise. This principle will be expanded further in Chapter Three. It should be noted that when Aries/Libra is intercepted, the repeating signs are not always Gemini and Sagittarius, as observed in Figure 3.

Vastly Unequal Houses

With interceptions, houses can be vastly unequal in length. Observe the extreme elongated and shortened houses in Figure 1, which is cast for a far northern latitude. Houses six and twelve each contain 143°42', whereas houses one/seven, two/eight and three/nine contain as little as 4°11', 3°43', and 4°24' respectively. The distortion is much less in Figure 3 in which the intercepted houses contain 55°20' and houses three/nine and four/ten contain 17°51' and 16°55' respectively. At a more mid-range latitude the distortion would be much less.

Effect on Quadruplicities and Elements

Another effect of interceptions in a chart would be the alteration in the structure of quadruplicities and triplicities. This will only be briefly mentioned here in order to remain focused on the amount of the chart affected by interceptions. It will be dealt with much more thoroughly in Chapter Six.

Without interceptions the quadruplicity on each of the four angles would be the same, creating squares to each other in succession moving around the chart (if not by degree, at least by sign). In *Preceptions of Astrology*, Bil Tierney calls this a natural tension. Noel Tyl calls it a developmental tension. Both are excellent phrases to describe the phenomenon. The natural developmental square between the Ascendant and Nadir or fourth cusp is the very reason why most of us develop a strong urge to leave the protective parental nest. There comes a time when we simply need to go out on our own. The natural square between the Ascendant and Midheaven creates the dynamics necessary for us to exert ourselves in the societal arena to fulfil our ambitions. A natural square also exists between houses four/seven, seven/ten and ten/one.

Without interceptions there would also be a natural square between the succedent houses of two, five, eight and eleven, which helps us to be aware of how important the development of our self-worth is in terms of experiencing romance, creating offspring, transforming our attitudes to mesh with others and enjoying a social life as we mix with others. The natural square would also exist between houses three, six, nine and twelve, which is where we gather information, develop skills, formulate our beliefs and gain wisdom through maturity.

In a chart with no interceptions, there is a natural creative flow for ease of expression occurring through the triplicities. When interceptions occur, this area is also altered to create a different type of psychological thrust. This can be significant in providing additional details into the dynamics of chart interpretation, and hence life (see Chapter Six).

Progressions

The progressed chart also reflects intercepted conditions in that a planet may enter or leave a natal intercepted house by progression. A person born with an intercepted Sun that progresses out sometime during the first thirty years of life is quite different from one who has it is in a non-intercepted position that progresses into an intercepted one. The natal intercepted position indicates that there is a fairly lengthy preparation time or inner development before the person is comfortable outwardly manifesting his/her Sun's expression. The number of degrees involved does not seem to make much difference in the length of time this could take. The intercepted Sun person appears more shy, introverted and self-conscious than if the Sun were otherwise placed. Whether this same Sun is angular, succedent or cadent also makes a significant difference. For instance, an intercepted Sun in the twelfth house is more internalized than an intercepted Sun in the first house.

If the Sun begins non-intercepted and moves into interception at some time m life, it indicates that a period of inner growth will be undertaken that will coincide with but not necessarily detract from the outward manifestation of the natal position. I will use my own Sun as an example. I have always led a public life, having been a child performer, a radio show panel anchor in my teens, later hosting my own television shows and much later lecturing in astrology. My Aquarius Sun is natally posited in my eleventh house, and at approximately age twenty-two, by progression, it went into Pisces, intercepted in my twelfth house. My public life continued with equal emphasis, but I began a personal search in another segment of my life for a deeper, more spiritual meaning to existence beyond daily activities, which eventually led to a career shift into astrology. It was a profound period of study, investigation and contemplation. The Sun has been out of its progressed intercepted position for the past several years, but those habits continue to permeate my life, as did the previous ones. The natal position or influence is not eliminated or nullified but added onto as the planets progress forward.

You might wish to observe the change in intercepted houses on a year-by-year basis by secondary progression or return charts. Observe the sign pair(s) and watch how you respond to this subtle shift in psychology when your needs related to those signs become more intense due to internalization. Also observe when any personal planets go into interception for this short period of time in the progressed chart. Their expression also will become more internalized, but only for a brief progressed period. For this observation, you might wish to set up a separate progressed chart as a subsidiary to your usual two- or three-wheel progressed chart, but we do recognize that the progressed chart is taken in context with the natal chart.

Transits

Transits weaving in and out of intercepted signs can create various effects. They can affect the thrust of the transiting planet as well as the temporary expression of the sign need by showing us different ways of expressing those needs. They can also gradually bring a deeper understanding of the needs indicated by the sign and how we can handle them more effectively. The transiting planet goes inward but it also gives an opportunity for an outward manifestation of the sign urge. Use keywords to develop your understanding of how this can be beneficial.

- The Sun illuminates
- The Moon sensitizes our emotions

- Mercury develops cognitive understanding
- Venus harmonizes
- Mars excites and activates
- Jupiter expands
- Saturn structures
- Uranus enlightens
- Neptune inspires
- Pluto transforms

Intercepted Planets Ruling Non-intercepted Houses

A planet may be contained within an intercepted sign and rule a non-intercepted house. That indicates a pathway of expression and integration. For instance, an individual might have an intercepted Mercury in the third house ruling the eleventh house. That person might be intense about reading, learning and studying in private life, particularly during the formal school years, but have a small circle of close friends with whom he or she develops comfort of self-expression that can eventually expand into other areas of communication and socialization. Confidence in self-expression develops as the individual gradually realizes he or she has something significant to say.

Summary

Listed below is the amount of the chart that is affected by an intercepted pair of signs.

1. Initially, six signs are affected by one pair of interceptions.

2. The rulers of the intercepted signs are affected in the way they function, particularly if they aspect each other.

3. One sign repeated on two houses, and the opposite two houses.

4. Houses are vastly unequal in size, changing their significance.

5. Houses of quadruplicities and triplicities are altered.

6. Progressions alter natal positions of both signs and planets.

7. Transits weaving in and out of intercepted signs, not only change the thrust of the transiting planet, but the fulfillment of the sign urge as well.

8. Planets may be contained within the intercepted sign, ruling a non-intercepted house and vice-versa.

CHAPTER TWO

Development of Interceptions

"There is a tide in the affairs of men, Which, taken at the flood, leads on to fortune."—William Shakespeare

Development by Transit

Transiting planets move around the wheel, each at its own rate, some fast and some much slower. The following is the approximate time a transiting planet spends in a sign. Its duration in a house will depend upon the number of degrees therein.

Moon	2½ Days
Mercury	Variable Days
Venus	Variable Month
Sun	1 Month
Mars	Variable Month (22 months for 1 revolution)
Jupiter	1 Year
Saturn	2½ Years
Uranus	7 Years
Neptune	14 Years
Pluto	12-25 Years

We will begin by examining the transits of the Sun. This sets up a yearly cycle of activity or a personal rhythm that each one of us can utilize to gain the maximum benefit from its sojourn. It would probably be useful to give a brief description of its transit through each house, bearing in mind that its duration in a house will vary according to the number of degrees contained therein. In the case of an intercepted sign, the Sun will illuminate an inner need for understanding and personal development; if the need is paramount you will reach outward for expression and attention. This will be according to the sign, through those particular house matters and where Leo is posited. You will seek to have the Sun shine on those endeavors. In your younger years this may be done somewhat awkwardly, but as time passes and experience is gained, you can do so more effectively. The aspects the Sun makes to natal planets will help in determining how crucial this action is. Some tension is exceedingly helpful in stimulating action and growth as long as it does not develop into immobilizing stress.

Yearly Rhythm of the Sun

First House: Since the Sun is illuminating self, this transit is a good time to review your attitude, style, presentation and physical sense. In an intercepted sign, for this brief period of time you may demand attention in less than subtle ways as you try new forms of expression.

Second House: Review your self-worth, earning capacity, budget and savings. In an intercepted sign you will likely take overt action in these areas. You may make a concerted effort to balance spending and earnings. You may seek additional income sources. Since this duration is short, many of these efforts will be experimental and fizzle out, but in the meantime, you are gaining valuable experience.

Third House: This is a good time to take a course, read a greater diversity of books, magazines, or periodicals, catch up on correspondence, renew contact with kin and neighbors, take a short trip. In an intercepted sign, you may sign up for a new course and not feel its benefit until several years later or you may sign up for a self-improvement course and thereby gain additional personal insight. You may take a pleasant weekend sojourn and vow to do it more often which usually does not manifest until the following year about the same time.

Fourth House: Pay special attention to home, family and heritage. It could be your annual house and/or yard clean-up and rejuvenation time. In an intercepted sign, you will likely deliberate deeply about contacting parents especially if a misunderstanding has occurred. Serious rifts take several years to heal and they requires overt action with courage and conviction to do so. The process is usually gradual.

Fifth House: This is an excellent time to seek more recreation, have more fun, take up a new sport, take a romantic holiday or get more involved with children. In an intercepted sign, the very least you may do is become more adventuresome and outgoing in expressing yourself which can increase personal attracting power.

Sixth House: This is a good time to organize and clean up neglected areas of your life and surroundings. The Sun may illuminate answers to old problems that you may have been avoiding. It is a good time to review work ethics and attitude; pay more attention to diet, exercise and rest. In an intercepted sign, the possibility of overt action is more apparent because the Sun encourages life and growth.

Seventh House: Pay special attention to your partner and your attitude towards relationships in general.

Eighth House: Assess your debts and credit card balances, investments and even your current insurance needs. In an intercepted sign, you will likely take overt action in at least some of these affairs, according to thoughts that have been gelling for the past year.

Ninth House: Take a trip, advance your education, review ethics and beliefs.

Tenth House: Find some way to shine publicly or in your career. Take a leadership role in a societal activity. In an intercepted sign, you may examine your reputation on an internal level and use the Sun's power to enhance your efforts. You may overtly seek some way to be noticed by your superiors, even if it is only smiling more often.

Eleventh House: Renew acquaintances, join a group, review goals and aspirations. In an intercepted sign, you may find yourselves being more social or more interested in group activities. This may be when you finally relent and agree to serve on a committee. By the mere effort of being more friendly, it is possible to meet an influential new friend. This month should be used to consciously extend your influence.

Twelfth House: Retreat, spend a little time alone, evaluate the past year's activities in a positive, complimentary way giving yourself credit for growth. Avoid a negative evaluation.

There is a very gradual development of being able to project yourself a bit more confidently as time advances, and being able to send your Sun's rays beaming toward others. At age twenty-five the Sun has transited through a particular sign twenty-five times. At age thirty-five the Sun has been in there thirty-five times, and so on.

Mercury

Mercury transiting an intercepted sign provides an opportunity for internal contemplation and cognitive recognition of how you can understand and express your needs in connection with the urges represented by the sign. The overt action might be as simple as finding a special book seeking information on a particular line of thought or even being willing to share some inner thoughts with someone else. In the third house you might phone kin with whom you have not talked for the past year, or uncustomarily pause and talk to a neighbor. In the fourth house you might feel the need to talk something over with a parent. In the sixth house you might confide in a coworker about a condition you have been putting up with for too long. In the ninth house, you might seek legal advice or spiritual counsel. In the eleventh you might confide in a friend.

If Mercury goes retrograde during this period, the internal process will be more pronounced and realization of the perspective gained usually does not occur until Mercury is once more direct in motion.

Venus

The transit of Venus through an intercepted house provides internal evaluation and a deeper understanding of relationships as well as aesthetic appreciation. Its effect is somewhat subtle and personal, and therefore not as noticeable as some of the other transits. I believe we might be more willing to give ourselves credit in the area where this transit is occurring.

Mars

The transit of Mars is highly significant in helping to express your interceptions more overtly. In fact, it might be the most significant transit of all in this process. When it goes into an intercepted sign, it energizes and motivates those needs and helps to provide outward manifestation. As an example, if Aries is intercepted and you tend by nature to be hesitant about taking the initiative and you are more Piscean in handling those house matters, when Mars goes into that sign it is as if some force inside is saying: "I am tired of not sticking up for myself. I am tired of making excuses or being taken advantage of. Why doesn't someone do something for me for a change? Why can't I just say no, I do not have either the time or the capacity?"

It is quite an about-face. The urge to be more forthright tends to be somewhat aggressive. Other people are surprised at such an uncharacteristic outburst. When Mars leaves the sign, you internalize again and wish that you had not spoken out so strongly or been so aggressive. You may feel guilty because you have upset someone or alienated an important associate, partner or coworker.

Eventually you learn how to stand up for yourself in a more gracious and acceptable manner without unduly disturbing your relationships. At about age forty-four, Mars has been in and out of that sign about twenty times, indicating that much has been learned about handling it appropriately. That is why I believe that interceptions begin being expressed more overtly around age forty. By that age we have surely gained some maturity and have become more skilled in handling ourselves.

The planet Mars seems to play a very big role in the development of intercepted positions. It is the action planet that links the inner or personality planets to that which is beyond self. If Mars happens to turn retrograde in the intercepted sign, its duration is extended up to three or five months and its effect appears to be more explosive when it is released.

Jupiter

Jupiter transits the chart in about twelve years, spending approximately one year in each sign. The planet of expansion and rewards, it provides an opportunity to gain wisdom, insight and growth in the area of its transit. As each planet transits into the intercepted position, it has the effect of bringing out the sign urge, while also going inward in comparison to its normal range of effect.

Saturn

Saturn provides an opportunity for structure and serious contemplation. However, we might feel inhibited, defeated, even useless in our effort to find fulfillment in the intercepted area where Saturn is transiting. This is about a two-and-a-half year period. We need to be assessing our needs in a cool, calculating, practical manner rather than feeling defeated or ineffective. This is certainly a time of evaluation and it should be done in as positive a way as possible without personal condemnation. I suggest observing if Saturn will make a square, opposition or quincunx aspect to the Moon while it is transiting an intercepted sign. This will warn you of times of discouragement and possible depression.

In my chart, Virgo is intercepted in my sixth house. I can recall clearly what occurred when Saturn was transiting there in 1978 and 1979. I was working exceptionally long hours and perhaps not devoting enough time and effort to diet and other health concerns, although it must be realized that Saturn illnesses are chronic in nature. In September 1979, the Sun, Mercury and Venus had joined Saturn in Virgo. In the middle of a very important schedule, I was rushed to emergency, suffered a week of distress and severe weight loss before an abdominal surgical procedure revealed an intestinal obstruction. Such correlations seem uncanny! Convalescence provided me with ample time to contemplate and evaluate how I was conducting my business and providing adequate backup in the event of an emergency. I was in my own television production business. Sun and Venus stimulated much support and assistance from associates.

Uranus

Uranus spends about seven years in a sign, taking about eighty-four years to complete its cycle. It can motivate you to sudden, unexpected, revolutionary behavior, and can dramatically energize a sign urge that is intercepted.

Many years ago, when Uranus was transiting Libra, I had several clients who had Libra intercepted in the seventh house and who had not been in a relationship for a long time and had even vowed to remain unattached. However, the transit brought a sudden love affair, an undying commitment, followed by an unexpected breakup when Uranus aspected a personal planet. It can be argued that Uranus transiting a seventh house without an interception might provide the same stimulation, but the most dramatic developments during that seven-year period seemed to occur with the people who had Libra intercepted.

Over the years I also have observed several clients who had been putting up with a strained relationship until Uranus transited an intercepted sign in the seventh house. The type of action taken and the resulting outcome had much to do with the sign involved as well as aspects. Uranus not only enlightens but it also helps to free us from conditions and situations that have become unbearably restricting.

Neptune and Pluto

The transits of Neptune and Pluto do not seem to be overtly expressive when they go into an intercepted sign. That is understandable when we realize how long they remain. I believe they provide deeper exploration of the respective needs.

Mars seems to be the prime developer of intercepted positions. It stays in a sign long enough to be useful but not long enough to cause much disruption or harm as we are learning to be overtly more expressive in those areas.

Development by Progression

As your chart progresses, so does the condition of interceptions. It does this in two ways. First, planets will progress in or out of your natal signs and houses and hence interceptions. Second, the progressed cusps will yield a variety of intercepted signs over a period of time, and hence planets as well. Many astrologers only consider the progression of the angles but I would encourage everyone to also include the intermediary cusps. This is the only way you will be able to observe the changes in intercepted conditions. The effect may be subtle but useful in your journey of self-awareness. I will deal with each of these situations in turn.

Planets Moving In and Out of Natal Signs and Houses

You start with a natal chart, but life is not static. It is an ongoing process of growth and development. You may start with a planet in an intercepted sign and have it progress out, or vice versa. Each provides a different growth pattern. As an example, if you have the Sun natally intercepted, it will take longer to overtly exhibit your Sun qualities and outwardly express your creative selfhood. You have a need to understand yourself very deeply at an inner level before feeling comfortable projecting your Sun needs and qualities outwardly. Naturally an angular position is less introverted than a cadent position. This certainly does not indicate success or failure. It merely indicates another way to develop. Inner growth is necessary before you are confident projecting your creative selfhood. I must warn you not to use only this as a signature of an introverted personality, although it often is. There is an adage in astrology that if a characteristic is prominent it will be indicated in the chart at least three different ways.

I know a gentleman who has an intercepted Pisces Sun in his twelfth house. As a young boy growing up he had a great desire to be in show business but felt awkward demonstrating the full scope of his talents in front of others. He studied various instruments but would not play publicly. He secretly desired to be an actor but would not do so. He painted in oils but would shyly show only a few people his canvases. However, he performed on stage throughout his teen years in pantomime and as a magician. As he grew up, his inner struggle and growth helped to sensitize his recognition and understanding of the talent in others. He became a very successful and notable television producer/director in the area of variety and fine arts. He helped others exhibit their talents.

I once read that the intercepted planet is released when it progresses out of the interception. I have not found this to be so. Using the above example, this person's Sun is at 29 Pisces 45, which means that by progression it went into Aries when he was less than a year old. By the time he was seven years old, his Sun had progressed to his Aries Ascendant and operated by progression from an angular position for approximately the next thirty years. He remained introverted until about age forty, when maturity helped him gain the confidence to be more outwardly expressive. Until then he preferred working behind the scenes. Again I will stress that an interception is not a barometer of success or failure.

The opposite scenario would have the Sun (or any other planet) move into interception by progression. In continuing to use the Sun as an example, this would not change the basic natal signature, but it would mean that you would go through a period of approximately thirty years of voluntary inner growth while still functioning in whatever outward way the natal chart indicated. Any outward joviality and social interaction indicated in the natal chart would remain, but there would be an inner intensity of searching for a deeper meaning to life. I have experienced this progression. My outward public life did not change, but inwardly I began a very serious, profound search for the meaning of what it is to be human in an earthly environment. In this case, the surface trappings of physical existence were not enough to satisfy the yearning of a progressed intercepted Sun.

By secondary progression, most of our outer planets will not move out of interception during this lifetime. That does not make them inactive. It merely means that those areas are highly significant according to the meaning of the signs, houses and planets. Mars can stay in an intercepted sign for a very long time, even if it does not change direction. Natal planets posited in interception will be dealt with in a later chapter.

Progressed Cusps

If you observe your progressed cusps over a number of years , you will notice that it is an ever-changing phenomena. Natally you may have an intercepted pair of signs indicating a particular psychological thrust and learning pattern. However, by progression this changes, presenting opportunity for growth of the natal position. It is another way to subtly give you an opportunity to experiment with different thrusts as signs change intercepted positions.

As an example I will use the chart of Wayne Gretzky. His chart has been progressed to the date of his official retirement from hockey. The transits are for the time and place this announcement was made: April 16, 1999, 4:00 PM, New York City. See Figure 5 for the complete three-wheel chart. Figure 4 isolates his progressed chart so that the cusps can be seen more clearly.

Hockey fans the world over watched that broadcast, and even those who normally do not watch hockey, tuned in. As he talked, in usual Aries intercepted fashion, his head was slightly bent forward, chin tucked in and he genuinely had trouble saying what he really wanted to say without feeling guilty about the number of people he may be letting down. He is called "The Great Gretzky" and is cited as being the greatest hockey player that ever lived. He is also called "Mr. Nice Guy" because he has never been a "mean" player nor been publicly rude to either the press or his fans. While he was living in Edmonton, Alberta, I occasionally associated with him in the television media and had the opportunity to observe how much difficulty he experienced in turning down personal appearances in spite of an overloaded schedule.

He had wanted to retire for some time. Looking at the position of his transiting Saturn in the first quadrant of his natal chart, an astrologer can understand why (see Figure 5). He was tired and needed a long rest. He has given a great deal to the game and to his fans, and now it is time for him to find out who he is as a person. He needs personal time to get in

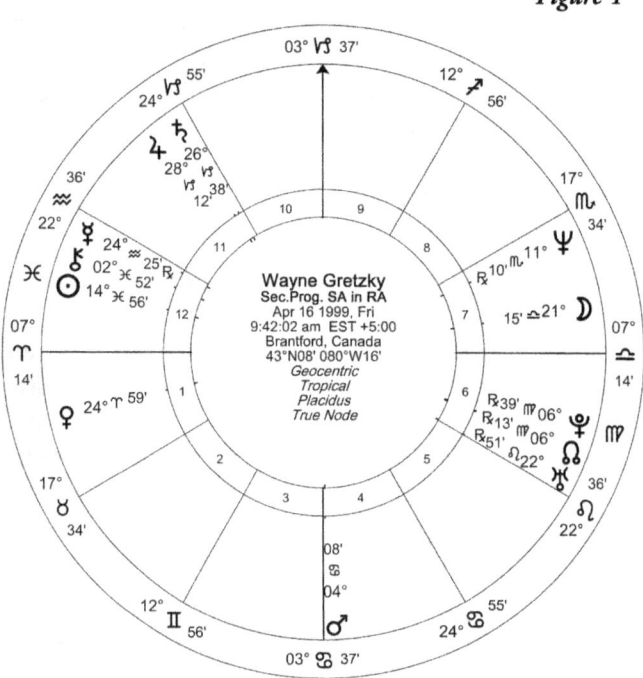

Figure 4

touch with his inner dynamics and Saturn in this quadrant helps to diminish career and societal activities to allow this purpose to fulfill itself. In *The Transits of Saturn*, Marc Robertson calls it a time of rebirth so that a new phase of life can open up. Gretzky's outer values or economics are already well established, but he has been in the public eye since his teenage years with many public demands and expectations, giving him little time to get in touch with himself deeply as a person. This transit is an inner compelling psychological urge that is difficult, if not impossible to ignore. He also wishes to spend more time with his wife and young family.

It is important to note that Aries/Libra is no longer intercepted in the progressed chart (Figure 4). This helped Mr. Gretzky with the task of initiating the action that was in his heart and mind. The intercepted pair is now Virgo/Pisces across houses six/twelve respectively.

In the three-wheel chart (Figure 5), the only progressed cusps printed on the second wheel are the Midheaven and Ascendant since they are of paramount importance. If you like, you can insert the eleventh, twelfth, second and third by hand from Figure 4. The change in progressed interceptions might be confusing for some of you to observe in a three-wheel format, so referring to Figure 4 should help. Please refer to both in order to follow what is being said.

As seen in Figure 5, Gretzky's Ascendant has progressed into the Aries interception in his natal second house. This further indicates his desire to retire and spend time on internal development,

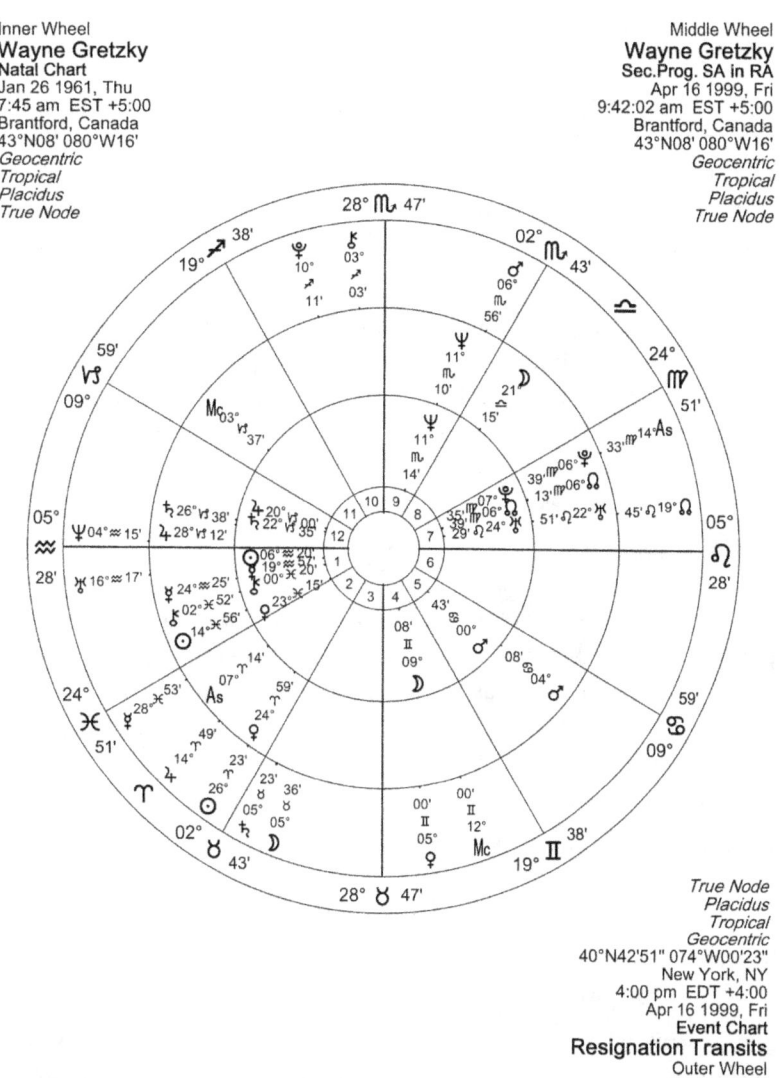

Figure 5. Wayne Gretzky's Chart progressed to time and place he announced his retirement; AA: hospital birth card (from him). Note: By progression, Aries/Libra is no longer in interception, which helped him do what he really wanted to do, which was to retire. It was a difficult decision and a difficult press announcement for him to make.

as already indicated by the transit of Saturn in the first quadrant. Also, his progressed Sun is now intercepted in Pisces, which is in the progressed twelfth house (more easily seen in Figure 4), a further indication that it is time to shift gears and retire from his high profile public position. He will not do this entirely because it is in his nature to be noticeable due to his angular planets, and the progressed Sun remains angular in relationship to his natal chart, as seen in the three-wheel structure (Figure 5).

Progressed Jupiter conjunct Saturn is now in the progressed eleventh house. Progressed Midheaven opposite progressed Mars gave him additional push to initiate action on his own behalf. This also puts his progressed Mars conjunct his progressed fourth cusp, which emphasizes home and family. His natal Mars is out of bounds (OOB) by declination and it is important to note that it remains out of bounds in his progressed chart. These figures are included in the boxes below the three-wheel chart.

For those unfamiliar with the term "out of bounds," I will offer a brief explanation. It is a planet in "declination greater than maximum declination of the ecliptic" as quoted from *Declinations: The Other Dimension* by Kt. Boehrer. It provides courage, energy and a sense of adventure beyond a normal range of activity. Many athletes or people who can move with extraordinary quickness have this, and others reach high in their goals and expectations of life.

I believe Mr. Gretzky's natal OOB Mars gave him extraordinary speed of movement as a hockey player and helped him project as he did even though it rules an intercepted position. We must also remember that an interception *internalizes* and *intensifies* the desires and needs indicated by the sign and/or planets. In this case it was his Aries needs that were intensified due to Mars being unfettered by the ecliptic. The fact that it is still OOB by progression, ruling his progressed intercepted Ascendant, helped give him the impetus he needed to do what he wanted to do and not what he felt his fans would like him to do.

- Natal Mars Declination: 27N09
- Progressed Mars Declination: 26N17
- Maximum Declination of the Ecliptic: 23:28

Summary

Another way we can gain experience in overtly learning to express our natal intercepted signs is by the constant shifting by progression.

There are certain years when we are capable of doing something related to our released intercepted positions that we may not otherwise have had the courage or desire to do. Also, other signs move into interception to provide us with the opportunity to more deeply internalize some of their needs. The universe is just. There is plenty of room for growth and development as long as we respond to the opportunities that continue to be presented to us. Astrology shows these to us.

CHAPTER THREE

Intercepted Signs

*"Forty is the old age of youth.
Fifty is the youth of old age.'* —*Victor Hugo*

WHEN ONE SIGN IS INTERCEPTED, the opposite sign by polarity is also intercepted. Neither one of these two signs is on the cusp or doorway of a house and hence in many ways they are not as overtly expressed during the first years of life, at least not until after the Saturn return, which occurs around age twenty-nine. When we internalize a basic need it gains a great deal of intensity and hence importance in our psychology. It becomes a need we struggle to fulfill in our outer experience. The operative phrase used in this text to describe the effect of an interception is:

Intensification Due to Internalization

It has been said that we do not comfortably and fully express our intercepted signs and planets outwardly until sometime in our forties. My observation indicates this to be largely true. The previous chapter gives an explanation for this reasoning.

The internal expression may create certain frustrations for a period of life and should not be considered an impairment or a personality flaw but an opportunity for internal growth and understanding in those sign urges. *This is not a punishment process but a learning one*. It is a process in learning the lessons the soul requires for its further development. There must be reasons why parts of our charts are internalized.

The concepts presented here are not to be taken as absolute in every chart. The purpose is to develop an understanding of the principles involved so that they can be applied to each individual chart. Other favorite keywords not used here can be applied successfully to expand the delineations. The ease or complexity of these developments in a single chart is determined by many other factors contained therein. The whole chart must be examined to see if these traits are supported elsewhere in the chart. They may also be softened or lessened. Furthermore, it makes a difference if the intercepted pair is in an angular, succedent or cadent position. There is a considerable difference if an Aries interception is in the twelfth or first house. The twelfth house would further internalize the process and the first would make it less introverted.

After the principles are understood, you will have to apply them according to the meaning of each house(s). Briefly, this is as follows:

First/Seventh Axis: Applied directly to our personal thrust and its effect upon relationships.

Second/Eighth Axis: Applied directly to our values and earning capacity as well as joint resources in a cooperative or competitive way.

Third/Ninth Axis: Deals with learning and applying the knowledge gained in a conceptual way, hence acquiring wisdom. Fourth/Tenth Axis: Deals with home and family which is the foundation from which we spring when we go out into the world, both physically and metaphysically.

Fifth/Eleventh Axis: Deals with love given and how it is received by others. It also deals with all of our creative endeavours and how they are appreciated by others.

Sixth/Twelfth Axis: One of solving problems both externally and internally. It is also the axis of logic versus faith.

After examining hundreds of charts of people with interceptions, notables as well as students and clients, another observation captivated my attention. There is often an outpouring of focused activity in one specific avenue of pursuit connected with the signs, while still retaining many of the inward characteristics presented in the following pages.

For instance, many athletes have the Aries/Libra pair intercepted. We have already observed this in Wayne Gretzky's chart. He is considered the world's greatest hockey player who, in spite of his sports prowess, also exhibits a shyness and sensitivity in his personality presentation. Other athletes in this category are as follows:

Dorothy Hamill, Olympic Gold Medal Skater: In order to practice more she dropped out of school at age fourteen and studied with a private tutor. This no doubt affected a normal growth in integrating and communicating with classmates.

Wilt Chamberlain, Basketball Star and Recordholder: He was 7'1" tall.

Herb Elliot, Record Runner: He broke the four minute mile record more than once.

Arnold Schwarzenegger, Body Builder, Actor and Governor: He won the Mr. Universe and Mr. Olympic titles many times. In the 1980s he became known as a movie muscle man. His most notable films include *Conan The Barbarian*, *Conan The Destroyer*, *Terminator I* and *Terminator II*. Then he began to project the softer side of his nature in *Twins* and *Batman and Robin* in 1997.

Robert Craig (Evil) Knievel, Motorcycle Stunt Daredevil: Lois Rodden called him a "modern day gladiator." Prior to his fame, he worked in the copper mines and became a safecracker and robber. He actually lived to retire.

With the Taurus/Scorpio group we find many financiers and people who enjoy gaining and manipulating resources. A notable example follows:

Merv Griffin, Talk Show Host and Financier: He made his initial money as a talk show host (Leo on his second and third houses) and then began developing television game shows, all of which led to great acquisitions of resort property. He was considered to be one of the wealthiest men in the world. In an interview on *Larry King Live*, he indicated that he did not need any more money but he enjoyed the game of making it.

Many authors, reporters, teachers and musicians have Gemini/Sagittarius intercepted.

Many restaurateurs, real estate agents or people involved in home-based businesses have Cancer/Capricorn intercepted.

In the Leo/Aquarius category there are many actors who feel more comfortable portraying someone else than being themselves.

In the Virgo/Pisces category there are people in medical fields, religious activities, and even atheists. Madalyn Murray O'Hair is a lawyer and professed atheist who for many years denounced organized religion. She won a case outlawing prayer in public schools.

Aries/Libra Intercepted

Aries is where we learn to take action on our own behalf in order to develop an essence of selfhood and build self-confidence as an individual. This process helps us understand who we are. With an Aries interception you have a tendency to be more condescending than forthright, directive or initiatory due to Pisces being on the cusp. You are more inclined to do what you feel is expected of you or what you feel you should do rather than what you feel is important or significant in your overall schedule of activities or range of possibilities. There is often an element of personal sacrifice and a strong sense of guilt if you do not comply with someone else's request or expectations.

You are sure to be more sensitive and prone to tears when you feel you may be letting someone down. I can still recall when Wayne Gretzky was giving a press announcement about his move to Los Angeles, tears were streaming down his face while the cameras rolled and literally millions of people watched. He was certainly reticent about moving to Los Angeles, and he knew how beloved he was in Edmonton where he first achieved fame and fortune. As the tears rolled and he tried wiping them with a tissue, in a shaking voice he said, "I promised Sather (his Manager) that I would not do this."

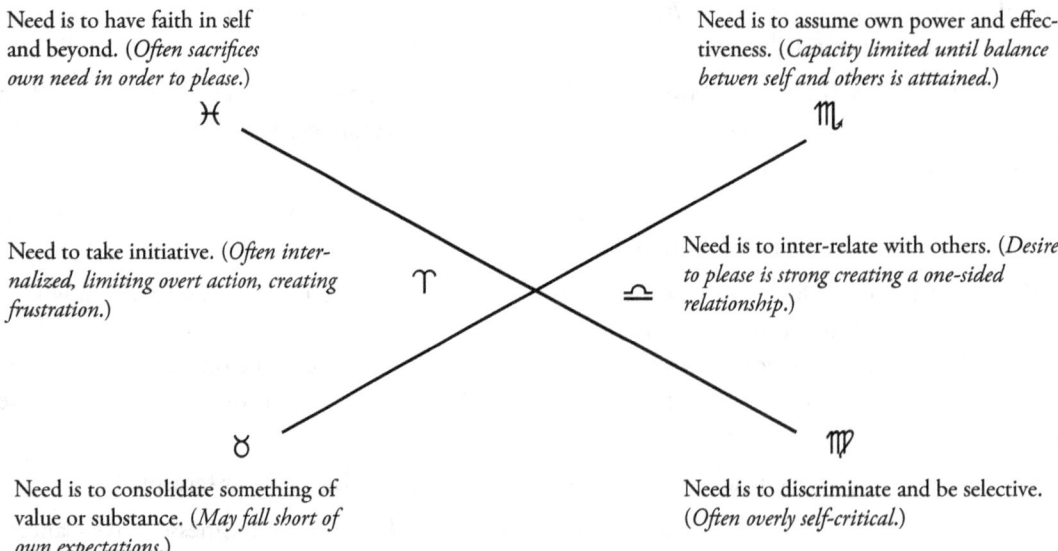

Figure 6. Aries/Libra Intercepted. Basic urge of each sign is indicated. The expressive needs of all six are altered by this one pair of intercepted signs. A key concept of the potential difficulty is in parenthesis. When Aries is intercepted, Pisces is on the cusp of that house and Taurus is at the end. This makes Libra intercepted with Virgo on the cusp and Scorpio at the end.

Taurus is our need to consolidate something of value or substance. It is a fixed earth sign and therefore our link as an individual to this planet is in a concrete, practical way. If we do a job well, get paid adequately and can look after ourselves, we develop a natural sense of self-worth and self-respect. However, if you have Aries intercepted, you may be unable to take enough overt action to develop your own talents and abilities in order to build adequate resources to take care of your own practical needs, which means you may fall short of your own expectations and can be disappointed in the results attained. This can in turn affect your personal self-worth and self-respect. I have often heard these people say that they are not getting paid what they think they are worth, and they do not know what to do about it. Many of them feel they are working just as hard, if not harder than their coworkers.

The number of degrees in Taurus does not seem to matter. It may be several or only a fraction. The possibility of personal disappointment exists until you learn to initiate action in order to develop a sense of selfhood. If the need to be of service to others is strong through an array of planets and aspects then a career in a service industry may be the avenue to pursue in order to attain the self-respect for which you are struggling. However, the mere fact of this interception being in a chart would not in itself be an indication that this is the solution.

The chart of Wayne Gretzky (Figure 5) has Taurus at the end of the intercepted Aries second house. He has amassed a fortune due to his great talent as an athlete, so monetary rewards are surely not a factor. However, what is a factor is his need to find a more equitable balance in his own life between what he gives his team and his fans, and what he gives himself and his family. Therein lies at least one facet of his Taurus self-respect. At the time of this writing, Saturn is transiting Taurus and he has retired from being an active hockey player.

Wherever the Aries/Libra axis is in the chart, we are constantly trying to find a harmonious balance between selfhood and cooperating with others as well as learning the true essence of compromise. Submission is not compromise. With the interception, the me/you psychology is often out of balance because of too many obligations and self-imposed responsibilities. It takes practice learning how to say, "no, I can't do that right now. My schedule is already overloaded. Perhaps I can offer a suggestion that may help you." Or words to that effect. Of course, there are times when being a helpmate is much needed and appreciated but we must also be careful not to rob someone else of his/her responsibility and self-sufficiency.

If you are overly helpful you may be considered a pushover by associates because you can readily be taken advantage of. You might invite this type of responsibility-abuse. Above all, you do not want anyone to think you are pushy, aggressive or selfish. You might be so concerned with what others think of you that you take on many responsibilities that could easily be shared by others.

Sometimes it helps to wonder why you do too much for others. Is it because you feel they are not capable of doing for themselves? Is it because you feel they genuinely need your help? Is it because you feel you would be better liked and admired? It is worth pausing on this thought for a moment.

Moving to the other side of the chart, you would have Libra intercepted. You may often find yourself in one-sided relationships because you do too much to please your partner, or you might couple with someone who is especially needy and dependent. Virgo is the leading influence in that area of the chart, and if it is manifesting in a negative way as it often does in this structure, you tend to be self-critical and wonder why anyone would like you or want to have a relationship with you. If you do not feel worthy, it is natural to try too hard to be accepted. Sometimes you worry so much about not being liked or doing enough for your partner that you actually become ill, particularly if displeasure is shown or a disagreement occurs. Virgo's basic need is to be discriminating, to be selective and to prioritize which, in the case of Libra intercepted, will eventually be a lesson learned through experience.

Where Libra is intercepted, Scorpio is at the end of the house, indicating a difficulty in perceiving the problem. When you lack personal appreciation, are self-critical and are overly condescending, it indicates you are giving someone else your personal power. This does not create a balanced relationship. One person has all the power and influence. This is an awesome responsibility and can easily be abused. If each person retains his/her own power and selfhood, and shares it with a partner, they both have the advantage of a combined effort. The highest level of shared energy is in the sex act. There is a moment of impact when both can share the very essence and creativity of life. If you have Libra intercepted, sexual gratification can be one-sided, belonging to the person who has the power.

With this axis intercepted, there is often the nagging thought in the back of your mind that you would like to be more forthright and wish you had the nerve to speak out on your own behalf. Various transits help in this learning process.

When the transit of the Sun moves into Aries for one month every year, something magical happens. The Sun is exalted in Aries and it helps to illuminate your personality. It helps to fire up a sense of personal ambition. It helps to understand your need to be more initiatory. You have the ability to say no without being offensive or feeling guilty. When the Moon is in Aries for a couple of days every month, this can arouse a sense of internal anger which may be outwardly expressed. Since it is such a short time, it is usually not disastrous unless accompanied by other stronger aspects.

Mars is a significant activator and stimulates aggressive energy. It is in its own sign in Aries but does require handling in a responsible fashion. This transit is a time when you might decide you are being taken advantage of. You can become aggressive, much to the dismay of your friends and associates who are not accustomed to this type of personality display in your otherwise more amenable nature. When Mars leaves, you usually return to your former behavior. However, by the time you are in your mid-forties, Mars has transited this position approximately twenty times and you have been gradually learning how to use this energy more effectively in an initiatory and less aggressive manner. It is a learned process that becomes more effective with the maturity that begins to develop after the Saturn return around age twenty-nine. One cannot state an exact age when this learning is complete because it is an ongoing process.

When intercepted Libra is stimulated by a transiting influence, you are learning how to relate with others more effectively. Transiting Mars stimulates activity. Saturn demands greater responsibility, reliability and timing. Saturn also can stimulate exceedingly frustrating events. In a lecture I gave once, a lady in the audience said that when Saturn was transiting her Libra intercepted fifth house, her former husband took her to court and took her girls away from her.

Uranus provides opportunity to liberate you from restrictions. I once heard Rob Hand refer to Uranus as the stick of dynamite that blows down the brick wall. If an existing relationship is secure, Uranus will give it greater freedom of expression. If it is already teetering, Uranus can blow it apart, but only to provide the freedom to move on. If you are not in a current relationship, Uranus can release the need and suddenly bring someone into your life.

Refer to Chapter Two for more details on transits.

This pair of interceptions requires developing faith in yourself (Pisces), learning to initiate positive action (Aries), in order to obtain results (Taurus), so that you can have a more successful relationship (Libra), by feeling worthy (Virgo), and sharing resources (Scorpio).

We will now look at some examples.

Figure 7

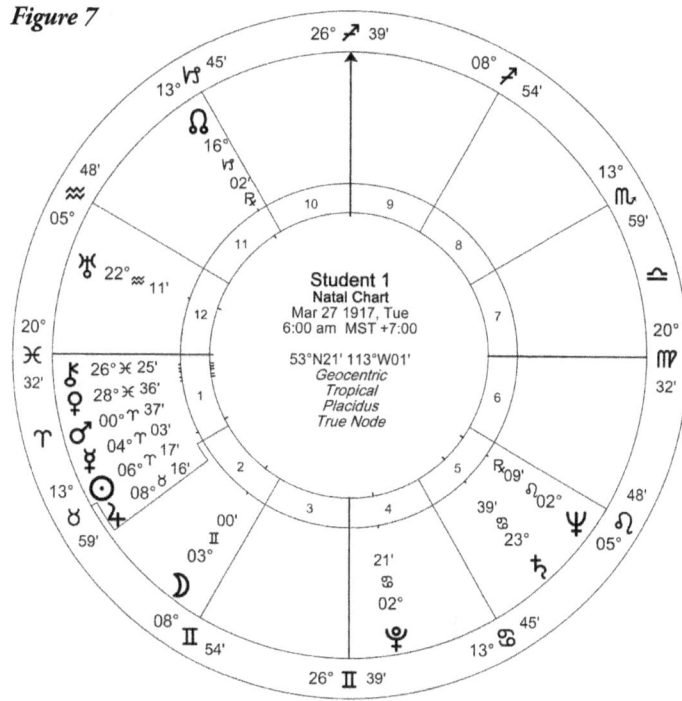

Student 1

Figure 7 is the chart of a student who studied with me many years ago. She is now deceased but her identity is being protected.

You will observe that she had five planets in the first house, three of them intercepted in Aries, including its ruler Mars. Libra is intercepted in the seventh house, and its ruler, Venus, is also in the first but not intercepted. These two rulers are conjunct each other but the intercepted position of Mars was more internalized, getting outwardly angry only on rare occasions. With the complexity of the first and seventh houses, she was more willing to please than to create a scene. Her relationship needs were strong, but due to the more negative expression of Pisces/Virgo, she felt she had to make many more concessions than her husband. We must also remember that she was brought up and spent most of her married life under a male-dominated marital philosophy.

She had been attending my classes for about two years, saying very little and nodding occasionally. When I began unraveling my concepts of an Aries/Libra interception, she sat upright, leaned forward and was anxious to share her story with the class. With great delight she verified everything I had been saying.

She was a very talented lady. Many aspects indicate this. She wrote radio scripts for children's broadcasts (Moon in Gemini, in her second house of income, ruling the fifth house of children), had written a book and also painted in oils. Otherwise she was a "dutiful" housewife and mother, to use her own word. For many years she tried to do her creative work at home, which her husband resented. He resented the time she took to do her writing and painting, and she felt guilty when she did it. It made her feel that what she was doing was not worthwhile. She felt insignificant. She tried constantly to find a balance between her own interests and being a good companion to her husband because she did not want to upset their relationship. She never worked outside of their home except for freelancing.

When she was in her mid-fifties, it finally became too much for her to bear. She knew she had to do something to alleviate her frustration. She went down the street and rented a studio. When she went there to work her husband did not resent it, but if she tried to do it at home, he became upset.

She said, "I cannot understand why it took me so long to initiate this action, but now that I have done so, I am much happier. I have greater respect for myself and I believe I am doing much better work." It certainly verified her chart for her.

Rex Harrison, Actor

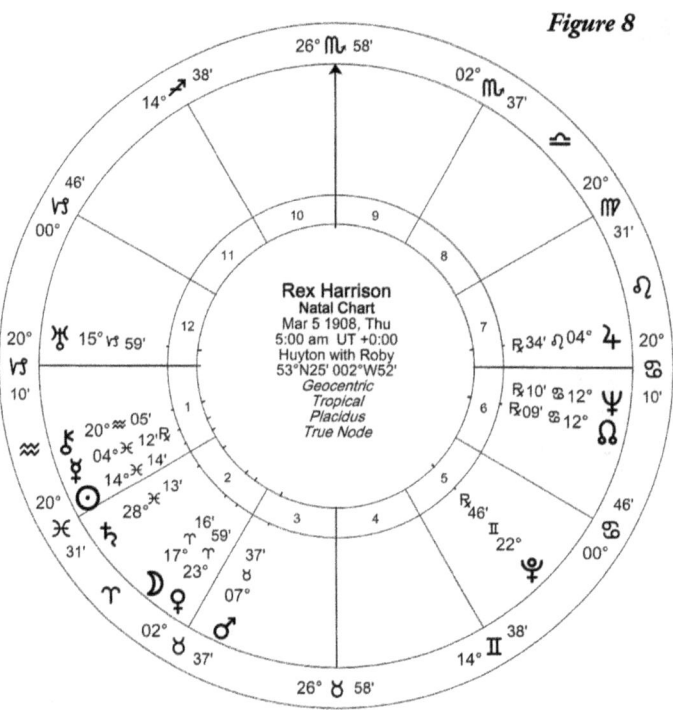

Figure 8

Rex Harrison's (Figure 8) most notable films are *My Fair Lady*, for which he won the Oscar for Best Actor, and *Doctor Doolittle*.

Note the Aries/Libra interception across the second/ninth axis, as well as the Leo/Aquarius interception across the first/seventh axis. His Moon, ruler of the sixth and seventh, is intercepted in Aries, as is Venus, ruling houses three/four and eight. This has high focus impact. By age seventy-one, he had been married six times. The intensity connected with this area apparently prompted him to keep trying to find balance and personal fulfilment in his life. He also has Leo/Aquarius intercepted across seventh and first. Ref: A: ABC

Liza Minnelli, Singer/Actress

Liza Minnelli (Figure 9) is the very talented daughter of Judy Garland. She won an Oscar for Best Actress in the highly acclaimed film *Cabaret*.

With seven cardinal planets she is highly enthusiastic and presents herself with great gusto. However, with three planets in the twelfth, including her Sun in Pisces and Mercury and Venus intercepted in Aries, she seems to spend a great deal of time in recluse away from public attention.

The accent on Aries/Libra across the troublesome twelve/six axis indicates relationship difficulties. She had a troublesome youth and has been married at least twice. She admitted herself to the Betty Ford Clinic for substance abuse. Ref: AA: PW

Figure 9

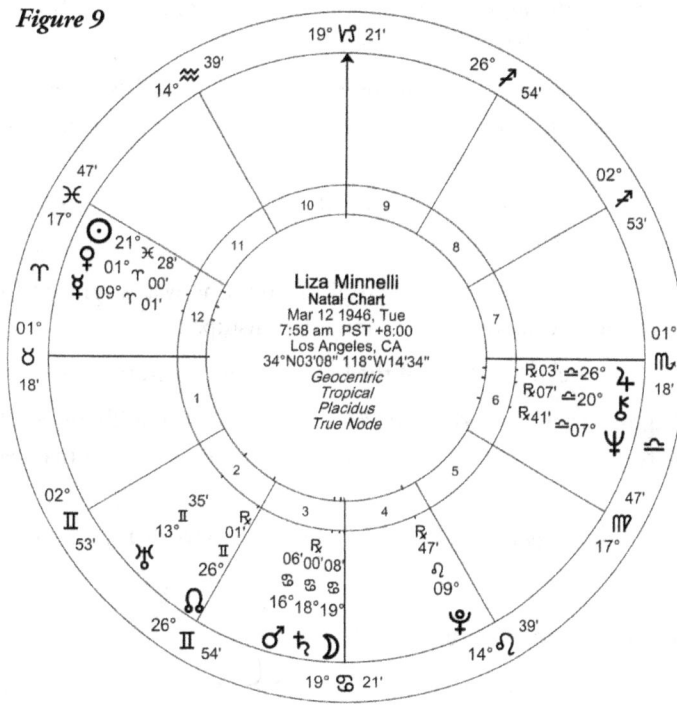

Other Examples

A lady in one of my lectures shared with the other people in the room that she had Aries/Libra intercepted across eleven/five. She was fiercely independent and in her maturing years had never been married. She rather bitterly stated that she had belonged to an organization, had worked on many committees, but never received the credit she felt she deserved. She had given it her all. When she ran for a key executive position and lost to someone she felt was less qualified for the position, she left the organization, never to return.

As previously mentioned, intercepted signs are often manifested through one particular avenue of pursuit while retaining the aforementioned psychological characteristics. Many notable athletes have been listed at the beginning of this chapter.

Enrico Fermi, Physicist: Across twelve/six. Known as the architect of the atomic bomb. This is highly applicable for someone in research solving intricate problems.

Michel Gauquelin, Researcher: Across three/nine. An astrological researcher who compiled massive birth data over many years in his desire to prove or disprove astrology. He experienced great disappointment when the scientific community failed to give him the credit he deserved.

Andrew Cunanan, Serial Killer: Across twelve/six. Serial killer who murdered at least four men, including designer Gianni Versace. Mercury/Jupiter/Uranus are conjunct in intercepted Libra in the sixth.

Carol Burnett, Comedienne: Across one/seven. Mercury and Uranus are both intercepted in Aries indicating intensity of creative expression. She has a genius for mimicry and an acute sense of timing for comedy. The rulers of her intercepted houses are in a trine aspect which helps the flow and may have helped her overcome her unhappy childhood. Both of her parents died of alcoholism. She is a perfectionist with three planets in Virgo in her sixth house. Other than her very successful comedy television series, she lives out of the spotlight.

Understanding Interceptions

John Denver, Singer: Across eleven/five with Neptune intercepted in Libra. Folk singer who had a complex love life, he died in a plane crash on October 12, 1997.

Mia Farrow, Actress: Across twelve/six with Venus intercepted in Aries opposed by Neptune in Libra. An actress, but perhaps more noted for her stormy personal life, including marriages to Frank Sinatra and Woody Allen.

Greta Garbo, Actress: Across twelve/six. An actress who chose a life of recluse and obscurity after she achieved fame. She spent her later years saving animals.

Tonya Harding, Olympic Skater: Across ten/four. An Olympic skater. She was disgraced for trying to win dishonestly. Scandals also include an abusive marital relationship.

Joseph Lyle Mendez, Murderer: Across twelve/six. One of the brothers who killed their parents.

Kim Novak, Actress: Across two/eight. Reached stardom in *Picnic* with superstar William Holden and then retired young to a rustic rural life on a farm with a menagerie of animals. She married her veterinarian.

Nicole Brown Simpson, Victim: Across one/seven. Murdered former wife of O.J. Simpson. Experienced intense personal relationships.

Taurus/Scorpio Intercepted

This is the axis of financial rewards, possessions and the resources we share with others. It is where we develop self-worth and learn to respect the efforts of others. The basic need of Taurus is to consolidate something of value and to turn abilities into tangible rewards. It enables us to be attuned to the practical reality of being an earthling in a three-dimensional environment. This is where we learn to be practical, realistic and steadfast. These qualities help to increase our earning capacity, help us take care of our physical needs and develop a sense of self-worth.

Where we find Scorpio we can expect complexities in our learning pattern. It is where we learn the true essence of cooperation through realizing that we must examine, understand and be willing to transform parts of our own ego to mesh with others so they too have an opportunity to grow. It is a painful process and hard to let go of fixed patterns even though they may prove useless in the pursuit of happiness and fulfillment. Quite often this axis creates a single-minded, selfish, driving attitude bent on serving our own needs. Transformation at the deepest level is often necessary if we are to achieve tangible results.

Taurus and Scorpio are fixed signs, thereby conferring self-will, tenacity and determination to succeed, which is more deeply emphasized when intercepted. The operative phrase being used repeatedly in this text is *intensification due to internalization*. If you have this pair of interceptions you may find it difficult to be satisfied with any amount of money that you earn or accumulate. With each phase of expansion there is always something else to covet. It is never-ending until your ego thrust begins the slow, arduous task of refining itself.

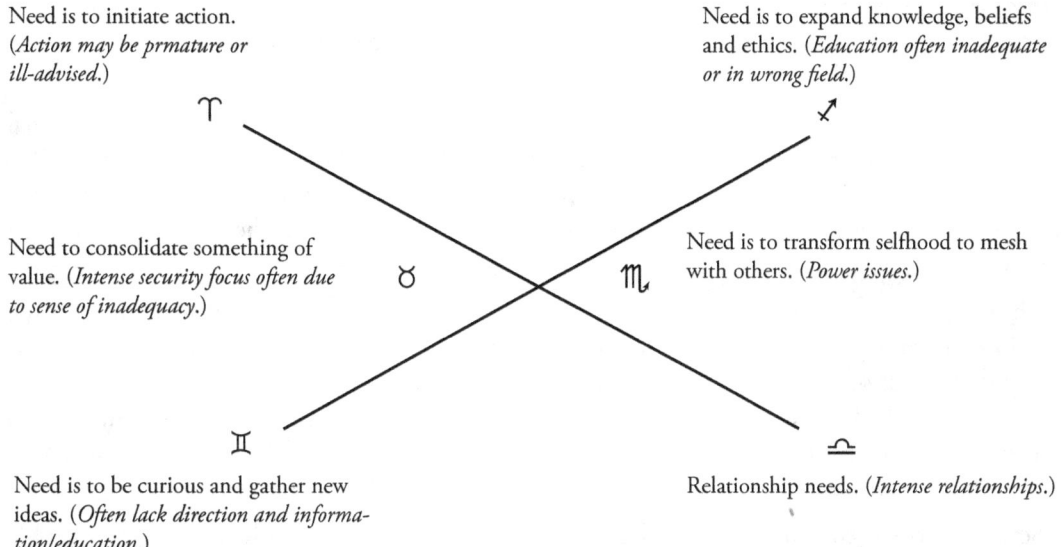

Figure 10. Taurus/Scorpio Intercepted. Basic urge of each sign is indicated. The expressive needs of all six are altered by this one pair of intercepted signs. A key concept of the potential difficulty is in parenthesis. When Taurus is intercepted, Aries is on the cusp of that house and Gemini is at the end. This makes Scorpio intercepted with Libra on the cusp and Sagittarius at the end.

Your desire for security may be so strong that you may be selfish, miserly and possessive in varying degrees depending upon the aspect between Venus and Pluto, as well as other placements in your chart. You may collect or horde and be extremely devastated if theft or personal loss occurs. You may be jealous and manipulative in an effort to gain control over others. You may dislike, be jealous or openly criticize those who attain what they desire.

Money and power are often viewed as being synonymous with each other. This might indicate the power to control other people, either personally or professionally, or to be as high-minded as gaining control and power over your own destiny. I once heard Zig Zigler, a motivational speaker, say, "power is to be assumed, not wielded." A dictator, bully or abuser wields power. When you assume your own power or the essence of your own selfhood, you do so with dignity and confidence without intimidation or conceit.

Aries on the cusp where Taurus is intercepted indicates that you may drive yourself feverishly either along one single path with fixed determination or in several directions at once with no apparent focus except to seek the elusive magic formula for success and fulfillment. Without a sense of direction, insecurity and inadequacy often prevails.

Gemini's function is to exert curiosity, gather knowledge, become informed, communicate with others and utilize the many resources available within the community, which in turn can help to increase earning potential and self-worth. If this energy is siphoned off and used in a feverish attempt to reach the golden ring, you might not tap the knowledge and resources necessary to increase your capacity to successfully achieve what you are striving for.

You might be one of the people who left school before you were fully prepared to meet the challenges of the competitive world. There might have been any number of circumstances propelling you to do so. It might have been due to oppressive conditions or simply an overwhelming desire to get out in the world to prove your worth. The following true story will help to dramatize this.

A client/student of mine had a younger sister, whom we will call Mary (not her real name). Mary left home at age sixteen before she finished school. Her education did not prepare her for any specific job. In order to make ends meet, she worked at two jobs, which indicates the intensity. While doing so, she was so unhappy that she continually talked about suicide. She felt she would always be a failure. She had Taurus/Scorpio intercepted across her twelve/six axis. Do not take this to mean that everyone with this intercepted position will be suicidal. By the time she was twenty-one, Mary was banking $1,000 a month to buy her own house, but she still felt very insecure.

Several years passed and I had completely lost track of both women. When I ran into the older sister in a shopping mall she told me that Mary did not commit suicide after all, but was still not a happy or content person. She had worked more than one job for many years and promotions came slowly. She now had her house, complete with beautiful furniture, fine china, silverware and everything else we call "creature comforts." I asked if Mary had anyone to share her life. She did not. She was afraid that someone else would scratch her furniture, break her china, mess it up or not value it the way she did. It was hers, she had worked hard for it and that was the way it was going to remain.

Libra is on the cusp where Scorpio is intercepted. The basic need of Libra is learning the art of interrelating. We would all be perfect if we lived on a deserted island by ourselves but the real learning begins when someone else reaches our shore. Scorpio indicates a need to transform and regenerate our own ego thrust so that it meshes more successfully with others. This is where we learn to appreciate others and how we each gain benefit from our joint efforts.

Where we have Scorpio we are learning the principle of transformation and regeneration. It is a fixed water sign and no other sign has greater determination or a stronger sense of purpose, particularly when intercepted. Ego development begins at Aries, and reorganizes and regenerates itself where we have Scorpio. Aries and Scorpio are in a quincunx aspect to each other. This often means changing an attitude, letting go of it or killing it off.

When Scorpio is intercepted, relationships are often destructive due to possessiveness. This means they cannot grow and develop, which is one of the functions of Sagittarius at the end of the house. If we are not willing to change, listen to reason and be honest and expansive, a relationship can die a slow and painful death. A Scorpio need that turns inward can become manipulative, and may not easily recognize a need to transform. A natural flow of receptivity may be blocked by selfish, possessive ideas.

Figure 11

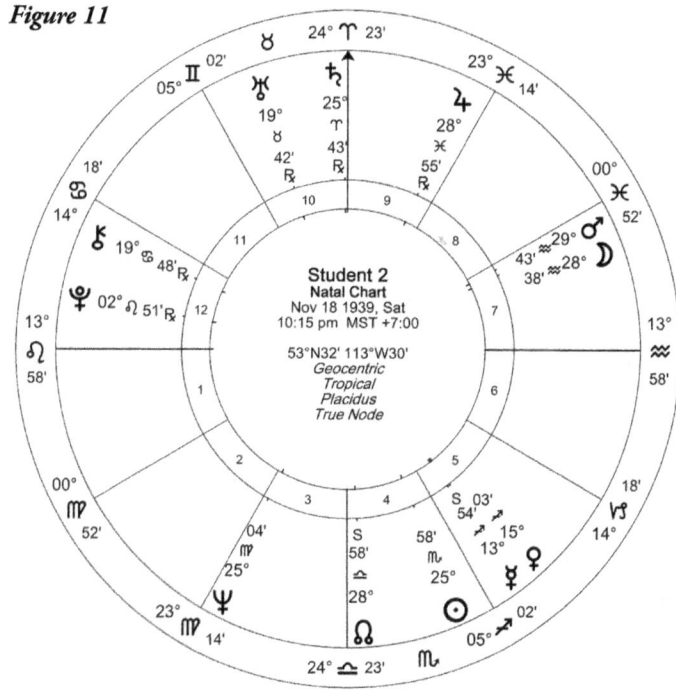

With Scorpio intercepted, power issues are often experienced. Gaining control over someone else or being unwilling to share power and resources in a selfless way impairs Sagittarian growth in understanding the principles of a successful and fruitful existence. Growth in this area is stunted.

In an effort to understand the complexities created by this internalization, I have seen many people develop a deep interest in metaphysics, astrology and self-help processes. They do this with the same intensity that others use to strangle their relationships or work solely for the purpose of personal material gain.

Student 2

I have had several students with this intercepted pair say, "I would love to study something that would help me be financially more successful, which would raise my self-esteem, but I can't figure out what that would be."

Figure 11 is the chart of a student who studied with me when I first began diligently pursuing the concept of interceptions. I shared my concepts with the class and then listened to their stories. Before I begin her story, let me point out a few pertinent points in her chart. You can study the rest later if you so desire. She has the axis of Taurus/Scorpio intercepted across houses ten/four. Uranus is in intercepted Taurus and her Sun and Fortuna are intercepted in Scorpio in the fourth. She has four planets in fire signs plus her Midheaven and Ascendant. This would help to give her the courage to do what she had to do in order to gain her own self-respect but opportunity had to present itself. She was studying astrology to help understand herself better and to find a way to boost her self-image. She felt her life was filled with hard work and little sense of satisfaction.

She was married, stayed home, and reared several children. She did her husband's bookkeeping but had no money of her own. She told the class that whenever he beckoned, she would respond. At the dinner table, if he wanted something, he would ask her to get it for him; she always complied. She cooked, cleaned, did the laundry and looked after the family without any assistance from him.

When Uranus was transiting Scorpio, which is intercepted in her fourth house, her husband lost his job and they did not have any other money. She was desperate. They had hungry mouths to feed and a mortgage to pay. No opportunities were in sight. She decided to do what she did best, which was to look after children. She opened a kindergarten. One day she came to class with a wallet bulging with bills and laid it on the table in front of her for all to see. With head held high (Leo Ascendant), she proudly declared: "Look at this! I earned this money. It is MINE. When he wants some he has to ask. When he asks me to fetch him a glass of water I tell him, go get it yourself. I am tired. I have worked all day."

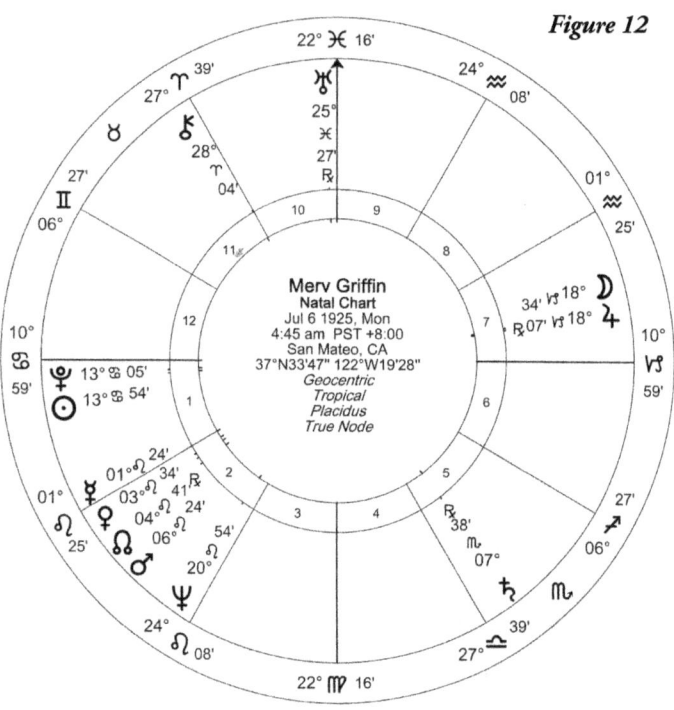

Figure 12

By the time Uranus had conjoined her Sun and squared her Moon, she felt liberated. She felt she had earned her self-respect. She also taught her husband to share the household chores.

When a Mars transit activates an intercepted Taurus, one is often motivated into aggressive action, which may not produce the expected results. If results are not forthcoming, the need becomes internalized once more, and it will take until the next transit comes along to motivate action. Eventually an action produces results and confidence begins to build.

The transit of Uranus often delivers surprising changes in financial status. These may be up or down, depending upon stability of the existing structure in that area. I do not believe the planets cause the problems. If matters are structured well and fulfilling an overall purpose in life, they will likely remain in tact. If not, a transit will time a change.

Saturn stabilizes efforts, particularly in Taurus because of the earth affinity. However, we often feel that Saturn is limiting because it seems to restrict our activities. In retrospect we often realize that the limitation was due to being on the wrong track in the first place.

Jupiter can expand either earnings or debts unless caution is exercised. One of the advantages of Jupiter transiting into an intercepted sign is that it gives you an opportunity to search your

Figure 13

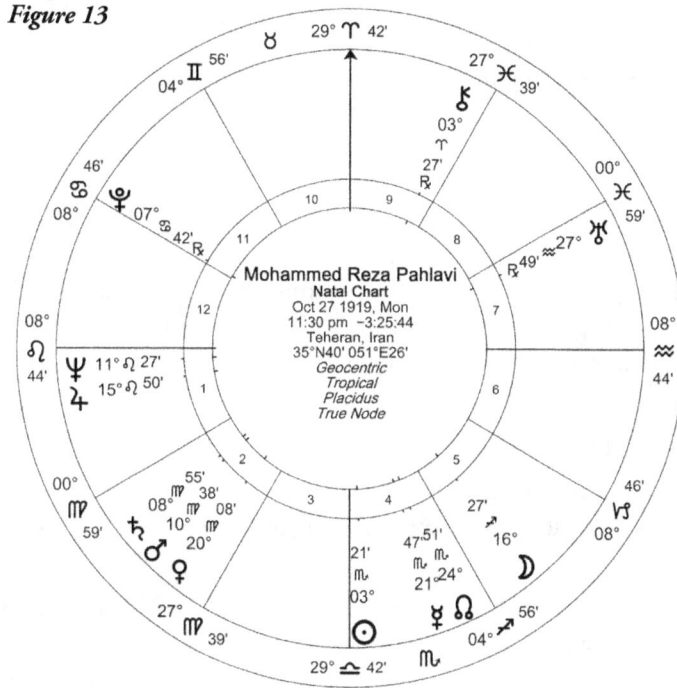

mind for a deeper understanding of life. It is also an opportunity to think deeply about ethics and morals. Your reading material will likely cover a broader range of subjects.

When Pluto was transiting Scorpio from 1983 to 1995, many Scorpios had deep and meaningful revelations with varying degrees of intensity, but few as vivid as those with Scorpio intercepted, particularly when planets were involved. Observe the years when your Scorpio moves into interception by progression. You can gain tremendous insight into your own nature, particularly as an astrology student with an understanding of the symbols.

Merv Griffin, Entrepreneur

Merv Griffin was first noted as a singer and pianist. He had no sense of purpose or direction until he became a talk show host. *The Merv Griffin Show* was highly successful for many years. He also created several highly successful game shows, including *Wheel of Fortune*. He accumulated numerous five-star resort hotels and was considered one of the richest men in the world. He was a sensitive, friendly, communicative, outgoing personality. His basic struggle during the first half of his life was to find a sense of self-worth. Once this was attained he enjoyed "playing" with money, manipulating deals and remaining active in the world of finance. At age seventy-four he said he had no intention of retiring because he is having too much fun; he died in 2007. Ref: *Larry King Live* television interview show; AA: ABC

Mohammed Reza Pahlavi, Shah of Iran

The thirty-seven year reign of The Shah of Iran came to an end by his exile on January 16, 1979 when he escaped from his country by flying to Paris. From then until his death he was a man without a country. This was preceded by months of violent demonstrations against his regime. The shah had lived in extreme luxury in the midst of abject poverty. His need for such riches would appear to stem from the intensification of his interception.

At the time of his exile, transiting Uranus was conjunct his natal Mercury intercepted in Scorpio. When transiting Uranus returned from its retrograde position once to more conjunct Mercury, the new Muslim religious leader, Ayatollah Khomeini, demanded the shah's return for trial but he never complied. Ref: F&WE; DD: Speculative

Other Examples

As previously mentioned, many people with the Taurus/Scorpio axis intercepted accumulate great riches. Part of this is the intensity to earn huge sums, and the other part is the tremendous determination and dedication to succeed. We could call it a "hot button" in the personality thrust. I believe this is a strong indication that interceptions are not an impairment, but they can be an asset by allowing a deeper than normal internal focus for some significant purpose. A few of these people are listed as follows:

Merv Griffin, Talk Show Host: See Figure 12

Bill Gates, Entrepreneur: Across eleven/five with the Sun, Venus, Saturn in Scorpio. He made his fortune through Microsoft. He lives in a palatial residence befitting his enormous wealth. He is also reported to have given billions of dollars to charity.

Ted Turner, Media Owner: Across six/twelve with Uranus in Taurus and Sun and Venus in Scorpio. He has often been called a broadcasting genius. He seems to have the Midas touch.

Ross Perot, Entrepreneur: Across eleven/five with Mars in Taurus. He used his wealth to pay for his campaign in the run for the United States presidency on an Independent ticket. His television advertising alone was enormously expensive, often running up to a half hour.

Bill Cosby, Comedian: Across twelve/six with Uranus in Taurus in a grand earth trine. His success came after he went back to university as an adult to obtain a Ph.D. in literature. At one point in his career he was the highest paid television star in the history of the medium.

Barbara Walters, Talk Show Host: Across eight/two. She was an obscure behind-the-scenes office worker for the first half of her career, gradually working her way up. In 1976, in her mid-forties she signed a three-year contract for $5 million, making her the highest paid broadcaster on television.

Nancy Reagan, First Lady: Across one/seven. One could say she married well. She spent lavishly on White House decorations and entertaining guests, and was reported to have been a loving caregiver to her ailing husband, who was afflicted with Alzheimer's disease.

Phyllis Diller, Comedienne: Across twelve/six. The first half of her life was spent as a housewife, but she had a deep longing to succeed beyond suburbia. At nearly forty, she became an almost overnight success as a comedienne.

Stephen Spielberg, Director: Across eleven/five.

Prince Andrew, Royal Family: Across ten/four.

Sir Arthur Conan Doyle, Writer: Across twelve/six.

Leonard Nimoy, Actor: Across twelve/six. Played Dr. Spock on *Star Trek*.

Norman Schwarzkopf, Military General: Across ten/four.

Ed Sullivan, Entertainer: Across: nine/three.

Eric Mendez, Murderer: Across nine/three.

Lee Harvey Oswald, Murderer: Across eleven/five.

Gemini/Sagittarius Intercepted

Gemini is a mutable air sign associated with the need to exercise curiosity so we can experience new adventures and develop mental perspective. A little child opens cupboards and drawers to find out what is inside and will climb a fence to run down the block to find someone to play with or cross the street to see what is over there. As the child grows, this curiosity is stimulated into a reading and study program at school that allows the student to gather a lot of information on a variety of subjects. As we grow further, we discover that there is also much information to be gained through communicating with people we associate with, where we work, where we do our personal business and in our neighborhood. We have newspapers delivered to our door, we listen to radio, watch television and may even visit our neighborhood library or cruise the Internet. By gaining knowledge and experience, more opportunities open up for us in our environment, thereby giving us more conscious choices in everything we do.

We can apply these curiosity needs in the house Gemini occupies in our own charts. If it is on the tenth cusp, we may pursue a Gemini-type career and read literature as well as periodicals connected with our business. If it is on the third cusp, we may be inclined to enjoy communicating across the garden fence or reading a great variety of subjects. If it is on the eleventh cusp we will likely have a great variety of friends that we enjoy communicating with and exchanging ideas.

If you have Gemini intercepted you have an abundance of thoughts and ideas that constantly tumble around in your head. However, you are often hesitant to say what you think for fear someone will think you are stupid, frivolous or shallow, which is far from the truth. You have a great inner desire to appear erudite, informed, intelligent and do not wish to risk appearing otherwise. This lack of security stems from the two signs on either side of the interception. One is Taurus which is afraid to upset the status quo or job security, and the other is Cancer which is struggling with varying degrees of emotional insecurity. You may have grown up in a household where children were to be seen and not heard, or where the parents were either of immigrant status struggling with the language or lacked education themselves. You will likely blush in school when asked to give an answer to a question or read an essay assignment. You may have been teased for one reason or another either because you had buck teeth, were too tall, lisped or your parents did not speak the language well or dressed differently. There can be other reasons, of course.

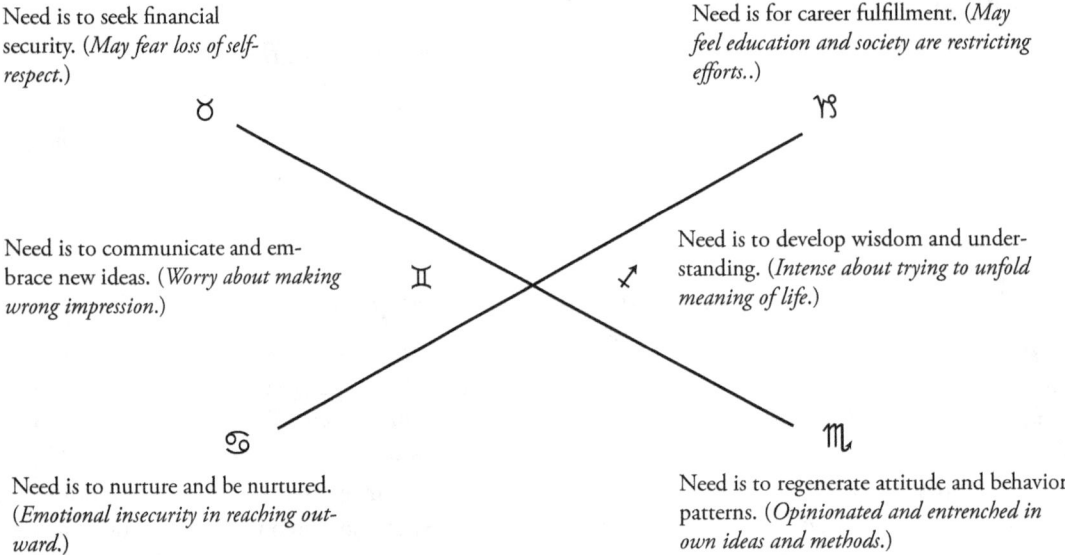

Figure 14. Gemini/Sagittarius Intercepted. Basic urge of each sign is indicated. The expressive needs of all six are altered by this one pair of intercepted signs. A key concept of the potential difficulty is in parenthesis. When Gemini is intercepted, Taurus is on the cusp of that house and Cancer is at the end. This makes Sagittariuis intercepted with Scorpio on the cusp and Capricorn at the end.

Up until around age forty, you may hesitate to say what you think, to express your feelings, submit your ideas or offer suggestions for fear of being ridiculed, ostracized or unappreciated but you will do so spasmodically as transits move in and out. One girl in my class said: "I say very little because no one listens to me anyway. Perhaps I don't know how to express myself properly. I may just as well keep my mouth shut, but boy, is my mind ever busy with what I would like to say. One day, when I get smarter, maybe they will all sit up and take notice of me."

With Cancer at the end of that house, you may find it exceptionally difficult to talk about yourself or how you feel.

It must not be construed that you are stupid or ignorant. An intercepted Gemini/Sagittarius has little, if anything, to do with intelligence. In fact, many of these people are brilliant writers, authors or teachers. A writer can "speak" on paper mull it over carefully, think about it and then make a decision about its quality. It also helps to get paid for the effort, which would give satisfaction through the Taurus sign leading into the interception. Such is not the case with the spoken word when expressing an opinion or an idea. A teacher plays a different role. A teacher gets paid for speaking to students on an informed subject that the students know little about which increases the teacher's confidence. This does not mean that all teachers lack confidence outside the classroom, but many with Gemini intercepted often do.

To move to the other end of the axis, Sagittarius is our need to freely experience what life has to offer. Without this capacity we limit our horizons. It is where we learn to conceptualize, to expand our intellect and our understanding of the world around us; whereas, Gemini is symbolic of what we learn from our immediate surroundings. Our early experiences and training from our parents or guardians provides us with a religious background and/or ethnic cultural understanding. Our understanding in this regard enlarges and expands as we mature and gain further knowledge and experience through our own perception.

If you have Sagittarius intercepted, you will likely undertake an intense search for your own philosophy of life, belief system or understanding of existence but will likely take great care to keep it secret. Sagittarius is bound in by the secretive nature of Scorpio and the structure of Capricorn. You keep it inside, at least for many years because these answers seem elusive and may take you down many paths until eventually it all comes together. The fear of embracing an idea prematurely exists.

You may be constantly seeking additional courses to upgrade your requisites and gain more respect from your peers. But you never seem satisfied that you have enough education and enough respect.

Scorpio, the sign through which we learn to understand the merits of other people, is on the cusp. Rather than assisting the Sagittarius needs, which happens more readily without an interception, the Scorpio intensity along with the Taurus need to be respected, creates a powerful internal driving force to be informed. With Capricorn at the end of the house you may feel you will never be successful in your career. You may also worry about your reputation. You may blame your family heritage or background, a lack of education, or simply being in the wrong place at the wrong time with little opportunity. Take heart, dear soul, because your time will come when your inner preparation is complete. Interceptions can manifest productively with a little maturity as long as you understand the needs of the signs.

With this interception, you may appear nervous or unsure of yourself and have a nervous laugh rather than having the confidence of a full fledged, heart-felt laugh. Perhaps you hold back in case you are the only one laughing. You may be one of those people who laugh with little sound. You may embarrass easily, particularly if you talk about anything personal. You are never sure if someone is joking or actually poking fun at you.

You have an insatiable appetite for information and knowledge, often studying unusual subjects, religions or philosophies that you keep secret from your business associates or everyone else except your closest friend. You are afraid of being ridiculed. Quite a few astrology students who have this feel it is better not to tell anyone they are even interested in astrology. They do not wish to defend their interest and are also afraid it will affect their reputation or even endanger their job. I had one student recently who said, "I study both astrology and Buddhism, neither of which I share with my business associates. I truly am afraid I will either be ridiculed, lose their respect, or worse still, lose my job. The only ones who know are my closest friends, my husband and my hairdresser who wants me to do his chart."

This student is a physiotherapist for a large corporation. She outlines and conducts programs that help to keep the workers physically fit. She also examines working schedules, routines and structures, and makes recommendations to management on ways to reduce accidents and improve job performance. She explained to the class that she had worked long and hard to gain the respect of top management, has made many sacrifices, and will not do anything to jeopardize this respect. She minds her own business at work, avoids office gossip and coffee clutches. Some of her coworkers may think she is aloof or introverted but keeping to herself does reduce her level of worry.

When intercepted Gemini is stimulated by the transit of Mars, you will surely decide it is time to speak out, say what you think, get involved, spout your knowledge or ideas and try to simulate into the group. Associates are surprised. You become embarrassed. When Mars leaves the sign, you examine the results of your effort and determine your degree of success or failure, which may often leave you feeling embarrassed that you acted out of character. After several of these transits, you begin to smooth out the rough edges of your ability to be an astute communicator. It will always take due thought and attention internally but confidence is developed gradually in developing the art of successful communication.

Many years ago I had a young student in her early twenties who had this interception. For several semesters she sat at the front of the room and said very little. On occasion when she did, her face would flush and she would feel uncomfortable. When I praised her for her astute observation she would blush even more and look around to see the reaction from the rest of the group. There were more than twenty students in the room.

One day we were talking about intercepted signs. When we came to Gemini, she listened intently, began leaning forward, and obviously wanted to say something. When I prompted her, this is what she said, "I know my face is turning red, but I am going to speak out anyway. You have just described me perfectly. I know I am smart but it seems like no one listens to me. They often butt in, over-ride my conversation or don't respond to what am saying. I get furious with myself when I speak out and furious with myself when I don't."

I looked at her chart. The transit of Mars was going through her third house Gemini interception. Once she had "broken the ice" with this particular group she continued sharing her insights with us even after Mars had moved on. She still had the challenge of working out her confidence with all the other people with whom she associated.

As for the other transits, the Sun and Mercury can be very helpful. The Sun puts the spotlight on you for a month. At times you will be pleased with what you say and at other times you may be embarrassed, but at least others see you in a more favorable light. Mercury helps you to objectify what you are trying to achieve.

Jupiter can help stimulate reading and understanding. You may seek to broaden your horizons, but more so when it goes through an intercepted Sagittarius. Saturn allows for depth of study and thought as long as you don't get discouraged or lose patience with yourself. I encourage you to undertake a serious pursuit and be content with gradual unfoldment. I remind you not to be critical of yourself. There is a tendency to put yourself down which is self-defeating. Uranus, of course, can stimulate unusual adventures that provide fodder for interesting storytelling as you recount these unusual experiences. It gives you confidence when others laugh with you and not at you. It is important to embrace the unusual but avoid being reckless. This can be a good transit for this interception but observe carefully the contact it may make with other planets in your chart to determine times of potential difficulty or danger. Other transits can be applied according to their nature.

When Sagittarius is energized you will get the urge to expand your knowledge and experience in some way. You may get the urge to travel, read exciting adventure novels, undertake a new study or even question your beliefs. Often ethical issues come to the fore. Saturn may stimulate an urge to study a subject that advances your career. You may teach, write or publish something you have kept hidden away in a box at the top of your closet. The transit of Mars can be an active period, but you must be somewhat cautious of the transit of Uranus. It is a creative force that can unleash bonds, but be careful you do not blast elements out of your life that you will later regret.

As I write this, Pluto is transiting early Sagittarius and I have not yet observed enough through my clients and students to find a strong enough theme to pass on to you. The complexity and diversity of dramatic changes that I have been witnessing are mostly occurring when planets are involved. It appears, from only a sign point of view, that fundamental changes are occurring at the deepest level of the way life is viewed. I have a couple of clients who have become disenchanted with their previously strong religious beliefs, but ingrained habits are not overthrown quickly or easily. It remains to be seen how drastic the change will become. One of these clients married into a very different culture and is attempting to absorb it so she can understand her husband better. Also, she is pregnant and will have to face the fact that her children will be brought up in a different culture as well as a different religion than her own, unless she changes. She is struggling with all of this in a very deep part of her consciousness. She must also deal with her own father who is staunch in his religion and critical of her action.

We will now look at some charts.

Bill

Figure 15 is the chart of a student's husband whom I will call Bill. As I recall, he was in his late twenties when I knew him. He was married, had a young family and a mortgage on a new home that he was very proud of. He did not want his wife to work because he needed to prove that he could take care of his family, all by himself.

Gemini/Sagittarius are intercepted across his twelfth and sixth houses respectively. He said, "One day I would like to set up my own business because I have a lot of great ideas but I don't have the confidence nor am I ready yet to gamble with my income."

In the meantime, he had a good job and was reasonably pleased with his accomplishments to date. However, he had one haunting concern that he knew he had to hurdle. He said he had a lot of great ideas he would like to share with his company, but he was afraid to say anything for fear his boss would think he was stupid or impractical. A few months later someone else would come up with the same idea, get praised or even get a promotion, and Bill would be angry at himself for not having the courage to speak out or the confidence of his own creative business ability.

He was proud of his house, the furniture, even the green grass in the front fringed by pretty flowers decorating the walkway, but he had a genuine fear of losing it. He felt this attitude was probably

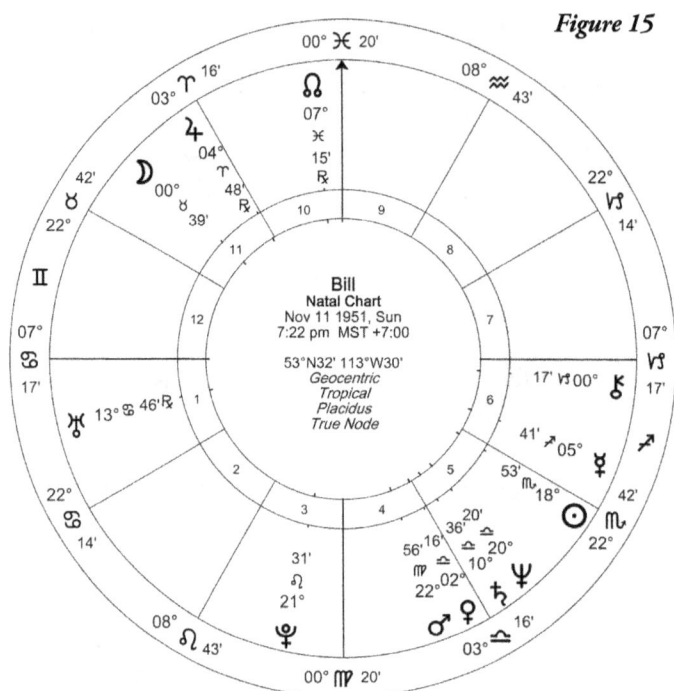

Figure 15

slowing down his own progress but was more comfortable biding his time and learning to be more confident than moving ahead too quickly. I not feel he was slowing down his progress. He had some internal work to do first. This twelfth house fear would eventually become the treasure chest of experience that he could draw from.

Woody Allen, Actor, Director, Scriptwriter, Playwright

In true Gemini/Sagittarius intercepted style he shows a strong inner need to say something, whether it is absurd and nonsensical or meaningful and clever. He expresses himself through his written word, then performs and directs many of his own films and plays. He began his career writing jokes for others, then started appearing in nightclubs with his own material. Biography.com said he established a persona and style that appeared in most of his work of a "flustered neurotic, obsessed with sex and death." Nevertheless, he won three Oscars with *Annie Hall* which he also wrote, directed and starred. It is said he is as neurotic in real life as the characters he scripts and performs. His personal relationship with Mia Farrow ended due in part to a bitter battle in which he acknowledged a relationship with one of her young adopted daughters. Ref: AA: DN#37

Agatha Christie, Mystery Writer

Agatha Christie (see chart on the following page) had more than seventy detective novels pub-

Figure 16

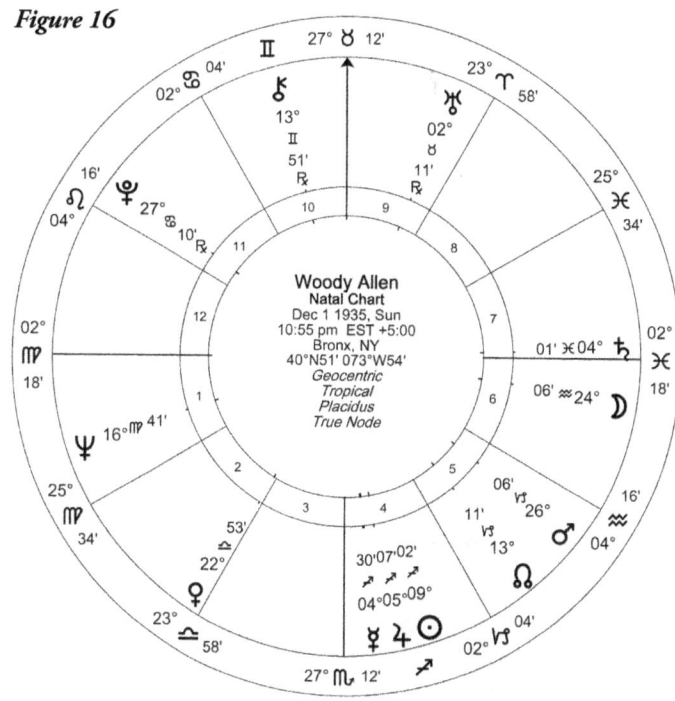

lished and translated into several languages; some became motion pictures and many were made into television dramas. You may be familiar with the motion picture adaptations of *Murder on the Orient Express* and *Death on the Nile*.

She immortalized two main fictional characters, namely, the natty, fastidious, Belgium detective, Hercule Poirot, and the English country lady, Miss Marpole, both of whom do more listening and observing than talking, which undoubtedly was a characteristic admired by the author herself. Poirot often used the phrase "the little grey cells, they are working," which is so characteristic of the author's Gemini/Sagittarius interception. In *Profiles of Women*, Lois Rodden said, "she germinated her ideas slowly."

The process of internalization due to interception can create frustration in certain areas of expression but I keep pointing out that it can also be very useful. It can help to develop a focalization that can lead to accomplishment. The Gemini/Sagittarius pair allows for deep contemplation. It must be stated over and over again that a whole chart must be considered because strong characteristics are indicated through more than one position or aspect.

Other Examples

The following list of people have a variety of vocations, but the number of writers with this pair of interceptions is remarkably high. Musicians are included because they communicate through their music. Gemini is also the sign of the inventor so take note of the number of people who have made remarkable inventions, and changed the opinion of the public in some way. My list of these versatile people is so long that it was difficult to chose how many and who to include.

Alex Haley, Journalist, Writer: Across eleven/five. Collaborated on *The Autobiography of Malcolm X*. He is best known for *Roots*, the story of an American family based on his own African-American heritage, for which he won a Pulitzer Prize. He spent 12 years doing the research. The book was scripted into a very successful television mini-series.

James Hilton, Novelist: Across eleven/five with Neptune/Pluto in Gemini, as well as Jupiter/Uranus/Saturn in Sagittarius. Many of his novels were made into motion pictures, the most notable being *Lost Horizon*, *Goodbye Mr. Chips* and *Random Harvest*.

Friedrich Nietzsche, Philosopher, Author, Critic: Across seven/one. He highly influenced existentialism as well as Nazism. His notable works included *The Birth of Tragedy* and *Thus Spake Zarathustra*. He suffered a nervous breakdown and died shortly thereafter.

Lord Byron, Romantic Poet: Across twelve/six. His early life was tragic and he had a club foot.

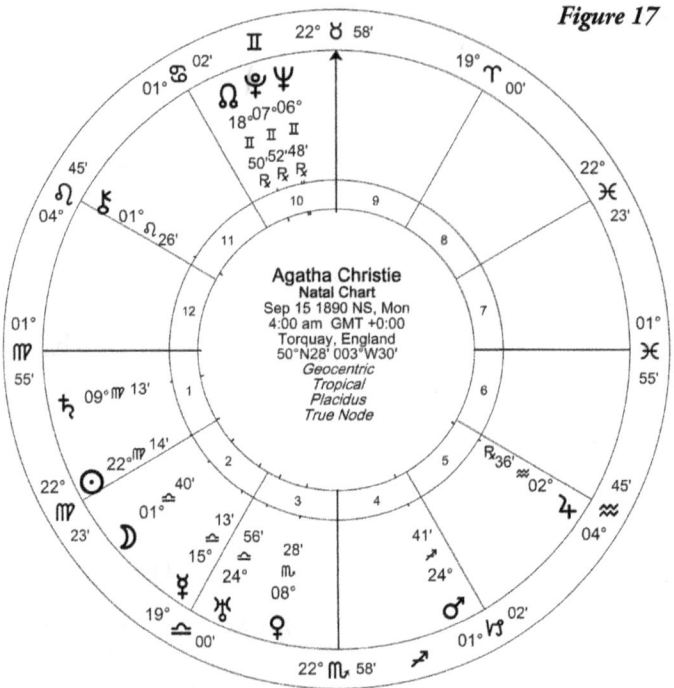

Figure 17

Nevertheless, he became "the darling of London society," and traveled extensively throughout Europe.

Jacques Cousteau, Oceanographer, Inventor, Writer and Filmmaker: Across nine/three with the rulers trine each other. He invented the aqualung for diving, and underwater television. He founded the Underwater Research Group and was commander of the research ship Calypso. His films will amaze and educate for years to come.

Antoine de Saint-Exupery, Pilot (commercial and wartime), Author and Air Pioneer: Across ten/four, with five planets intercepted. Opened commercial flight routes.

Louis de Broglie, Pioneer Physicist, Author: Across twelve/six. He was awarded the Nobel Prize for his work on the wave nature of the electron which is called "de Broglie waves."

Honore Daumier, Painter, Lithographer and Caricaturist: Across eleven/five. He satirized government corruption which was an unpopular concept in the nineteenth century.

Leonard Bernstein, Conductor and Composer: Across ten/four. As well as a brilliant career as a conductor, he composed three symphonies, three ballets, two operas, the Broadway musical *Fancy Free*, as well as the highly claimed *West Side Story*. He was active musically until his death in 1990.

Mick Jagger, Musician: Across eleven/five. Formed the famous Rolling Stones rock group. He presented an unconventional image both on and off the stage that was appealing to the rebellious youth of the 1960s. Decades later, the group is still touring and producing music.

Keith Emerson, Musician: Across eleven/five. He played many instruments including two guitars at once.

Virgil Grissom, Astronaut: Across nine/three. One of the seven original American astronauts.

Guy Ballard, Cult Founder: Across seven/one.

Prince Charles, Royalty: Across eleven/five. Appears to be late in fulfilling his destiny as the future king of England. His first wife, the late Princess Diana, accused him of being uncommunicative and distant.

Copernicus, Astronomer: Across ten/four. He is considered the father of modern astronomy. He challenged a great body of learning when he purported that the Earth rotated about its axis daily and around the Sun yearly. He literally revolutionized the Western world of thought which became known as the Copernican Revolution.

Galileo, Astronomer, Mathematician, Writer: Across eleven/five. His public support of the Copernican theory brought him a prison sentence which was commuted by the Pope. In 1993 his scientific work was formally recognized by the Roman Catholic Church. He is considered a genius inventor and mathematician. He spent his later life writing.

John Dillinger, Bank Robber: Across eleven/five. The FBI declared him Public Enemy #1. He was killed by in a shootout. He lived fast and died young at age 32.

Hugo Black, Senator and Supreme Court Justice: Across seven/one. One of the most distinguished jurors in American history. He was noted for sticking to the letter of the Constitution, especially those rights written in the First Amendment.

Cancer/Capricorn Intercepted

Cancer is a cardinal water sign associated with our need for security, protection and a safe place to be. As children growing up we need to be nurtured, loved and protected so that we can carry that sense of security into the adult world. As an adult we also need to be nurtured by someone with whom we feel safe. In your grown up years, have you ever stood in the middle of the floor with your arms wrapped around your lover and found that the two of you began rocking to and fro? If you have never done so, you may wish to try it. The feeling that accompanies it is one of emotional security and contentment, even if only for that brief moment. It stirs up unconscious memories of having been rocked as a child. So as we were nurtured, we have an adult need to nurture others. It may be our partner, our children, our friends, the people we work with and even our pets. Gardening is also a form of nurturing or caring.

You need to have a safe place that gives you comfort. Perhaps it is your domestic haven or one particular room or chair, it may be your desk at the office or corner work place, it may be at the

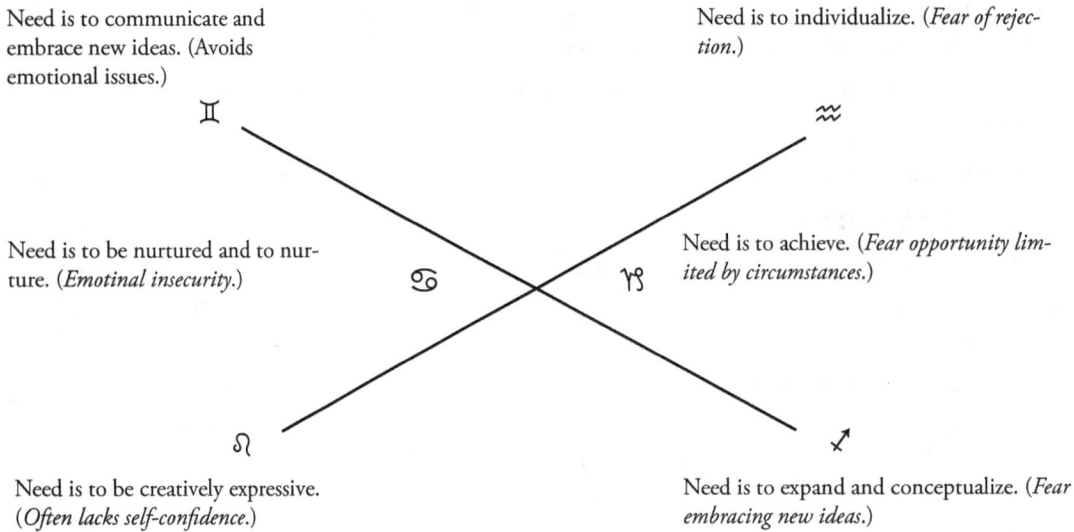

Figure 18. Cancer/Capricorn Intercepted. Basic urge of each sign is indicated. The expressive needs of all six are altered by this one pair of intercepted signs. A key concept of the potential difficulty is in parenthesis. When Cancer is intercepted, Gemini is on the cusp of tluu house and Leo is at the end. This makes Capricorn intercepted with Sagittarius on the cusp and Aquarius at the end.

local bar. A metaphysical safe place may be deep inside in an area of your psyche that you are unable and unwilling to share with others except on very rare occasions when you allow yourself to be vulnerable. It is a tender area where you can feel pain, sorrow and even happiness. That is where you really need security so that you can go out into the world more comfortably each and every day to meet the challenges of the outside world and your career, which is where you experience and develop your Capricorn urges.

Capricorn is an extension of Cancer. It is a cardinal earth sign associated with our need to achieve, to be recognized, to contribute and be part of a larger social flow. In a way, we take our Cancer shell of protection with us because Capricorn is where we stake our outer territory in as small or large a zone as we feel comfortable operating in. You may be highly ambitious or just content to carefully guard whatever you have at the moment.

The amount of security we feel where either of these two signs are posited depends on whether or not they are on the cusp of a particular house(s) or intercepted, if there are planets in those signs, and the condition of their rulers to each other as well as to other planets. The planets are the access to our basic needs and what we need to be aware of in order to be fulfilled.

If Cancer is intercepted, the need for emotional security is intense. It may have been missing in childhood and sought in a private corner of the house, or the neighborhood, or even in the far re-

Figure 19

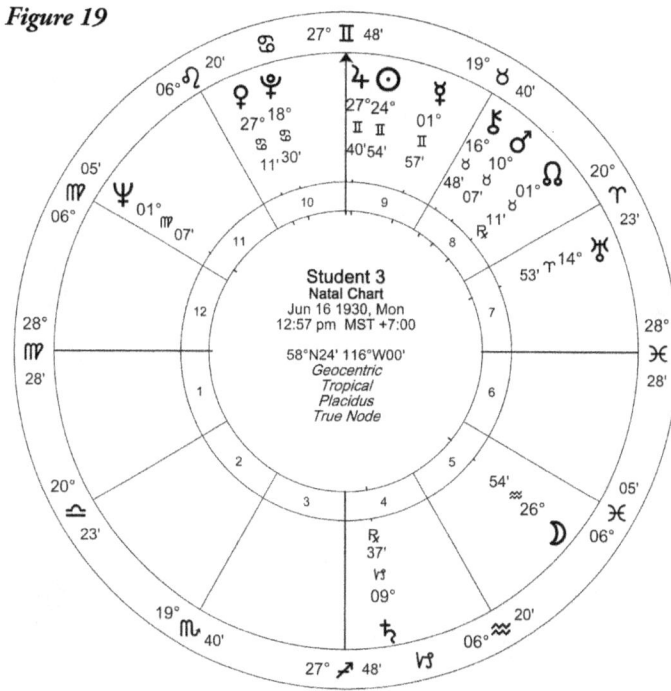

cess of your mind, longing for the day when you could feel secure, loved, nurtured and appreciated. You may grow up unable to trust anyone. There may be issues with mother, or a female guardian. You may have been brought up in a large family where chores were more important than being cuddled on mom's or dad's knee, making you feel like a servant or even a commodity. You may have had to share your room with other siblings who were always prying into your possessions depriving you of privacy. You may have come from a broken home or a foster home and may continue to feel like you do not have any roots or connection to anyone meaningful. In more extreme cases of emotional fear and mistrust, there may have been abuse and/or neglect. There are many potential scenarios. Each one is slightly different but the results are similar.

Student 3

Figure 19 is a chart labeled Student 3. She was in her mid-fifties when she decided to study astrology but had previously studied many different metaphysical and healing subjects including gemstones, herbology, psych ism, etc. She was a delightful, eager student of mine for about four years. When we came to the semester dealing with interceptions and the Cancer/Capricorn pair, she was eager to share her story with the rest of the class.

She was born out of wedlock at a time when there was a stigma against both the person born out of wedlock and the mother. She was bounced from foster home to foster home, ridiculed by classmates, did poorly in school and dropped out as soon as she could get away. For years she wandered from one menial job to another, sometimes living on welfare. She was lonely, depressed and felt like she did not belong anywhere or with anyone.

After years of loathing and self-pity she decided that if anything was going to change she would have to do it herself so she undertook the responsibility of restructuring her life. She went back to grade school and eventually attained admission into a technical school where she learned how to repair sewing machines and other small appliances. She established her own small business and bought a modest home.

She hosted many open house parties for friends who had various metaphysical interests. I was proud to be invited. She had collected a group of interesting people and hoped that through her others would connect. She was very proud of how she had changed her life and finally found a place for herself in the world. She was so grateful that astrology had given her a focus of understanding and that she could see it in her chart. I remember her saying, "It is a great comfort knowing that I did everything right after all." My eyes still moist over when I think of her.

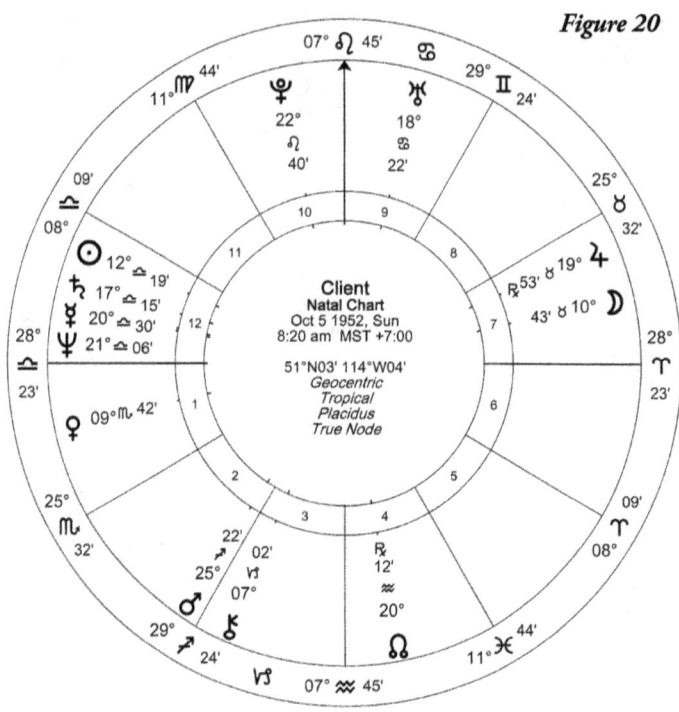

Figure 20

Cancer intercepted makes it difficult to trust anyone because you feel vulnerable to hurt and betrayal, so you keep your feelings locked inside until you have sorted them out and realize that you must find an inner security level inside of yourself before your feelings can be released. Even without being intercepted, at the slightest provocation, the crab pulls into its shell. This security may come well after your Saturn Return when you realize not everyone is out to hurt you. However, it is difficult to make a commitment unless you have known someone for a very long time. In the meantime, that person may get impatient and move on, which reinforces your sense of insecurity.

You may have been brought up by a demanding mother. I was doing a one-day workshop on interceptions with our own astrological group and we were sharing experiences. I mentioned that some people with this interception may not be able to stand up to mom until well into their adult years. One girl started chuckling so I knew she had this set of interceptions. I asked how old she was when she was able to stand up to mom. Continuing to grin, she confessed, "Oh, about 31." That was the beginning of the maturation process and it would still take time for her to be able to stand up to her mother with comfort and confidence without undue guilt.

Where Cancer is intercepted, Gemini is on the cusp. Gemini is the need to communicate and be involved with interesting activities, but insecurity makes it difficult to talk about the personal side of your life or how you feel. As soon as the conversation switches to you or your inner feelings, you switch it to someone else, change the subject or begin chattering about frivolous matters. One young girl in one of my classes, who was in her late twenties said: "I know what you are saying. I really am much more sensitive and caring than people think I am. They don't seem to take me seriously but it's probably my own fault. I guess I am a little flippant at times."

This internal intensity of seeking inner personal contentment can then make it difficult to develop a sense of security in your creative self-expression which is Leo occupying the end of the house. This is where you develop self-confidence, which takes longer to develop when you are emotionally insecure. There is an internal fear of being put down, not being accepted, or even being ridiculed. This also makes it more difficult to develop a loving relationship. Rejection is painful. The crab pulls its vulnerable parts in.

Moving to the other side of the interception we have Capricorn. This is where we have a need to go beyond ourselves into the larger social sphere and make a contribution, or achieve status and recognition for ourselves. When intercepted, you may limit your goals because you are insecure in your individuality and creativity. Your territorial boundaries may be small until other facets of your development occur. For instance, you may feel that your education is insufficient to meet your goals or to give you equal opportunity with others, so you may need to reinforce it by taking additional courses or seeking a degree. Even then, you will probably never feel that you have enough education to be competitive. You may gravitate to self-help books and classes on personal development.

Client

I had a client with this across his ninth and third houses. His chart is presented in Figure 20. He was exceedingly ambitious, worked very hard and definitely felt a lack of education. He spoke well, dressed well, and appeared to be successful as a sales executive with a residential development organization. He did not want his wife to work because he measured his success with his ability to provide well for his family. He felt his father had never had a chance to be successful so he set him up with some "business deals." I was later to learn that his father was a front person or name for some of his own personal under-the-table deals. When they lost money or he fell into debt my client never told his wife because he did not want to worry her. This can be seen with Libra on his twelfth and first. Duplicated houses will be dealt with in Chapter Four.

One day I received a call from him asking if he could come over for an immediate consultation. He was on the brink of tears. I knew something terrible had happened. Within the previous hour he had been fired from his job for a questionable business deal, which also involved his father. He needed to talk to someone and was not ready to go home. The transit of Saturn was in Pisces forming an exact quincunx to his Natal Sun, and would go on to trigger his Saturn, Mercury and Neptune. Transiting Uranus and Neptune were traveling together in Capricorn (1994) in his intercepted third house exactly conjunct his Progressed Mars and exactly quincunx his Pluto/South

Node in the tenth. This is a good example of transits going into an intercepted house and activating it in an overt way.

A court battle followed and he lost everything. I had given him plenty of warning about the upcoming aspects and what they could mean but his intense need to be successful overwhelmed his common sense and good judgment.

I have heard a number of clients and students with this pair of interceptions say that they feel their family background or family heritage is a drawback in their rise to success. You may be embarrassed by the way your parents dress or speak. They make speak with a foreign accent or lack education to speak the language well. As much as we do not like to admit it, some communities have negative attitudes against certain cultures. Sometimes it is not the community fostering the problem, but an embarrassment stimulated from your own parents who feel they do not fit in.

I had a woman in one of my classes who shared the way she was experiencing her Cancer/Capricorn interception. She was tied to her family business, which was a chain of restaurants owned and operated by aunts, uncles, cousins and other assorted relatives (Cancer). They were all involved. She didn't feel she had any choice but to remain loyal to the family, but in essence this actually gave her much needed security. She had taken several other courses (Gemini) before she came into astrology. She wanted to understand life more broadly (Sagittarius). Her entire identity seemed wrapped up in the whole family group and she longed for the freedom to find her own individuality, (Leo/Aquarius). She said, "There is so much I would like to try. I would like to explore more of my own creativity but I am afraid they will laugh at me and I will lose face. They will all talk about me behind my back."

When she checked their charts, she was amazed at the number of her family group who had Cancer/Capricorn intercepted. Many of them also felt trapped and buried in the group identity.

When you gradually begin to feel emotionally less vulnerable, you will be more creative and allow your own individuality to emerge which is Leo/Aquarius at the end of each house. Everyone of us has a very special, unique, creative gift to give the world that cannot be given by anyone else. How wonderful to be able to experience and release it!

These people have often said to me that they do not understand why everyone else gets promotions and they do not, yet they feel they work just as hard and have equal experience. Perhaps the lack of self-confidence and creative challenge is obvious in their aura. Many feel intimidated when they are face to face with an authority figure.

There can also be a cleavage between your personal and professional life. It may be hard to find a balance between the two. You may work very hard at your career in an effort to get ahead, and thereby neglect your family. Or perhaps your family obligations are so strong that you neglect your work. This could happen if your spouse or a child is ill requiring some form of special attention. I know several single parents with this pair of interceptions who experience continual daycare problems that conflict with career advancement.

Sagittarius is a need to expand. Aquarius seeks freedom of expression. However, Capricorn's interception indicates internal intensity in wanting to achieve but feeling trapped or paralyzed due to circumstances. This internalization is actually a preparation time for emergence rather than a lifelong threat of loneliness and sense of failure. Being more informed or educated in many areas is certainly one path to freedom of expression and self-confidence which can lead to fulfillment and success. Timing is important. Do not let anyone rush you. Do not compare your progress with anyone else.

Different cycles of varying lengths are experienced because interceptions change and planets progress in or out and transits move through these intercepted degrees. You may be hesitant to have a relationship because you fear that someone may find out your deepest secrets, or you fear being hurt. When an activating transit moves through Cancer, you may decide to try a live-in relationship. You may try many relationships over a period of years before you feel secure enough to make a more solid commitment. When Saturn moves into your intercepted Cancer, you face new responsibilities within yourself in trying to understand the root of your discontentment. Of course, you will feel lonely, misunderstood, and depressed but that is part of the process. However, you may decide it is time to put down roots and buy a house. You may feel it is time to see a therapist. You may examine your heritage more closely by taking a trip overseas and visiting relatives you have never seen. It is a time when family albums come out and sometimes you find out about a relative you never knew you had. There is much to digest. You can judge other transits by their nature, duration and the aspects they form to natal positions.

When an invigorating planet moves into your Capricorn interception, you will likely feel particularly ambitious. You will likely take a keen look at your situation and decide how you can better yourself. It may be a time when you find the courage to ask for a raise or something as small as asking for better light or ventilation in your working area. I do not mean to sound frivolous, but sometimes small achievements can make a big difference in your slow steady climb to the top. When the Sun is in your intercepted Capricorn once a year this is the time to make small improvements. Sometimes a transit can really shake you up as in Figure 20 with the Uranus/Neptune transit in Capricorn during the early 1990s. Some of you have interesting stories about what happened in your life with that duo. I have clients who were so discontented that they stormed into the boss's office and quit on the spot. Others were involuntarily downsized and lived the trauma of feeling they were a failure. Yet others received promotions beyond their expectations. The type of aspect can certainly make a difference as to how easy or difficult a change will be.

Student 4

Figure 21, Student 4, is the chart of a young man who first came to see me as a client in his mid-twenties and then became a student. He went through several of my semesters. He said the study of astrology and particularly the study on interceptions helped him understand himself a great deal better. At that time he was also completing a four year University degree in business.

He was living at home but hated his mother. I asked why he did not move out and he said, "I can't afford to but I live in the attic, which gives me some peace so I can study. Besides, I have to stay home to protect my sister."

When I asked him what he had to protect his sister from, he said "our mother." I never did find out what his mother did that had wounded him so badly. In spite of this inner turmoil he had a ready smile and a friendly greeting for everyone. He was doing a coverup with Gemini on the cusp.

When he finished university, his first job offer was in Europe. He really wanted the job so he could get away from everything

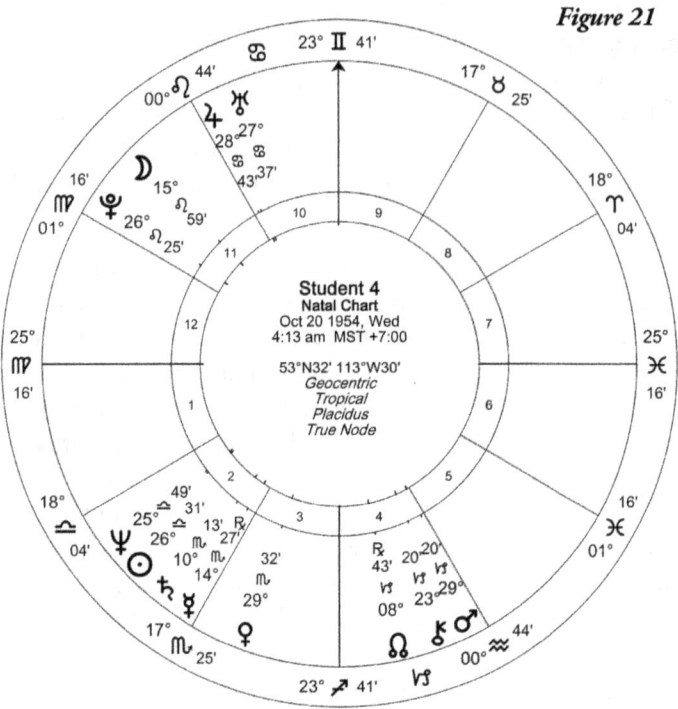

Figure 21

and thought the adventure would be exciting, but he said he was terrified to leave the country in spite of the allure. That is his ten/four Cancer/Capricorn interception with planets and the Nodes contained therein. It is also part of a T-Square but that is not what we are delineating at this time. He took a job locally as office manager for a food processing plant. Isn't that amazing synchronicity?! We both laughed about it at the time.

When he finished my astrology classes I did not see him for several years. I ran into him on the street one day and we stopped to chat. I asked him if he had been out of the country yet and he said no. He had not even traveled south into the United States for a holiday, which many Canadians do regularly. He was still afraid to leave his homeland in spite of all his rational thinking. He still thought a lot about going to Europe to work but did not have the necessary courage and inner security to do so. He lamented that his first job offer was a lost opportunity. At that point he was still not sharing his life with a partner.

Several more years passed, he was now in his forties when I ran into him once again. He still had not left the country and still longed to do so. He could easily afford it because he did have a good job. He was still living alone. He still had a mother problem. He said rather wistfully that he was still looking for himself. I told him not to fret because most of us were also on a personal quest of self-discovery.

Figure 22

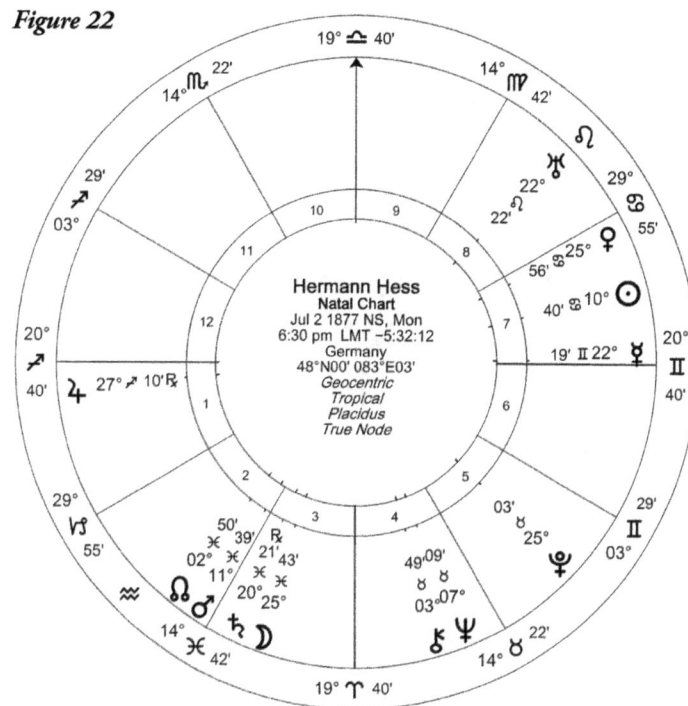

The following pages show charts of celebrities who have this pair of interceptions. As previously pointed out, the intercepted signs are only a part of the chart delineation and will be mitigated by other factors, including the rest of the intercepted interpretation itself. Some of these people made obvious contributions connected with their interceptions, which indicates intensification due to internalization. It is important to note that in most instances we do not know the early background or family life of these people, which is where this pair of signs would have the greatest significance. Also, people with this axis tend to keep their personal lives private.

Hermann Hess, Novelist and Poet

Hess's formal education was spasmodic. He left several schools before completion and then further educated himself. Among other adventures, he studied Indian mysticism. The *Funk and Wagnalls Encyclopedia* states his earlier works were characterized by "an atmosphere of nostalgic melancholy." His novels include *Damien*, a psychoanalytical story; *Sidhartha*, a search for spiritual happiness; and *Der Steppenwolf*, a violent criticism of the modern world lacking in spirituality. Lois Rodden says he suffered from depression, hypochondria, suicidal tendencies and alcoholism. He received the Nobel Prize in Literature in 1946. Ref: F & WE; AA: *Portrait of Hesse* by Zeller "Mother's Diary": ABC.

John Logie Baird, Electrical Engineer, Television Pioneer

John Logie Baird was a pioneer in the development of television for home entertainment. This was a wonderful use for his Cancer/Capricorn pair of interceptions. I could not find any information about his personal life. He began his research in 1922 at age thirty-four. In 1926 he gave his first demonstration of a television picture image. He created color images in 1944 which he projected onto a screen. He developed stereophonic sound. He also did research in radar. Ref: Biography.com; F&WE; AA: F/N: ABC.

Jimmy Swaggart, Evangelist

He was not only a charismatic, dynamic speaker, but an astute business man who amassed a fortune from his followers until his downfall. He was caught in a cheap hotel with a prostitute. On television, in front of millions of people, with tears streaming down his face, he asked for forgiveness, but his credibility was ruined. DN#13: BC.

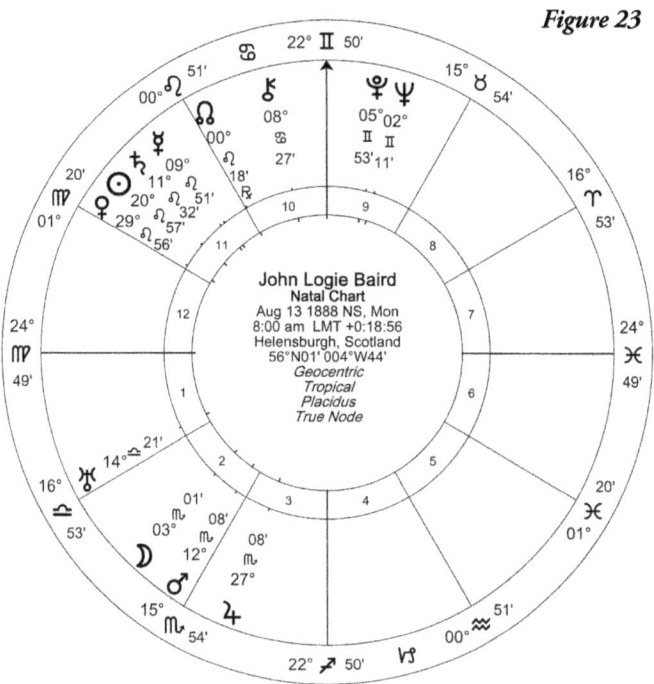

Figure 23

Other Examples

Among famous people there does not seem to be a noticeable vocational trend in a way that can be seen by some of the other intercepted pairs, perhaps because it indicates emotional needs and drives more than the others. However, as previously indicated, the attraction to food and home industries is more apparent. The need for personal recognition and achievement is also apparent.

Princess Ann, Royalty: Across nine/three. Only daughter of Queen Elizabeth II and Prince Philip. She grew up largely isolated from her parents, yet highly disciplined and regimented. She experienced a lonely youth. She is in her second marriage.

Mary Baker Eddy, Founder, Christian Science Church: Across seven/one. She tried marriage three times, each ending with the death of the husband. She gave up her son from her first marriage to foster parents. She was sickly and emotionally unstable as a child and as an adult her medical and psychological problems left her in a poor physical condition. She as been described as being psychosomatic. She was constantly involved in lawsuits, some against her and some she generated.

Henry Mancini, Musical Arranger: Across seven/one. Many of his musical scores are well known including *Moon River* and *Days of Wine and Roses*. He won an Oscar for *Victor/Victoria*. I personally worked closely with him on a television program and found him to be cooperative, but distant and difficult to talk with.

Oscar Levant, Pianist, Composer, Actor: Across ten/four. He was a close friend of George Gershwin and became the foremost Gershwin interpreter. His most memorable film was *An American*

Figure 24

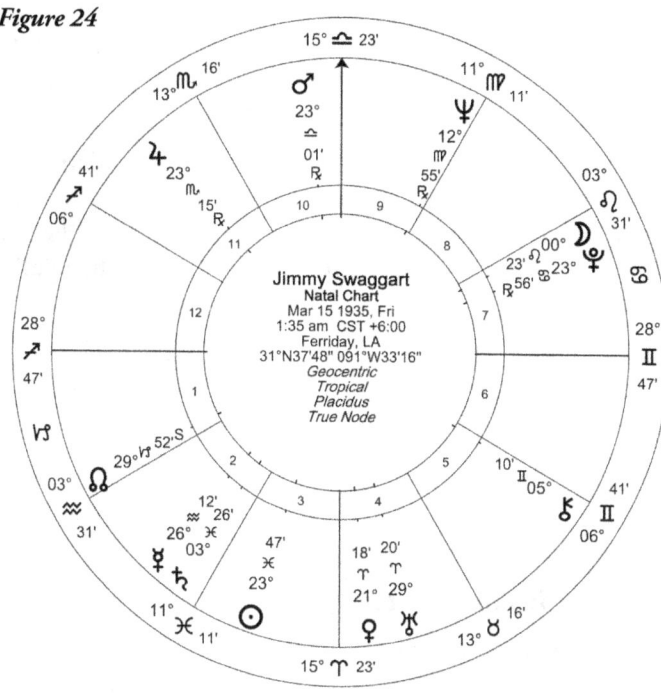

in Paris. His neurotic behavior was openly displayed and publicly acknowledged which became more acute as he got older.

Hans Christian Anderson, Poet and Author: Across seven/one. Some of his most notable works are *The Tin Soldier* and *The Ugly Duckling*. He grew up in poverty with little education and few associates. He was not taken seriously in his public life during his lifetime and had little personal esteem.

Julie Andrews, Singer, Actress: Across ten/four. Rodden quotes from *People* magazine (1977) that as a child "I loathed the singing and resented my stepfather." In her adult life she underwent intensive therapy. She won an Oscar for Best Actress in *Mary Poppins*, and received a further nomination for *The Sound of Music*.

Ava Gardner, Actress: Across twelve/six. Her most notable films include *Mogambo, Night of the Iguana, Barefoot Contessa, Snows of Kilimanjaro,* and *Earthquake*. She was married to Mickey Rooney, Artie Shaw and Frank Sinatra, and preferred a life of obscurity in Spain.

Bette Davis, Actress: Across eight/two. Her acting achievements are enormous. She won two Oscars for Best Actress and was nominated ten times. She brought tremendous emotional power to the screen. In her personal life she was married and divorced four times.

Bobby Fischer, Chess Champion: Across twelve/six. At fifteen he became the youngest grandmaster in chess. He lived most of his life in Europe and was wanted in his own country for tax evasion and violating U.S. economic sanctions against Yugoslavia. He seems to have had a quarrelsome nature. He died in Iceland in 2008.

Anne Frank, Diarist and Concentration Camp Victim: Across twelve/six. Lived with her family for two years in complete concealment supported by friends and then was betrayed. She wrote a diary of her experiences and feelings that was later published.

Hermann Goering, Nazi Politician/Military Leader and German Patriot: Across eight/two. His rise to power was swift and his administration brutal. He commanded the "Death Squadron"

Understanding Interceptions

in the First World War. After joining the Nazi party he was given command of Hitler's Storm Troopers before founding the Gestapo, and setting up the infamous concentration camps. He was later made Marshal of the Reich. He was convicted at the Nuremberg War Crimes Trial but committed suicide before he could be executed.

Shirley MacLaine, Actress, Author, Political Campaigner: Across ten/four. She acted in a great variety of dramas and comedies. It was a good way to explore her own feelings. With her Moon in the twelfth house (ruling her tenth house Cancer interception) and three planets including her Sun in the eighth, she searched for the deeper meaning of life. In spite of some ridicule, she publicly espoused her believe in reincarnation and spirituality.

Frank Sinatra: Across nine/three.

Ivana Trump: Across eight/two.

Danny de Vito: Across seven/one.

Grace Kelly: Across nine/three.

Dr. Walter Koch: Across ten/four.

Leo/Aquarius Intercepted

Leo is a fixed fire sign through which we are endeavoring to unfold our creative potential. Fire leaps and dances, sometimes beautifully, sometimes ferociously, and at other times it can be reduced to a few smouldering embers waiting to be revived. When intercepted, you may have great creative urges that are *intensified due to internalization*, but some form of inner development is necessary before you are willing to let others enjoy the warmth and light of your fire.

Aquarius is a fixed air sign and it is where we release our individuality for others to accept or reject. If they accept us, it can bring friendship and happiness to those who are involved. If they reject, us we are often left feeling humiliated and unwanted. Our individuality is actually the release of our creativity, the essence of our self-expression and the genius we are trying to express. The ultimate freedom is the ability to be ourselves and have the confidence to give the world our particular gifts or talents which cannot come from anyone else.

If this pair is intercepted, some inner development is required in order to experience this form of release and freedom. Self-confidence may be low for a variety of reasons. When we are children we need to be encouraged to explore different avenues of self-expression and creativity. With this pair of signs intercepted, you may have been continually put down or unduly restricted in expressing yourself. If you were laughed at or had a finger pointed at you disdainfully, you would soon shrink back into yourself. Your fire would sputter, smoke and be reduced to a few smouldering embers waiting to be revived.

Maybe your parents did not know how to praise your efforts at self-exploration or were critical of everything you did. Your lack of self-confidence may have resulted from a school teacher who

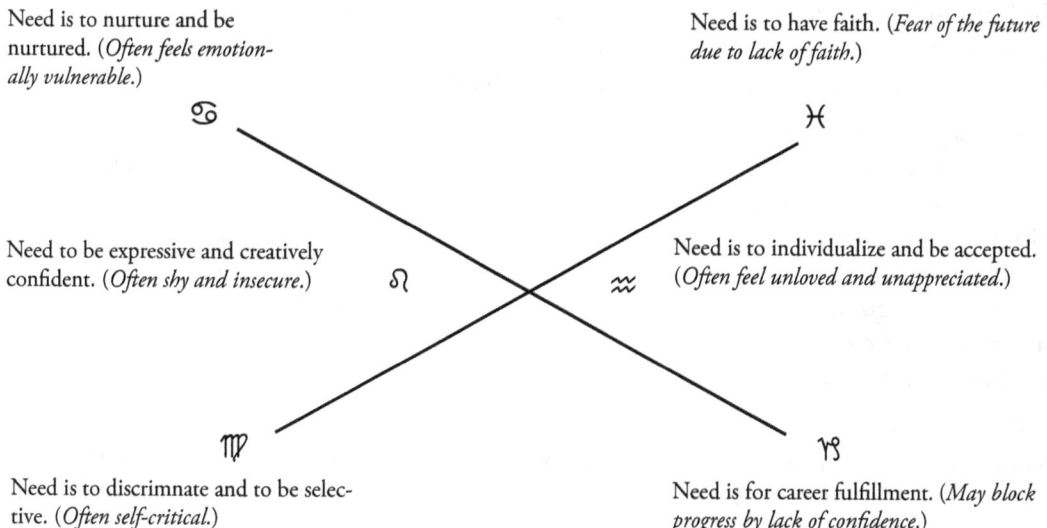

Figure 25. Leo/Aquarius Intercepted. Basic urge of each sign is indicated. The expressive needs of all six are altered by this one pair of intercepted signs. A key concept of the potential difficulty is in parenthesis. When Leo is intercepted, Cancer is on the cusp of that house and Virgo is at the end. This makes Aquariuis intercepted with Capricorn on the cusp and Pisces at the end.

continually put you down, rebuked your answers or told you that the colors you chose in your art work were silly and that trees are not purple. Art is subjective. It is either liked or disliked. I had one client who was brought up in a musical environment, loved music and joined the glee club. One day, in front of the whole group, he was told not to sing a particular song because he was off-key. He was so embarrassed that he left the glee club and never sang in front of anyone ever again, even in a group. After he grew up, he said he would only sing with his car stereo or whenever he knew he was all alone, and even then sometimes his throat would just tighten up and ugly sounds would come out. Not everyone has to be a Caruso to enjoy singing. There is an old saying that "everyone in Italy sings opera but not necessarily well."

You may have grown up in a family where one of your siblings had an extraordinary gift that was admired by everyone and developed with great pride and financial sacrifice. Your talent may have been overlooked, not encouraged or developed. One of my clients with this interception had this experience. She had writing talent that was not encouraged in her growing up years. As an adult she developed it herself. Her family had devoted all their time, money and interest to her sister's singing lessons, pretty clothes and public appearances. My client said it took her a long time before she would let anyone read what she had written because she was afraid they would show little interest. I believe both time and her astrologer helped her realize how very talented she was and that she did not have to continue living in her sister's shadow of achievement. I felt that the internalization of the interception was so powerful that it created an even greater need for her to develop her writing talent, almost in spite of her family, because it was not anything she took for granted. She is now over 50 years old and is finally proud of her own achievements.

You may have come from a large family, have been more sensitive than some of your other siblings and received very little praise or attention. Sometimes a sibling can be unintentionally intimidating, even cruel or perhaps sarcastic at your every attempt to be pleasant. If you grew up with hand-me-downs, you may have felt that you could not look your best and that your friends would recognize your outfits from another time, another place. Children are tender little people, and when they go to school they are attempting to function in a social and learning environment far larger than their small family unit. Parents are not always aware of their struggle but need to be continually on the lookout for this type of problem to develop.

With this interception, you may have trouble accepting a compliment. When your new outfit is admired, you may pretend it is old, or you may tug at it somewhere, or get red in the face. You may reply, "Oh, this old thing. I just stuck it on this morning because I couldn't think of what else to wear."

Heaven forbid that anyone should know that you just bought it yesterday. This is because Aquarius is also intercepted, and this is the sign indicating the need to be accepted. You may always feel like the odd man out. You may be on edge for fear other people will not accept you, may not like you or may criticize something you say or do. This is particularly difficult for people who draw, paint, write poetry, create music, do crafts, etc. A client once told me about a childhood experience that she has never forgotten and I believe it is symbolic in itself. She had spent hours creating a wonderful sand castle and when she ran off to fetch her parents to show it to them, someone had stepped on it, right in the middle. Her parents carelessly said, "Don't worry about it, dear. You can build another one," and they walked away.

They missed the whole point. This was the one that counted. She thought the person who stepped on it did so because they thought it was too ugly for anyone else to see.

With this interception, you may dress plainer than your heart would desire because you may be concerned that someone will think your colors clash or your outfit is inappropriate. You may be concerned that someone is starring at you for these reasons rather than because you look attractive or interesting. Your inclination is to think the worst of yourself.

Cancer is on the cusp of the house where Leo is intercepted, and you may feel more comfortable at home or in a familiar environment rather than in social surroundings, particularly with new associates. As an adult you may need a lot of cuddling and nurturing. You may have carried your "security blanket" longer than other children. Your need for assurance could be exceptionally strong. In a love relationship, you may need to be told over and over again "I love you, I love you, I love you." You may give many gifts to your lover in order to hear those magical words of love and adoration.

Virgo at the end of the house can indicate a strong degree of self-doubt. You may be highly critical of yourself. You may wonder why someone would want to love you. You are likely to feel unworthy when you are loved and oppressed when not. In time, however, when you accept your own creative self, have the courage to project it regardless of the feedback you receive, you will be a much more confident person in a highly competitive world. With this interception it is difficult to realize that you will probably not be liked and appreciated by everyone you meet. There are bound to be clashing aura colors and planetary positions.

Aquarius is where we release our creativity and receive acceptance or experience rejection. If it is intercepted, you will likely be bound by the tradition of Capricorn and preset territorial boundaries. You may feel you need to conform to someone else's dictates, ideas or patterns. You may not realize that you can add spice and flavor to your life as well as to the lives of others by allowing your own unique individuality to emerge. With confidence of your own expression and the proper amount of discrimination, you can greatly expand your horizons and enhance your growth. It will happen in time, but realize that you have some inner growth to do first.

Pisces at the end of the intercepted pair is where you will learn to have faith in yourself as well as a higher power, faith in your creative endeavor, faith that many people will like you for whom you are, and faith that your life will continue to unfold in an ever increasing upward spiral. There is a point at which you need to let go, to stop analyzing, categorizing and shredding an issue and put your faith in a power beyond yourself with the knowledge that you have done your best. Self-acceptance is a big issue with this intercepted pair. Learn to compliment yourself.

When Leo is stimulated by an energetic transit, you may search for ways to draw attention to yourself. You may dress more flamboyantly or buy a piece of gold jewelry. You may brag about something you have done. You may be confident enough to fall in love. You will want to let go, have some fun or experience some new form of entertainment. You may radically change your taste in music, literature and motion pictures. You may notice that you crack more jokes, laugh louder, and even say "hello" more loudly than usual. Look for indications that you feel more expressive and outgoing. If you feel a little foolish, you will simply pull back and regroup. You will vow to express yourself differently, and you will try again. This uncertainty will not last a lifetime. It is a learning pattern with deep significance.

When Aquarius is stimulated, you will be prone to eccentric or outlandish behavior. This may reflect in your dress, your manners or your attitude. If you are dissatisfied with your job, you may stomp up to your boss and quit on the spot. Both Uranus and Neptune are in Aquarius as I write this, and I am getting reports about just such reckless behavior. There is a very strong desire to express one's individualism, voice opinions and allow your personality to burst forward. Neptune sends out a message for you to make sure it is what you really want. Your new reality may be a dream come true or a nightmare.

You may find yourself making new friends or looking up friends you had abandoned a long time ago. You may join a new group in order to meet new people. You may decide it is time to accept a nomination for an executive position in an organization in which you have kept a low profile. A little bit at a time you will release old patterns of behavior so that your true individuality can emerge.

Up to our Saturn return, we are usually trying to be what others expect us to be. Both our parents and the school system put their stamp upon us. After the Saturn Return we must begin responding to the voices of individuality inside that are speaking louder and louder demanding attention. We must undertake this development without the guilt that we are not living up to someone else's expectations.

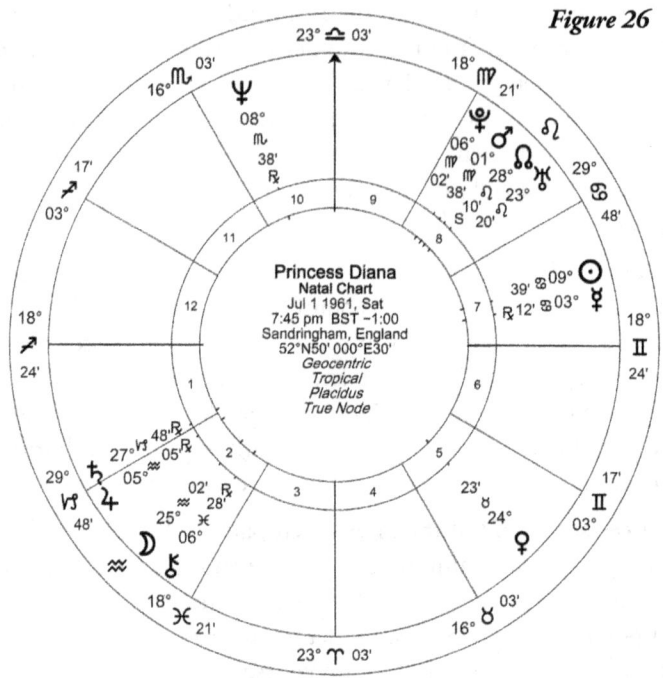

Figure 26

Princess Diana

The chart of Princess Diana (Figure 26, M/H) is being presented as a good example of someone with a Leo/Aquarius pair of interceptions who struggled with the concepts outlined in this text in spite of her privileged birth and circumstances.

Princess Diana was deeply loved and admired by millions of people all over the world but her early personal life and her life in the palace were far from idyllic. Her mother left the family when she was very young. Her husband and the rest of the Royal Family did not seem to give her the support she needed in order to feel loved and wanted. She was sweet, charming and had a habit of slightly bowing her head as an expression of shyness. I have seen this trait in other people with this pair of interceptions.

Student 5

Student 5 (Figure 27), is a lady who studied with me for only a couple of years when she was in her late twenties. She was married, had two small children and a mortgage on a new home. She did not have a career or job beyond her family.

She had pleasant features, poor complexion and did not wear makeup. She had a friendly, un-

Figure 27

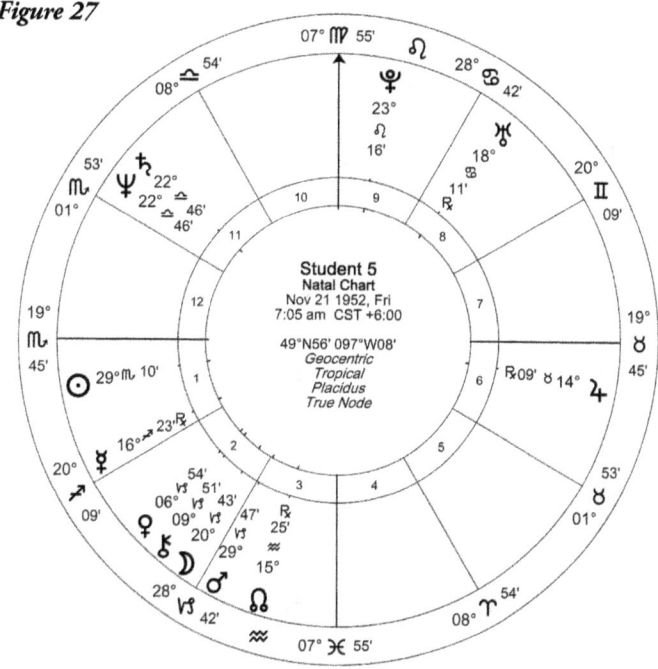

assuming personality, was soft-spoken and rather quiet in class. This would not be unlike a Leo/Aquarius interception. She did not wish to draw attention to herself.

She did not have any college or university education but had a thirst for knowledge as well as a deep yearning to understand life at its deepest core. Her intercepted pair is across her ninth/third houses. Her Mercury trine Pluto indicates intellectual creativity, a depth of understanding, as well as a fascination for the unknown. Her Mercury is out-of-bounds or beyond the ecliptic at 24S21 indicating it is not bound by traditional patterns of learning and curiosity. Her perception is excellent with a fast birth Moon at 14:05:32.

When we were studying this pair of interceptions in class she said, "I long to be a writer. I feel I could do great things and be a truly creative thinker but I really do lack self-confidence. I need a constant prod. I need positive feedback and lots of praise. First I want to raise my family and experience more of life so I have something to say. I know it is in there."

With Cancer on the cusp of the house containing her Leo interception, she felt she had to rear her children and even see them educated before she undertook the pursuit of her own creative needs, although her children were also part of her creative need. I suggested perhaps she could do both.

I asked if she did any writing now just to exercise her skill. She said at this point that she could not think of anything to write about. I told her if she wanted to be a writer she should write. She could keep a diary. She could write about her children, her family, incidents in her neighborhood, anything, just to be exercising her skill. Many writers keep notes on characterizations and humorous incidents. My contention is that if you want to be a writer, you write. In the beginning it does not matter if it has any commercial value. It is merely a way to gain experience and gradually gain the confidence needed for later.

Student 6

Figure 28, is the chart of a young man who was first a client and then became a student. With his permission I am presenting his chart under the name of Student 6. He hopes it will help someone with similar circumstances and the same struggle to find some form of comfort and understanding.

He was brought up in an abusive environment and has struggled long and hard to gain his self-confidence as a person. He moved to new schools and neighborhoods often. All through his growing up years he voluntarily went to Sunday School, Bible camps, religious seminars all in

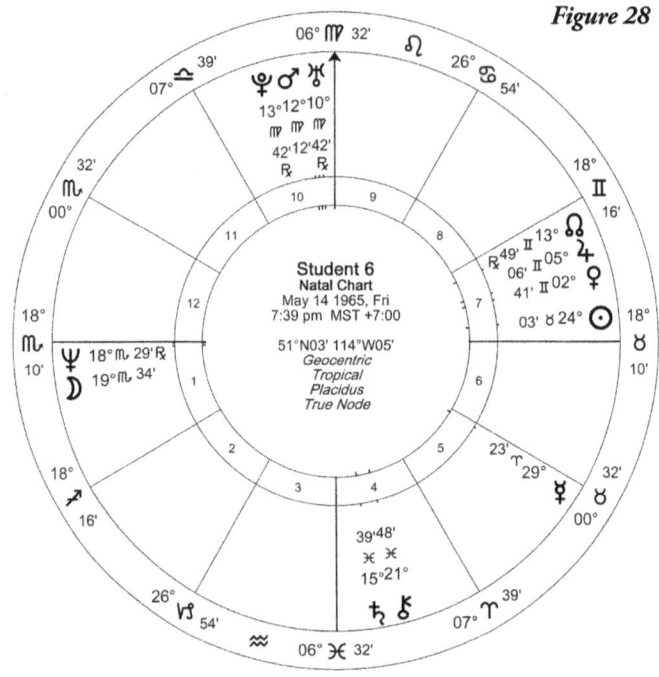

Figure 28

different denominations. He was convinced he was going to hell and was searching for salvation wherever it might be found.

With his Leo/Aquarius intercepted, he presents a bravo type of attitude with a wide open smile and a quick easy chuckle, which is often a nervous laugh so people will not see he is "sweating." He is a talented singer but does not feel he has enough training to sing in public. When told by a music teacher that he had an exceptional talent, he was so self-conscious that he did not believe her and quit taking lessons. In his thirties he still wanted to take lessons and pursue a singing career.

Note that this axis is across his ninth/third houses. His university is incomplete. He left because he felt stressed out and thought he was going to "mentally explode." He then took several years off from formal study, during which time he became my client and astrology student. He recently completed a two-year college course, which he also found very stressful. Both of these courses were being taken in French immersion which was exceptionally difficult for someone whose basic language is English. He has not rationalized why he was attracted to this foreign study program except to undertake a challenge and boost his sense of accomplishment.

I asked him how he felt in group participation. He was quick to reply, "Oh, groups are my death!" This was spoken through his Scorpio Ascendant! He will put himself into a position of speaking in front of a group, but he does stammer and is very nervous. He even has trouble reading his own notes. He would feel more comfortable burying himself in the group identity but he struggles to

Figure 29

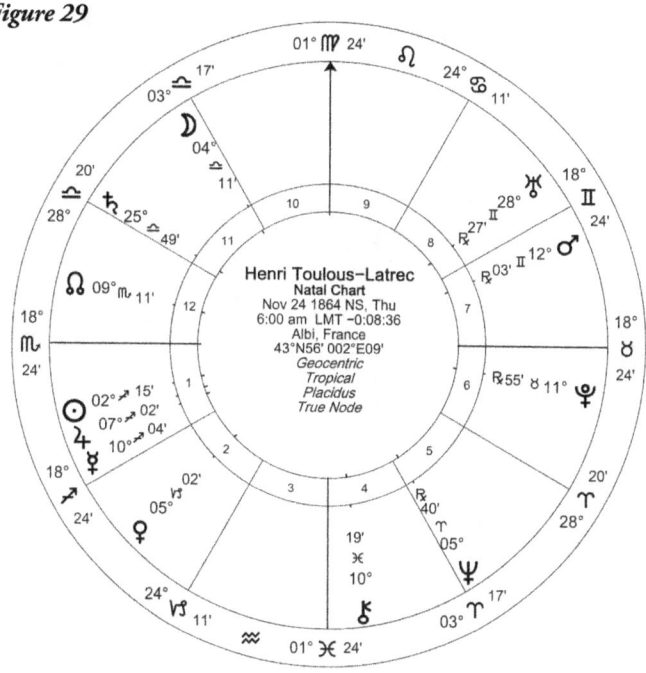

have his individuality emerge as a separate entity. He often feels his ideas are ridiculed. This is the intensity of his third house intercepted Aquarius.

He confessed that he has trouble seeing his own accomplishments until they are written out, preferably by someone else. This was a stark experience for him when he had a resume professionally written. He said, "Hey, I really did that. I could own it when I saw it written."

Henri Toulous-Lautrec, Painter, Lithographer

Toulous-Lautrec was born into an influential family of Parisian Bankers. An accident left him badly crippled and in severe pain. He shunned his heritage and lived a bawdy life of drinking and carousing in the artists' quarters of Paris. His most famous work depicts dance hall girls lifting their skirts and legs in the can-can dance. This was outrageous for the time. Both his creativity and bohemian life style are befitting someone with a Leo/Aquarius intercepted. Ref: Biography.com; AA: Gauquelin #1078: ABC

Hal Holbrook, Actor

Holbrook's (see chart on the following page) identity struggle would have begun at a very early age when he was abandoned by his parents. His acting career never took off with any great success until after his Saturn Return when he found a very unique act that had never been previously attempted. He became Mark Twain talking to the audience from on stage. He was highly acclaimed for this portrayal and accumulated over 2,000 performances. It was undoubtedly the most successful one-man show in the history of theater. Ref: Biography.com; AA: ABC

Other Examples

Following is a list of other notable people who have Leo/Aquarius intercepted in their charts. I will endeavor to give you as broad a mixture of personalities as possible but my own list contains an unusual number of actors/actresses. Because of my own television and motion picture production career, I had an opportunity to talk at length with many of these performers, and they told me repeatedly that they were more comfortable portraying someone else than revealing themselves. Acting out different characters, in different costumes and make-up gives them an opportunity to explore many of their own inner dimensions that they may otherwise hesitate to explore.

As well as actors and actresses, many enormously talented artists, poets and musicians also have this pair of interceptions. Directly prior to a performance they seem to need an extra boost of confidence from backstage personnel. Their physical appearance is also very important. Of course, there are always other facets of the chart indicating the same creative outpouring, but people who have this intercepted pair do it with an intensity that is due to its internalization.

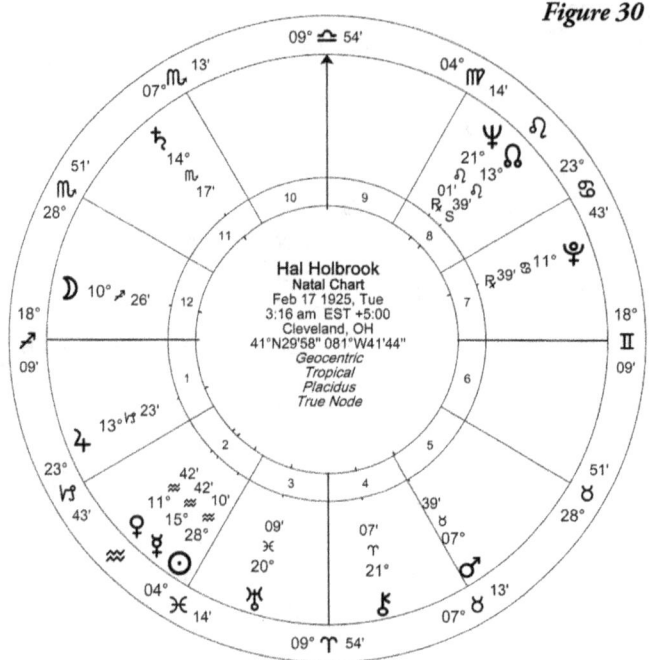

Figure 30

Sara Ferguson (Fergie), Royalty: Across nine/three. Duchess of York through marriage to Prince Andrew. They divorced in 1996 after many years of scandal. Fergie, as she became known, experienced an identity crisis throughout her marriage into the Royal Family.

Lenny Bruce, Comedian, Social Satirist: Across eight/two. He was known for his outrageous conduct and comment. His work was called both obscene and radically relevant. Because of this he was banned from performing in some cities and countries and was even arrested once in New York for public obscenity. He died in 1966 of a drug overdose. Some critics say he liberated a whole new generation of comedians.

Dr. Louis Berman, Endocrinologist: Across eight/two. He came from a very poor Jewish background which may have given him a driving need to succeed and overcome a deep inferiority complex. With a Leo/Aquarius interception, it is amusing, if not applicable, that one of his books was entitled *Glands Regulating Personality*.

Sean Connery, Actor, Politician: Across seven/one. It is ironic that the role of a suave, virile secret agent 007 James Bond is a role he grew to hate, although he did six episodes in all. In his earlier days he was a man of many trades, from bricklayer to lifeguard, to model of bathing suits to body-builder. He is also a notable politician in his homeland of Scotland.

Jack Paar, Television Host: Across seven/one. He quit school at age sixteen and became a radio announcer. After World War II he went back to radio, then to television where he hosted NBC's *The Tonight Show*. It was later renamed *The Jack Paar Show*. He was a natural interviewer and conversationalist but after about six years he wanted to get out of the spotlight so he retired from public life and bought a local television station. His feuds on and off the camera were well known.

Giacamo Puccini, Operatic Composer: Across ten/four. His operas include *Manon Lescaut*, *LaBoheme*, *Tosca*, and *Madam Butterfly*.

Erwin Johannes Eugen Rommel, Field Marshall: Across seven/one. He was commander of the Afrika Korps where he achieved great success. He was born to command and winning was not an option but a necessity.

Auguste Rodin, Sculptor: Across seven/one. Best known for his work *Le Penseur* (1904) (The Thinker) which stands in front of the Pantheon in Paris.

George Sand, Author: Across six/twelve. Her identity struggles must have been difficult. She left her husband and family to live the life of a free-spirited Bohemian. Her numerous love affairs and personal attire were scandalous for the day. In *Profiles of Women*, Lois Rodden writes, "Though she suffered a lifetime of periodic depression and passionate idealism, Sand was at heart an optimist."

Anna Mary Robertson (Grandma Moses), Painter: Across seven/one. She reared 10 children and then became a painter at seventy-eight. Two of her most notable works are *Hoosick Falls in Winter* and *Thanksgiving Turkey*.

Queen Elizabeth II, Royalty: Across seven/one. She was crowned queen of England on June 2, 1953. She is a conscientious and dedicated ruler who does her duty well but seems to prefer a quiet life. The public has often wondered if she will ever give up her throne to her son, Prince Charles, who is surely very disappointed that his destiny seems to have been delayed.

Brigitte Bardot, Actress: Across eight/two. After a few films, she left the glare of the spotlight at thirty-nine to live a quiet life in Paris. She went from sex kitten to recluse to animal rights activist.

Helen Gurly Brown, Author, Magazine Editor: Across eight/two. Her father died when she was ten. She was a very unattractive young girl who grew up to be a sophisticated, accomplished woman. Rodden quoted her as saying, "I have been mildly terrified from the day I was born and still am." She wrote a book entitled *Sex and the Single Girl*, a single woman's guide in a society where sexual identities were being uprooted and women were confused about their identity and conduct. It was an immediate bestseller.

Joanne Woodward, Actress: Across nine/three.

Linda Ronstadt, Singer: Across seven/one.

Carol Channing, Actress: Across eleven/five.

Emily Dickinson, Poet: Across nine/three. Lived a reclusive life.

Virgo/Pisces Intercepted

Virgo is a mutable earth sign, concerned with practical issues and solutions which require selectivity and flexibility. It is ruled by Mercury which is the messenger through which we seek knowledge in order to harvest the ensuing wisdom, understanding and trust. This is where we find order in the midst of chaos, where we take information and categorize, analyze, sort and organize it as a tool for efficiency and problem solving. It is where we separate the wheat from the chafe and discard useless, redundant straw that stands in the way of supplying food for the soul.

This is where we put effort into something that will produce tangible results. We work to take care of ourselves, to help others in need and to relieve their suffering. That is our duty in a three-dimensional world of necessities and obstacles. We must learn to take care of ourselves with discrimination and not drive ourselves into exhaustion for the sake of duty because each of us is needed in so many ways.

There is a point at which we have done all we can to help someone or bring a matter to fruition, and we must back away and have faith that it will be all right. We must have faith that the universe unfolds in both a personal and common destiny. We are learning to do this where we have Pisces in our charts and through its ruler Neptune. However, we must be careful that Pisces does not become a place where we escape for a long time if reality becomes too dense. It is a great place to go for a rest, for contemplation and spiritual understanding. Much wisdom, compassion and understanding develops where we have Pisces and this usually happens in our quiet hours, in the recluse of our own mind. Strong Piscean characteristics do create the artist, poet, musician and dramatist who helps others escape toil and concern if even for a short while.

The Virgo/Pisces polarity is where we seek to find a balance between the everyday work-a-day world and the world of universal understanding and spirituality. This is a very common pair of intercepted signs which symbolically means that many of us want more out of life than getting up in the morning, going to work, coming home, relaxing for awhile in the evening, going to bed and then starting the process all over again. We crave the peace that comes from knowing there is a reason for earthly existence and that something lies beyond all that. Even if there is no tangible proof, at least we can trust that there is.

In my lectures I have often called this the axis of "paralysis by analysis." Aries is the last sign in the string of six involved in this pair of interceptions and it is where we learn to take the initiative. I hope to point out in the following few pages that if any of the other sign fulfillments in this particular group are being inhibited while we are developing some of our other needs, then we cannot expect to make as much outward progress as someone else, unless Aries is on the Ascendant. Let us not be hard on ourselves by comparing our progress to others. Our school system teaches us to judge in this way. If we do not complete school in the prescribed number of years then we "fail." It should not matter if it takes longer as long as the goal is met. We are expected to go to college or university right after school rather than when we are thirty, thirty-five or forty. I know a gentleman who became a lawyer in his mid-fifties.

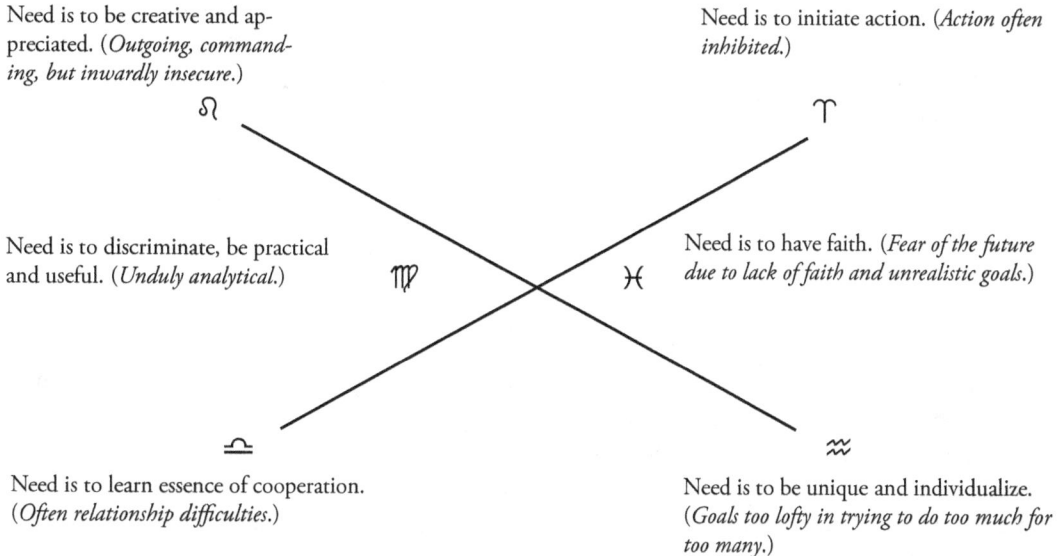

Figure 31. Virgo/Pisces Intercepted. Basic urge of each sign is indicated. The expressive needs of all six are altered by this one pair of intercepted signs. A key concept of the potential difficulty is in parenthesis. When Virgo is intercepted, Leo is on the cusp of that house and Libra is at the end. This makes Pisces intercepted with Aquarius on the cusp and Aries at the end.

The *intensification due to internalization* of this pair of signs indicates a struggle with faith versus logic. Both my husband and I have this pair and every time I relate one of the significant ways we both experienced it, many people in the audience nod their heads or murmur "me too," so I will include it here.

I was brought up in a very regimented home. My father passed on when I was only three months old. My mother was not deeply religious but was determined to make sure that my brother and I were going to grow up with good moral values. She was a Pisces with a Virgo Ascendant and Moon! We belonged to the United Church of Canada. I went to church three times on Sunday, once to sing in the choir, once to play the piano for Sunday School and again in the evening to keep an attendance record of young people from Sunday School. I went to Bible School in the summer. Whenever I would ask our minister various theological questions he would simply say, "You ask too many questions. All you need to do is believe. The Bible is not to be questioned. It is God's word."

Thus began my intense struggle with faith versus logic. I needed a spiritual base for my life. I searched far and wide in my adult years, including a study in comparative religions. For a while I was even a borderline atheist and that hurt my conscience even more. It was through the study of astrology that much of my spiritual understanding developed or was reinforced. I do not mean to indicate that astrology is a religion but the magnificent order of the universe that I began to see through astrology, helped me to realize that such a magnificently conceived order must be Divine. In any ordered environment there is a hierarchy or steps of authority indicating the possibility of a Supreme Being, Higher Power or God. Religion had thus, for me, been transformed from words on a page into a reverence I had not previously experienced.

Through Virgo we need to see things in real, practical terms, and Pisces is where we learn about faith and where we experience inspiration. In our everyday affairs, there is a point at which we need to feel we have gathered enough information in order to make a logical assessment leading to a firm decision or conclusion. If this axis is not in balance, we may waft from our decision or continually wonder if we have made the correct one.

If you have Virgo intercepted, with Leo on the cusp, your confident exterior can be undermined by self-criticism. Thus, a lack of inner confidence may be the culprit preventing assimilation of all significant data necessary to make a good decision or to feel confident that the correct decision has been made. You must also be able to forgive yourself if you do make a mistake. *To err is human*. It has been said that you can measure the success of a person by the number of mistakes he/she has made. With this interception you may worry excessively about making a mistake. This is where faith in yourself can help relieve this burden.

If you are a perfectionist, express false pride, worry incessantly, relationships can also be difficult, which is the sign of Libra at the end of the house. You may then be the type of person who is constantly correcting your partner, criticizing his/her action and endlessly foisting your opinions on others. Also, in an effort to be appreciated and loved (Leo) you may take on too may obligations and try to be all things to all people. If so, it is time to pause, reflect and learn how to prioritize and be selective. You must learn how to take care of yourself so that your battery of human energy does not run down. Many of us with this interception have periods of serious health problems and hence become very diet and exercise conscious popping vitamin pills by the handful in order to have enough health and energy to inflict ourselves with another heavy load of responsibility. We thrive on the accompanying praise.

If this axis is across your sixth/twelfth houses, you will likely have a very strong work ethic and will do your best when praised and appreciated. It is often helpful to have a job with a creative outlet so that you can exercise your creative gifts with more confidence. You may have a tendency to work so hard, take on so many duties, always be the one to volunteer for overtime, that coworkers become less cooperative and resent you. The resulting unpopularity is a jolt to your pride.

Moving to the other side of the axis where Pisces is intercepted, you may be torn between two different avenues of intensity. Pisces is two fish tied in the middle. One is struggling to swim up into the sunlight for enlightenment, and the other wants to hide in the darkest, deepest corner of the pool. The enlightenment you find in the sunlight is filtered and assimilated in the inner recesses of your mind until it becomes a principle you can work with in your everyday life.

Aquarius on the cusp of the house may indicate a strong humanitarian need to help others in the

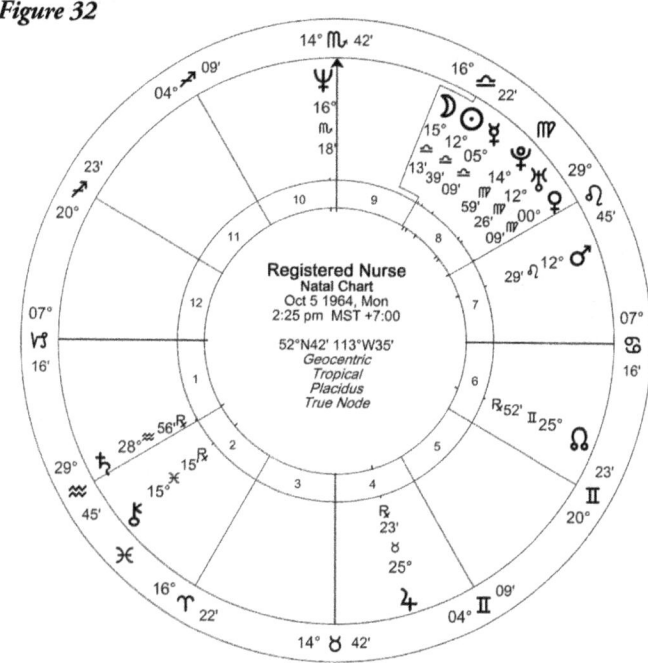

Figure 32

path of your own self-discovery. However, you must be aware not to drown yourself in the problems, sorrows and needs of others without the discrimination to know if their need is genuine or if it is your own need to be accepted and honored. Through this axis you can either be inspired into worthwhile action (Aries) or burden yourself needlessly (Pisces). You may then need to learn how to handle the ensuing guilt as you encourage others to do for themselves rather than being too willing to do their job for them. It reminds us of the old axiom, *You give a man a fish and you feed him for a day. You teach him to fish and you feed him for a lifetime.* This is why many people in the nursing, healing, or social services have this axis intercepted. Remember that Aquarius is where we learn to release old patterns including guilt.

Registered Nurse

Figure 32 is the chart of a registered nurse. You will note that she has twenty-nine degrees Leo on the cusp of a house containing six planets, three of which are intercepted in Virgo. Every fall, as transits move into this house, she "gets frazzled." It is a difficult time for her. However, even at thirty-four years old she must have achieved much satisfaction and fulfillment particularly in her Virgo intercepted houses due to some form of intense need to heal and serve mankind, to transform their lives so that hers may also be healed and transformed in some mystical and spiritual way.

Her parents divorced when she was twelve years old, and there is no doubt that she witnessed the breakdown of their relationship. She started living with her mother and then ran off to live with her father. Her father remarried, and she spent her 'teen years attending Baptist and Pentecostal church services, which included witnessing the dramatic activities that occurred regularly. She was disillusioned by the whole process because she felt the church was teaching one thing and living another.

After her school years, she became a single mother. At this point she must have recognized a strong Virgo/Pisces need within herself because she struggled through the arduous task of obtaining a nursing degree while caring for her baby. She received financial aid through a government program. I cannot imagine how difficult this was for her. She is now a registered nurse who receives much praise for her work in intensive care. This is a great use of her intercepted signs and planets.

Mario Lanza, Movie Star, Tenor

Mario Lanza was discovered while singing in his family's grocery store. His movies include *The Great Caruso* and *That Midnight Kiss*. His most notable song, "Be My Love," literally tugs at one's heart strings. He was not a well disciplined artist and was noted for his extravagant, self-indulgent personality and eating habits. He

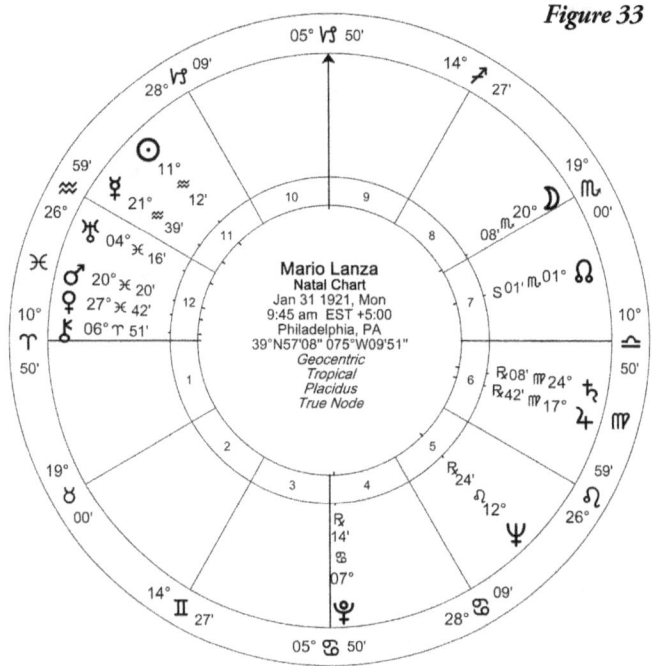

Figure 33

died of a heart attack in Rome, after overeating. Note the conflict between the planets in both intercepted houses, across six/twelve. Ref. Biography.com; AA: BC

Dr. Tom Dooley, Physician, Humanitarian

This is the chart of a man who dedicated his life to the suffering and healing of others. He started his medical career in the United States Navy on a ship helping Vietnamese flee from the north to the south. He then set up a refugee camp and wrote his first book, *Deliver Us From Evil*. After he resigned from the navy he went back to Laos and established clinics for the wounded and dying. He raised money by writing another book, *The Edge of Tomorrow*, plus his lecturing. He was a co-founder of the Medical International Cooperative Corporation. He also wrote *The Night They Burned the Mountain*. Ref: Biography.com; AA: ABC

Billy Graham, Protestant Evangelist, Author

Billy Graham's (see chart on following page) chosen profession is in the field of organized religion. He became a fundamentalist at age sixteen and was ordained as a Southern Baptist minister in 1940, at age twenty-two. With Mercury in Scorpio he is a persuasive, magnetic speaker. He claims to have converted literally millions of people to Christianity, and is the author of *Peace with God* and *World Aflame*. Ref: Biography.com; AA: BC

Figure 34

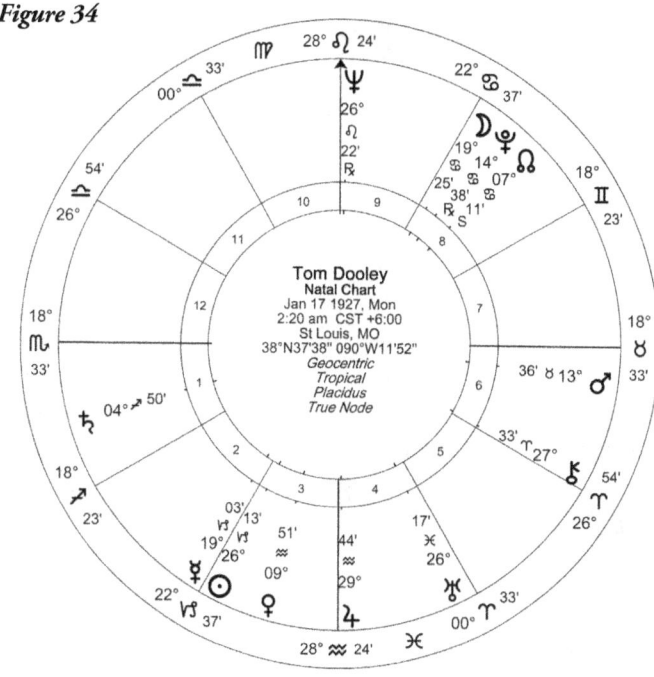

Other Examples

There is a great variety of people who use the intensity of this pair of signs as teachers, authors, preachers, humanitarians, doctors, researchers and artists. Virgo is the ability to create order from chaos and give form to inspiration, creativity and spirituality. I have repeatedly stated that every part of the chart must not be taken as a separate portion, but as part of the whole mosaic. We are all complex individuals, each responding to the pulse of the universe in a different way. We also share similarities.

Abraham Lincoln, President of the United States, Humanitarian: Across seven/one. He was born in a log cabin and lived a simple rural life until he undertook the study of law on his own. He entered politics and proved to be an extraordinary leader, not only politically but morally. He crusaded against slavery as well as for the preservation of democracy.

Emmaline Pankhurst, Suffragette: Across seven/one. With Moon opposition Neptune, she had a dream. With the help of her barrister husband and her own intensity from the interceptions, she was not about to give up until she elevated the status of women and gave them the right to vote. She was prepared to use any means to gain attention for her cause, even to the point of being jailed. She lived to see some fruits of her labor.

Annie Besant, Activist, Theosophist: Across six/twelve. She was a woman of strong beliefs. She married a minister, left him and became a social activist and an atheist. She was arrested on a morals charge for circulating birth control information. After studying theosophy and meeting Madame Blavatsky, she became a devout follower and went to India where she became president of the Theosophical Society.

Clara Barton, Founder of the American Red Cross: Across six/twelve. She was a tireless, dedicated worker in the battlefields of life, both during wartime and civilian catastrophes, yet she never felt she had done enough. She founded the American Red Cross and wrote three books about its history, as well as *The Story of My Childhood*.

Herman Melville, Writer: Across five/eleven. He had Mercury in Virgo, and many of his books were based on his sea travels, including *Moby Dick*, which has become a classic both as a book and as a motion picture. He was not greatly acclaimed during his lifetime. He died in obscurity as a poor man. After his death he was recognized as one of the greatest creative artists in the history of American literature.

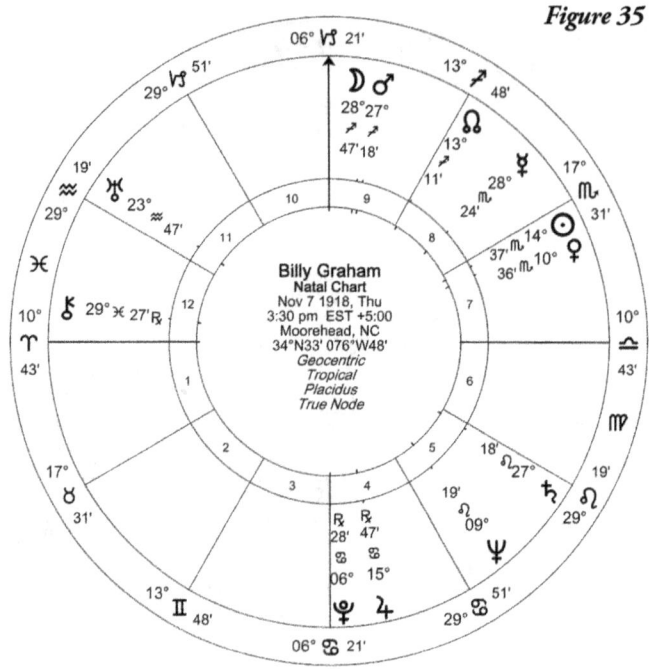

Figure 35

Janis Joplin, Rock Star: Across seven/one. This is an example of someone with this pair of intercepts who must have had a great deal of inner turmoil that never had a chance to be resolved. She lived hard and fast, and died by a heroin overdose.

Elizabeth Arden, Cosmetics Entrepreneur: Across six/twelve (Aries Ascendent). Virgo is often prominent in the charts of people in the fashion and cosmetic industries. The interception gives it intensification. Leo of flare opens the house and Libra of public relations is at the end of the same house. Her early life of poverty undoubtedly held secrets she was trying to overcome (twelfth Pisces intercepted). Aquarius was her need to break from her past. Aries on the Ascendant was the personal initiative to drive forth. The planets, of course provide the action.

Lois Rodden, Astrologer, Author, Lecturer: Across seven/one. Her development must have covered many colorful stages. She became a professional astrologer in 1967 at age thirty-nine. With her sense of precision and powerful analytical skills, she is renowned for her dedicated work in categorizing and cleaning up incorrect and misleading birth data so that our research and study could provide more accurate results. She compiled five books of charts, wrote *The Mercury Method of Chart Comparison*, *Modern Transits* and *Money, How to Find it with Astrology*, and published *Data News*. Her chart collection, which is regularly updated, is available at www.AstroDatabank.com.

Orson Welles

William Butler Yeats

Barbra Streisand

CHAPTER FOUR

Repeated Signs

"Self-confidence is the first requisite to great undertakings."—Samuel Johnson

WHEN WE HAVE ONE PAIR *of intercepted signs in a chart, we will also have another sign elongated to stretch over two houses that are next to each other. That would put the opposite sign on the opposite two houses.*

This phenomena of an elongated sign certainly does not diminish its importance in the chart by extending those particular sign needs over a larger area, but it does mean that we work through those needs in both houses. They are linked in their effect. Their rulers also govern both houses. I have been able to observe instances where all four houses were contingent upon each other, and in other cases this did not seem as obvious. Also, bear in mind that this will have a more noticeable effect in some people's lives than in others. As always, we must look to the whole chart to determine what type of lessons, as well as growth and development, are paramount in the life.

The number of repeated signs depends on the number of interceptions. One pair of intercepted signs yields only one set that is repeated. However, in Figure 1, Hartwell Plane Crash, you will observe there are three signs intercepted across houses six and twelve respectively, creating the same sign on four houses, plus the opposite sign on the opposite four houses. This is indeed a complex situation. In this instance, the intercepted pair usually encloses the greatest number of planets.

There also appears to be a sequence of development. It is often more successful to develop the necessities of the first house in the sequence of duplicated signs than the second. I have even found it useful to follow the sequence of understanding and development through a specific order of A, B, C and D, as seen in Figure 36. You will observe this in some of the delineations in the following pages.

A transit going through the sign also links the two houses. It will spend the same amount of time as usual in the sign, but less time in each house.

I emphasize once again that no part of the chart should be considered an impairment. Every chart indicates an individual approach to development and growth.

Same Sign on First and Second . . . Seventh and Eighth Houses

Two houses following each other are always linked, but in the case where the same sign occupies the first and second houses there is an exceptionally strong relationship between your ability to project your identity with honesty and confidence . . . and your self-worth which affects your earning capacity. This can play out in several different scenarios.

The Ascendant or first house cusp is what you show others, whether it be through energetic Aries, determined Taurus, outgoing Gemini or sensitive Cancer, etc. Whatever sign you project here, you need to do it with an honest representation rather than shrinking from it or over-emphasizing it negatively. Your ability to do this is related to the success or frustration of your second house fulfillment. You literally must learn to sell yourself.

You may try many different approaches in learning to project yourself in a comfortable, positive fashion. Sometimes there is an extensive trial and error period, which is assisted by the ever changing opportunities presented by your progressions and transits. (Progressed cusps change intercepted signs even if only briefly. Transits stimulate activity.) You need to examine your image carefully and ask if others would find you appealing or appalling. Does your image match the type of job you are seeking? Your style of presentation may be important. The way you carry yourself physically can also be significant, such as slouching or standing up straight, shuffling or walking with a sense of purpose.

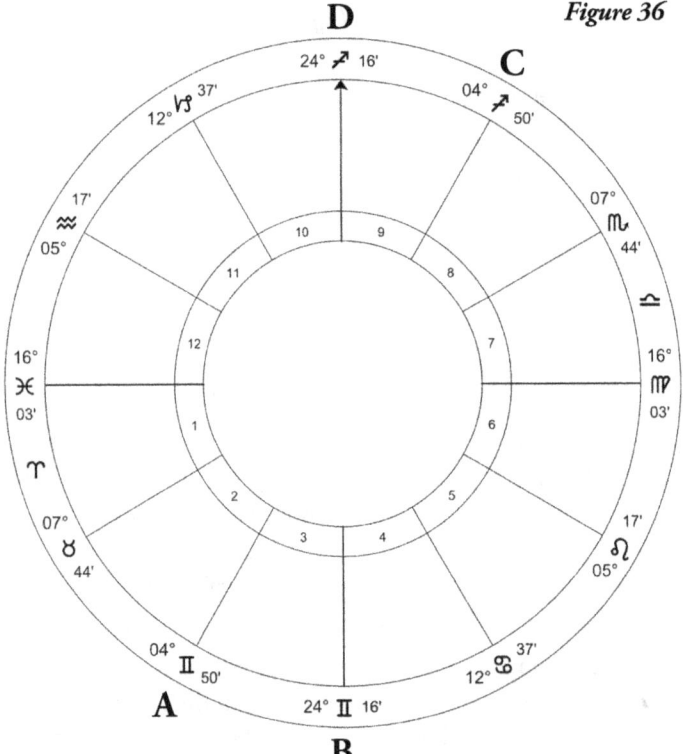

Figure 36

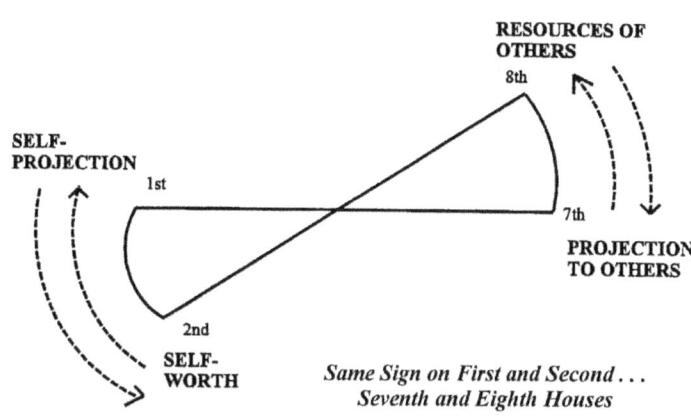
Same Sign on First and Second... Seventh and Eighth Houses

The attitude you project also sends out messages. If you are disheartened, disenchanted and disillusioned with your job status, it can pull you down. You may need to form new habits of presentation. There is an old adage that says, "fake it until you make it." In most instances, failure can be turned around by positive action brought on by a positive attitude.

In other words, with these two houses coupled, your image can either help or detract from your ability to earn the amount of money you feel you deserve or would like to have.

I have known many clients and students with this position who left home early to go out to work. Some were forced out by difficult or even abusive conditions. Some left simply because they could not wait to get out on their own and have money in their pocket. They were anxious to take on the world as an adult but soon discovered that it is much more competitive than they first realized and that the job at the local beanery was all right when they were in their teens but not adequate enough to provide for a home and family. Then comes the time of disappointment, bitterness and resentment that can turn to failure and a lack of motivation. However, never forget that there can be a turnaround period and a restructuring of attitude and presentation, as well as increasing job requisites. Many people in this situation take night courses while continuing to work at a menial job. Others quite their job, take out a student loan and complete a degree in a minimum length of time. It also means undertaking a large financial burden.

By Polarity Same Sign on Seventh and Eighth Houses

The seventh house is our interrelating needs and skills. The eighth is where we receive support from others and learn the benefits of shared resources. This may be economics as we learn the principles of cooperation and compromise. It also includes sharing ourselves physically as in the sex act.

Linking this to the first and second houses, I have known some people who married young, hoping that the combined income of two people could give them the self-respect they craved. Quarrels over money problems soon predominated because like attracts like. Many of them ended up coupling with someone in approximately the same income bracket which is little help considering the additional expenses. Invariably one of the two is out of work, which makes matters even worse. The trap is set deeper if a pregnancy occurs.

With money problems eroding the relationship, sexual incompatibility usually follows. The stage is set for a break-up. However, if a relationship is going to grow, the eighth house is where we make changes in our own understanding and personality thrust so that relationships can work more smoothly. In the natural or basic chart pattern, it is in a quincunx or reorganization aspect to the first house of self.

The same sign on the seventh and eighth houses, is truly a lesson in learning how to integrate with a partner personally, financially and sexually. The needs of your partner must be carefully understood and integrated with your own.

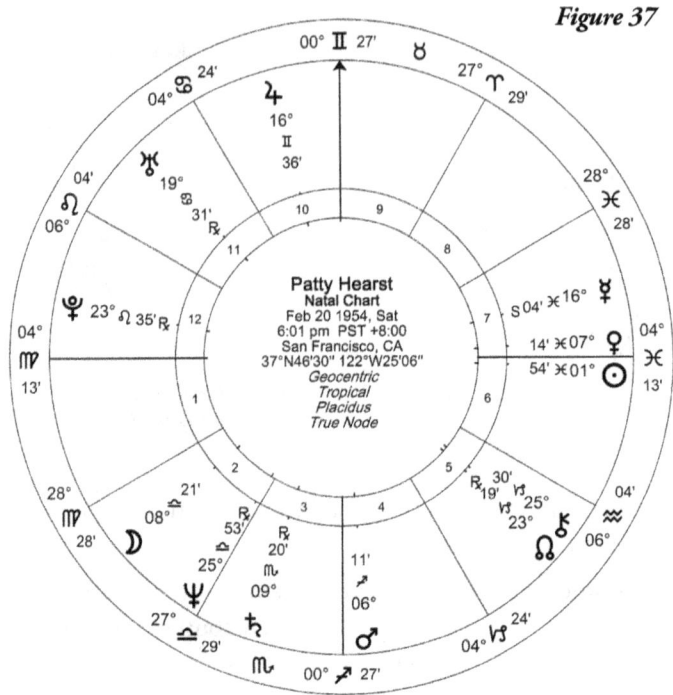

Figure 37

I have also known others with this combination who were able to successfully sell themselves (first and second houses) to others (seventh) as financial advisers, bankers, insurance representatives, sales people and even counselors (eighth).

Patty Hearst, Heiress

Patty Hearst is the granddaughter of newspaper giant Randolph Hearst. She was kidnaped on February 4, 1974, by the radical Symbionese Liberation Army. She went through a complete identity change as a result of brainwashing. She changed her name, denounced her heritage, her wealth, and became the lover of the leader. After seven months with the gang, she was caught during a robbery and sentenced to prison. She earned parole and married her bodyguard. Her road back to recovery was difficult and confusing. Both changes could be called a metamorphosis. This is a dramatic example of duplicated signs on houses one/two and seven/eight. AA: PC/BC

Other Examples

Prince Charles, Royalty: Leo first and second/Aquarius seventh and eighth. He married one lady because she was acceptable by heritage and could give him a suitable heir to the throne, but he loved another. I would suggest that in lieu of the long wait to fulfill his destiny he has had to search deeply for his own self-worth.

Alex Haley, Author: Leo first and second/Aquarius seventh and eighth. His most notable work is *Roots*, which became a popular TV mini-series. His Gemini/Sagittarius interception across the eleventh/fifth added to his creative writing skills as well as the desire to do so. The duplicated signs no doubt created the necessity to find his own identity and self-worth through his ancestor who was captured in Africa and sold as a slave in the United States.

Elizabeth Taylor, Actress: Libra first and second/Aries seventh and eighth. Her movie *National Velvet* thrust her into the role of celebrity at the tender age of eleven. She has been considered one of the most beautiful women in the world. It must be difficult to know who you really are in the midst of constant adoration. Her several marriages, including twice to Richard Burton, attest to her personal struggle.

David Berkowitz, Serial Killer: Scorpio first and second/Taurus seventh and eighth (Gemini/Sagittarius across eighth/second). He killed five people, plus six known to be wounded. Known as the Son of Sam, he never knew his parents and was adopted at seventeen months. His mother died when he was fourteen. He was known to be strange, and hit and pushed people for no apparent reason.

Woody Allen, Writer, Actor, Director: Virgo first and second/Pisces seventh and eighth. It is said he is as neurotic in real life as some of the characters he has scripted and performed. His relationship difficulties are legendary.

Barbara Walters, Broadcaster, Interviewer: Libra first and second/Aries seventh and eighth. With her Taurus/Scorpio intercepted, she has been driven by a strong need to make something of herself. She honed her appearance and presentation to perfection in order to utilize her talents into a marketable skill.

Greta Garbo, Actress: Gemini first and second/Sagittarius seventh and eighth (Aries/Libra intercepted across twelfth/sixth). She made several movies before retiring at a young age to devote her attention to the welfare of animals. (The chart I used in this analysis is in the realm of DD.)

Ed Sullivan, Television Host: Virgo first and second/Pisces seventh and eighth. He showcased the talents of others, and is credited with helping hundreds of talented performers attain stardom.

Henry Kissinger, Statesman, Professor: Cancer first and second/Capricorn seventh and eighth.

Timothy McVeigh, Murderer: Gemini first and second/Sagittarius seventh and eighth. He was convicted for the devastating Oklahoma City bombing on April 19, 1995 at 9: 10 AM CDT, which killed 168 people.

Same Sign on Second and Third . . . Eighth and Ninth Houses

When we have the same sign on the second and third houses, the needs of that sign link their growth and development over a larger than usual area. Our self-worth and earning capacity is directly linked in some significant way with our early education, relationships with kin and neighbors, and our ability to adapt to our immediate environment. Conversely, the stimulation of our curiosity to learn new ideas, new skills and the confidence to be an integral part of our community does, in some significant way affect the development of our talents into tangible economic results. You may do this through outgoing Aries, resourceful Scorpio, practical Capricorn, curious Gemini, etc. When making your initial assessment, never forget to include the sign on your Ascendant because, as previously mentioned, it is how you reach outward to the rest of the world. Each sign flows in magnificent harmony to the next one, all around the wheel.

You may be continually assessing your self-worth in a very conscious fashion. For instance, if you have an earth sign, particularly Taurus, on both of these two houses, you will certainly check the stub of your pay cheque carefully, check your bank book every time you make an entry, and be reluctant to spend money on anything except an educational book, a trade journal or another short course that increases your repertoire of skills.

You may combine the two houses in the way you earn your money. I have known quite a few people with this combination who earn their living through communications such as teaching, writing, acting or selling. Among my clients I have a truck driver, a teacher, a receptionist and a postal worker. I know some with this combination who work in the broadcast industry. You might be a traveling salesperson. Refer back to the story and chart of Student 2, Figure 11. This is the lady whose husband lost his job, and she was desperate for a way to feed her young family. She had a wonderful idea to start a kindergarten in her neighborhood. It turned out to be very lucrative and fulfilling for her.

There are also several ways that your income may be temporarily thwarted due to third house situations. Your parents may move into a new neighborhood so often that your educational structure is poor, requiring development in your adult years in order to increase your earning potential. Some form of third house responsibility may limit your early education hence your earning power. I knew one fellow who had a younger brother who wanted to go to law school very badly but his parents were struggling farmers with a large family who could not afford to send any of their children to college or university. The older brother, whom I will call Frank, sacrificed his own education, took two jobs, and put his younger brother through law school for seven long years. Frank had frayed cuffs on his shirt and jacket while his brother was well dressed. Frank deferred his own marriage plans until his brother graduated. Frank was very proud of his brother and loved to boast about his achievements. I have known them both for 45 years and they are still very close in their love and appreciation for each other. As a postscript, over the years Frank has been very involved with many community efforts in raising money for playgrounds facilities for underprivileged children and whatever else the community needs. He is retired now but is a fund raiser for cancer research.

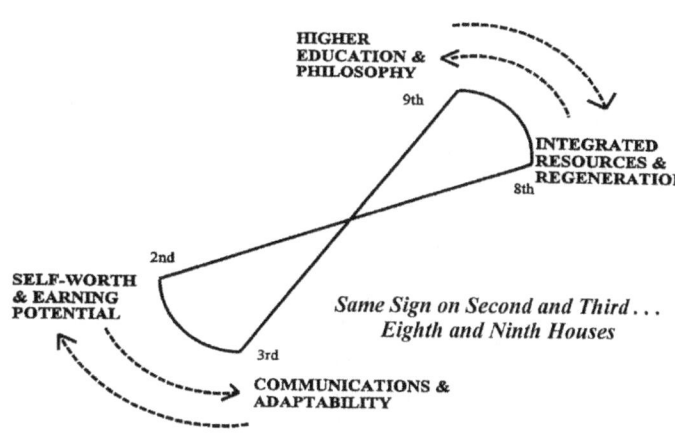

Same Sign on Second and Third... Eighth and Ninth Houses

I have great admiration for this man who was exceptionally successful in using this combination without regrets or remorse. He always has a warm greeting for everyone he meets.

I had a student who kept taking one short course after another at our community college. She ended up in my astrology class and that kept her occupied for several years. One of her challenges was to overcome her shyness so she could be more communicative because she felt that may be the key to a promotion and a higher income.

By Polarity Same Sign on Eighth and Ninth Houses

The eighth house encompasses all the resources we share with others, which would include our immediate partner, the bank, the government and even the natural planetary resources. It is also where we go deep into ourselves to plummet the meaning of life. The ninth house encompasses all the issues of the higher mind, including the beliefs and ethics we form from all our experience, diligent research, investigation and adventure. Combining these two can produce many different scenarios.

You may have had to borrow money or take out a student loan in order to advance your educational desires and needs. Mutable signs here may cause you to worry about paying back such an exorbitant sum, causing sleepless nights and even nightmares. One client of mine wanted to quite her studies and give the rest of the money back. She was having a reoccurring nightmare that she was drowning in a sea of money and was powerless to spend any of it. With the sign Aries on her 10th house cusp, she would never feel good about herself if she did not take positive steps to improve her position. She continued her studies and the nightmares finally stopped.

I had a lady who came to see me one day because she was deeply troubled and very frustrated because she wanted to go back to university and complete her degree. She had reared her children and now wanted to do this for herself just to feel a sense of accomplishment, whether she ever used it or not. Her husband said she could do it if she wanted to, but he would not spend his money on educating her at this time in their lives. He was more interested in developing their future retirement. When I ran the chart through my computer, I smiled to myself when I saw Cancer on both of these two cusps with Leo on the Midheaven and Sagittarius rising. I asked her if he would mind her going back to university if she paid for it herself. She said he would not mind as long as

Understanding Interceptions

it didn't cost him any money. She was delighted when I suggested that she take a part-time job and be a part-time student.

You may experience this position by feeling that your partner will not support your beliefs, your astrology studies or your metaphysical interests. He/she may even resent any money you spend on courses or books. I knew one girl who left her husband because he ridiculed her astrological studies. She was tired of hiding her books, lying about where she was going and sneaking a little of her grocery money to buy another book. Of course, there were other underlying causes but that was the proverbial straw that broke the camel's back.

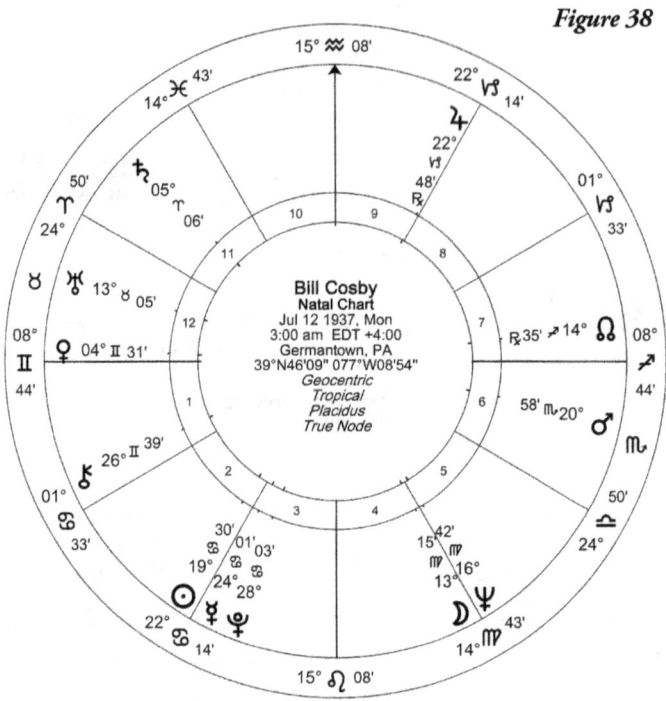

Figure 38

Another client had raised her family and now had a great yearning to travel. Her husband was at the age when he was still too deeply engrossed in his career to travel with her. He said she could travel all she wanted as long as she paid for it herself. He considered it an unnecessary extravagance. I suggested she take a part-time or seasonal job, earn her own money, see the wonders of the world, and bring back a lovely gift for him wherever she went. That is precisely what she did.

In terms of higher-minded pursuits, you may have a very strong investigative mind that questions everything you hear, everything you read, and whatever someone is trying to teach you. I have students who hopped from one faculty to another at university because they questioned everything too deeply and were not satisfied with a formal approach to study. They were reluctant to abandon their studies completely because attaining a degree was a goal instilled in them by their parents. Their weaning process at the Saturn return could be traumatic.

There may be lessons in ethics connected with investments and handling other people's resources, particularly for someone who is trying to get money the easy way.

Bill Cosby, Comedian, Author, Television Producer

According to Biography.com, "rather than repeat Grade X, he left school and joined the navy." He later continued his education and earned an M.A. and Ed.D after many years of dedicated

Figure 39

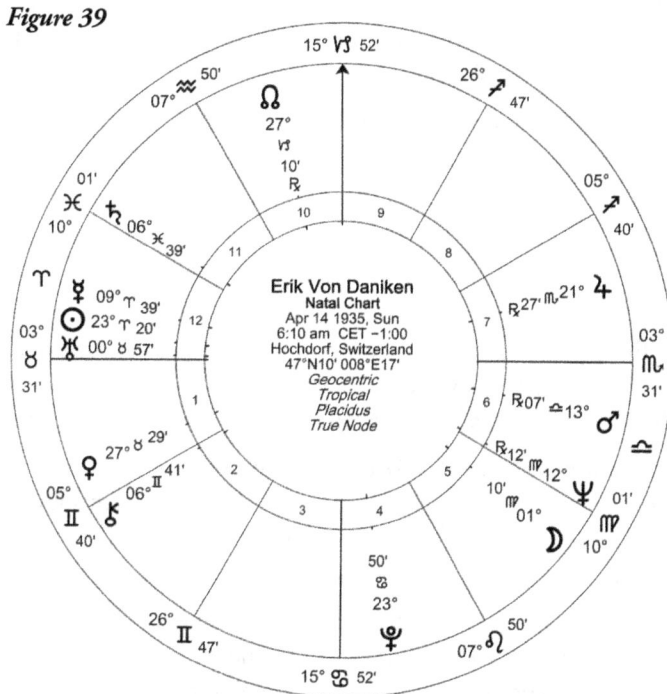

effort while pursuing his career and fathering five children. This is an excellent example of someone who educated himself in his adult years. He has starred in several television series including *The Cosby Show*, in which he played an obstetrician. With his Taurus/Scorpio intercepted across twelfth/sixth respectively, he overcame his personal demons, and used the powerful internal need to succeed. He become one of the wealthiest performers in the entire American television industry. His son Ennis was murdered in 1997. B: DN#18

Erik von Daniken, Adventurer, Author

Erik von Daniken gave me his data many years ago when I was working on a television production with him. We had many a delightful conversation as we waited for the crew to complete their various set-ups. His books include *Chariots of the Gods*, (1969), *Gods from Outer Space*, 1971 and *The Gold of the Gods*, (1973). He was perhaps one of the most controversial authors in the early 1970s with his revolutionary theories of prehistoric visits from astronauts 40,000 years ago. He asks questions that do not have answers based on present day knowledge and theories. His books have sold millions of copies in 32 countries, and his exploits have been documented in a television documentary which has aired many times.

For him to have such a dramatic and compelling need to investigate the past, and stake his reputation in front of the world, there must be an accumulation of chart evidence coming from different sources. His need was no doubt partly due to the intensity of the intercepted Aries/Libra across the twelfth and sixth houses respectively, containing his Sun, Mercury and Mars. Observe also the T-Square stemming from his Pluto in Cancer in his fourth house squaring both his intercepted Sun and Mars. This interception creates Gemini spanning the second and third houses, as well as Sagittarius spanning the eighth and ninth houses, which indicates living up to his beliefs in spite of the financial and legal concerns. The ninth is also the house of publishing.

He was seriously ridiculed by the scientific community. His world exploits to gather evidence for his claims, as well as offsetting lawsuits, bankrupted him personally. He had previously owned a prosperous hotel in Switzerland. This was many years ago and I have no way of knowing to what extent he recuperated his losses and what his personal status is today.

Only recently I saw a television rerun of his dramatic documentary with himself as the commentator.

Other Examples

It is interesting to note that many people who make their living in the entertainment business have this combination.

Merv Griffin, Talk Show Host, Entrepreneur: Leo second and third/Aquarius eighth and ninth. Leo on second and third describes perfectly how he made his initial money. His multiple and complex financial holdings are indicated by Aquarius repeated on eighth and ninth houses.

Sir Arthur Conan Doyle, Physician, Author, Father of Forensic Medicine: Cancer second and third/Capricorn eighth and ninth. Creator of Sherlock Holmes mysteries. First, his main source of income was his writing. Second, one can easily see the forensic inclusion in his work through the combination of eighth and ninth houses.

Steven Spielberg, Writer, Director, Producer: Leo second and third/Aquarius eighth and ninth. He certainly had a calling. He began making films as a child and became one of the youngest television directors in the industry, prior to making motion pictures. Most notable films are *Jaws, Close Encounters of the Third Kind, ET, Raiders of the Lost Ark, Indiana Jones and the Temple of Doom, Hook, Jurassic Park* (plus sequels), *Schindler's List* (for which he won the Oscar for Best Director) and *Saving Private Ryan* (won the Oscar for Best Director).

Arnold Schwarzenegger, Bodybuilder, Actor: Leo second and third/Aquarius eighth and ninth. Most of his starring roles have been as a muscle man; these include *Conan the Barbarian, Conan the Destroyer, Terminator 1* and *Terminator 2* and then on the lighter side, *Batman and Robin*. He also served as the governor of California.

Phyllis Diller, Comedienne: Cancer second and third/Capricorn eighth and ninth.

Leonard Nimoy, Actor: Cancer second and third/Capricorn eighth and ninth.

Liza Minnelli, Actress: Gemini second and third/Sagittarius eighth and ninth.

David Frost, TV Interviewer: Leo second and third/Aquarius eighth and ninth.

Ross Perot, Entrepreneur: Leo second and third/Aquarius eighth and ninth.

Same Sign on Third and Fourth . . . Ninth and Tenth Houses

The third and fourth houses are linked by the needs of the sign thereon. Your communicative needs, early education, relationships with kin and neighbors and ability to adapt to your immediate environment are often dramatically linked with your home environment and parental influences.

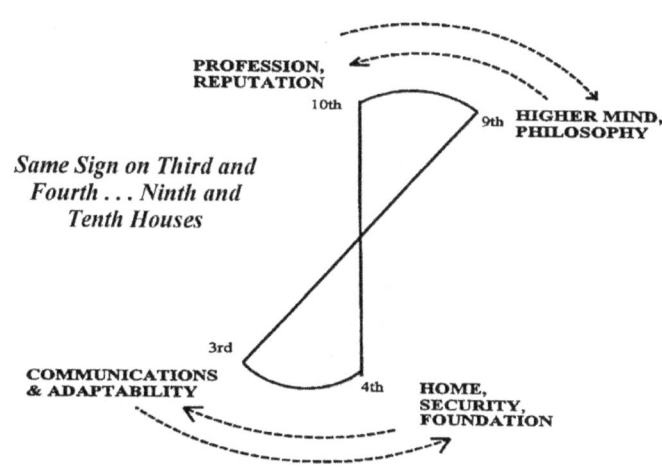

Same Sign on Third and Fourth ... Ninth and Tenth Houses

Conversely, the general condition of your home environment, be it supportive and inspirational, or upsetting in some way, has an impact upon your ability to express yourself, to learn and to function each and every day that you venture forth into your daily activities. The combination may be helpful, expansive and encouraging, or it can be stifling until an inner security is developed. In other words, your mental perspective relates directly to your emotional well-being. Whether we have this cusp condition or not, we can all contest to the fact that if we have a dispute with someone in our family in the morning before going to work, it can take at least part of the morning to regain our emotional equilibrium. Imagine what this would be like if you grew up under those conditions day after day.

If you are not nourished both physically and emotionally, it can affect your learning ability in school, your relationship with your teachers, as well as other students. I have known many clients with this situation, and they have had to search for inner peace, as well as restructure their early education. It may create a personality that is self-protective or hesitant to exert influence in some way. Refer to the chart of Student 1, Figure 7. I do not know her early parental influence, but I do know that she did not want to express her feelings and needs to her husband because she did not want to disrupt what she felt was a secure home and marriage within which to raise her two daughters. After moving her studio down the street in the same neighborhood, he ceased resenting the time she spent at her work. Eventually she published some of her work, and gained a significant reputation. (Sagittarius on both ninth and tenth houses.)

I had another client many years ago who attested to a very difficult childhood. She was abandoned by her mother and grew up in a series of foster homes with little care and attention paid to either her physical or emotional needs. For many years she was filled with anger and resentment because she did not feel she belonged anywhere or that anybody cared what happened to her. Shortly after her Saturn return, she decided that she could not keep blaming society anymore. If anything was going to change she would have to be the one to do it. She restructured her education, which took many years, but finally landed a good job and bought a new house. I will never forget when she finally understood her life from her astrological patterns. She clapped her hands and said, "I really did do it *right* then, didn't I? I took charge of my life, took responsibility and gained my self respect and inner security. It took a long time, but I did it! I feel so fulfilled."

Understanding Interceptions

In another scenario, you may have been a student who needed constant attention and comforting from your teacher, as an extension of mother in the classroom. Perhaps you were an only child who was doted upon or who had a childhood illness and received much attention from mother and other care-givers. This attention seeking can foster many different attitudes from sweetness to misbehavior. If teased unduly, these children may run home often or seek refuge in a secret hiding place. It may be a physical hiding place, or an emotional one, creating a shy, insecure personality.

There are also people who would prefer not to use either their family or given names and may chose a nickname, or change either one or both completely. Bela Lugosi did this for the stage in his homeland of Hungary before going to America.

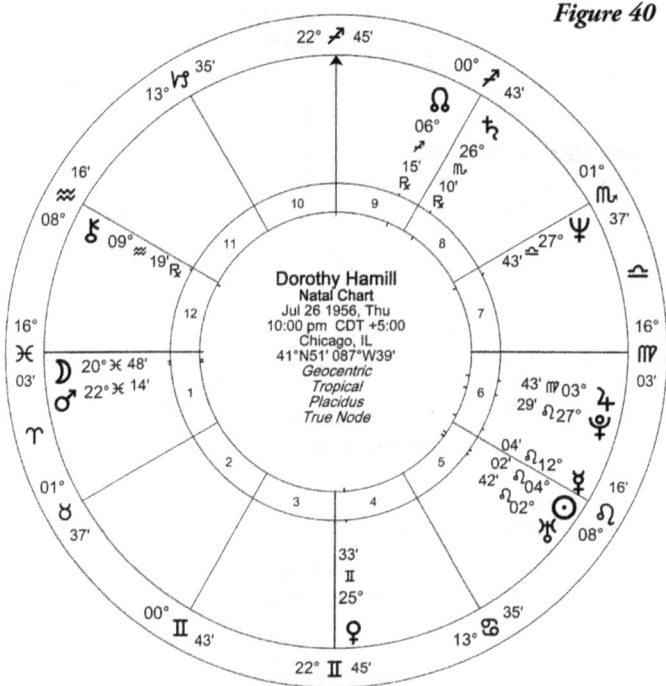

Figure 40

When the same sign appears on the ninth and tenth houses, the amount and quality of education or preparation past grade school relates directly to your career and the security found as you project outward into the realm of contribution and achievement. Of course, this is so in everyone's life, but is often more emphatic in some way when the two houses are linked by the same sign. Many times these people will backtrack in their adult years, improve their prerequisites, and enter college, a technical institution or university. The goal is long-range but the benefits are extremely gratifying.

The two houses may be combined in the career such as educators/professors, clergy, people in the travel industry, as well as import/export, or in the publishing business. William F. Buckley is a perfect example. He is the founder and longtime editor of a magazine called National Review. He often appears on television discussion programs, and has written several books including spy thrillers. According to Biography.com, he is known for his "sesquipedalian vocabulary" (which means using long words that are often humorous).

This combination would not be uncommon for people who teach astrology in an adult extension department at an educational institution, who write magazine articles and eventually publish at least one book that commands attention in their chosen field.

Figure 41

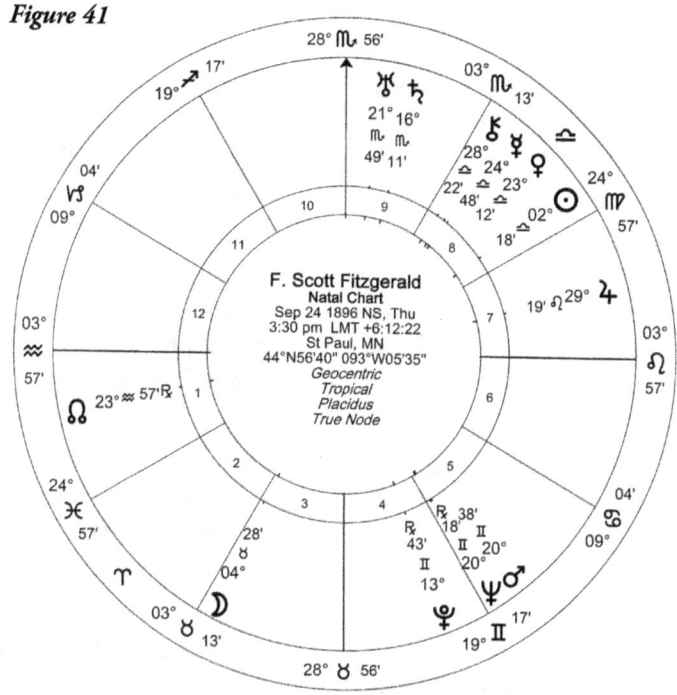

It is also prevalent in the charts of people who are restless, travel a great deal or are involved in multi-cultural activities. Refer to the chart of Dorothy Hamill, Figure 40. She traveled a great deal due to her skating career. You may travel in search of a philosophy or a guru as you pursue different belief systems, which eventually can change the path of your life. I have a client with Sagittarius on the ninth and tenth who changed her religion because she believed it would further her career and standing in the community.

There can be a link between your ethical/moral conduct and your reputation and/or career advancement. Joseph Lyle Mendez is a stark example. He has Capricorn on his ninth and tenth houses. He and his brother Erik have both been convicted of murdering their parents.

Dorothy Hamill, Gold Medal Ice Skater

Every scenario is different. Dorothy Hamill has Gemini on her third and fourth/Sagittarius ninth and tenth. She left the formal classroom at age fourteen to practice more and study at home with a tutor. I cannot say whether or not her education was compromised, but she would certainly have had different community experiences than if she had attended school in a more diverse environment with her peers. A: ABC

F. Scott Fitzgerald, Author

He left Princeton University before graduating to join the army during the First World War. His writing shows great psychological insight. Perhaps his best known work is *The Great Gatsby*, which was made into a motion picture. It is the story of a man who was materially very successful but destroyed himself and everyone around him in the process. Fitzgerald and his wife Zelda lived a life of extravagance, and alcoholism, leading to debts. Zelda was institutionalized and Fitzgerald had a mental breakdown. He is considered to be one of the great American writers. B: ABC

Understanding Interceptions

Other Examples

Linus Pauling, Chemist: Gemini third and fourth/Sagittarius ninth and tenth. He received his Ph.D. at the California Institute of Technology where he also spent most of his professional career, successfully combining the ninth and tenth houses. He was the first person to receive two Nobel prizes: one in chemistry for his work on molecular structure and, the Peace Prize for his effort in banning above-ground nuclear testing.

Alexander Graham Bell, Inventor, Educator: Gemini third and fourth/Sagittarius ninth and tenth. He worked as an assistant to his father at University College in London, in the field of speech physiology where he conducted his own research into teaching the deaf to speak. He later obtained his own professorship at Boston University. He invented the telegraph and telephone, later establishing the Bell Telephone Company. He was also keenly interested in aviation. We see many links between these houses in his whole life pattern.

Christopher Isherwood, Novelist, Scriptwriter: Leo third and fourth/Aquarius ninth and tenth. He was born and educated in England, taught in Germany, traveled to China and emigrated to California. He inspired the musical *Cabaret*, wrote *Journey to a War*, as well as *The World in the Evening*, *Down There on a Visit* and several more. He was deeply involved in Hindu Philosophy, and was on a constant search for the meaning of life.

Orson Welles, Actor, Director: Leo third and fourth/Aquarius ninth and tenth. He was no doubt conditioned by his varied early life. His mother died when he was ten, he toured with his father who was a concert pianist, attended a private school, and then his father died when he was twelve. He became the ward of a physician named Dr. Maurice Bernstein. He turned down college and went to Ireland where he acted in the famous Gate Theatre. Much later, with John Houseman, he founded the Mercury Theatre, which broadcast the famed radio dramatization of H.B. Wells's *War of the Worlds* that was so realistic that people all over the United States fled to the streets in panic. He went to Hollywood and made *Citizen Kane* which was not appreciated or acclaimed for many years. For many years he was ostracized due to his erratic attitude. He was divorced several times, was grossly overweight, failed at many projects, but eventually was honored as one of the true film-making geniuses.

Bela Lugosi, Actor: Gemini third and fourth/Sagittarius ninth and tenth. He played on the Hungarian stage under an assumed name before going to Hollywood, where he played a villain in many B-grade motion pictures. He constantly had money and marital problems, and became a drug addict. When he died he was buried in his Dracula cape.

Carol Burnett, Comedienne, Actress: Gemini third and fourth/Sagittarius ninth and tenth. She had a very unhappy early home life. Her parents were alcoholics who kept separating and reuniting. She was virtually brought up by her beloved grandmother. After her parents died, she took care of her twelve-year-old sister. In spite of this, she had a brilliant career as an entertainer, due much to her very mobile facial expressions and mimicry.

Mia Farrow, Actress: Cancer third and fourth/Capricorn ninth and tenth. Born of show-business parents, she spent several years in a convent and at one time even considered being a nun. Acting had greater allure. Her most notable films include *Rosemary's Baby* and *The Great Gatsby*. She was married briefly to Frank Sinatra, had twins with Andre Previn and a notorious relationship with Woody Allen.

Ringo Starr, Drummer, Singer, Songwriter, Actor: Gemini third and fourth/Sagittarius ninth and tenth. He had a difficult childhood and left school at age fourteen to earn a living.

Same Sign on Fourth and Fifth . . . Tenth and Eleventh

The fourth and fifth houses are linked by the needs of the particular signs thereon. Our early nurturing, conditions surrounding our home environment and our emotional security are dramatically linked with the release of our creativity, ability to take a chance, fall in love, have fun, enjoy a healthy relationship with our children and even to bear children. Conversely, the ability to release our creative flow is in relationship to our early guidance. This is true in all of our lives but more so in some remarkable way by this double occupancy of signs.

I have a client with Cancer on both of these houses who can attest to all of the above. I will call her Jane for the sake of convenience but that is not her real name. Jane was brought up by a single mother who was very protective and over-powering. As a youngster she showed great talent as a musician and dancer but her mother did not consider these important activities. Both the music teacher and the dancing teacher gave Jane free lessons for a couple of years to try and convince her mother of their value. She performed in her local community at many functions. Her mother was proud but unyielding in the further development of these talents. At about age nineteen Jane fell in love and wanted to get married, but her mother blocked the arrangement with so many emotional tantrums that the young girl gave up the relationship thinking that her mother may have good reasons. Her mother later regretted her actions.

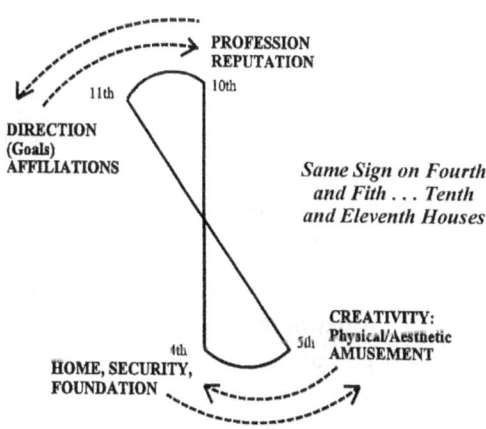

Same Sign on Fourth and Fith . . . Tenth and Eleventh Houses

Several years later, when Jane fell in love once more, her mother was supportive this time but tried to convince her she was not strong enough to have children. She eventually did have a son and grandma finally released hold on her daughter by enjoying the grandson.

Mario Lanza, Figure 33, also had Cancer on the fourth and fifth houses. His enormous talent was not fostered as a child growing up. It was only when he was working in his family's grocery store, singing most of the time as he worked, that he was discovered and taken to Hollywood. However, his life continued to be an emotional roller coaster. It seemed difficult for him to adjust to his success. Perhaps he was insecure in accepting his talent and never felt he was as good as his publicity indicated.

Such was not the case with Liberace, a child prodigy, who had Taurus occupying his fourth and fifth houses. He developed into a gifted, flamboyant performer and was also a self-professed mamma's boy. He never found lasting personal happiness in his search for a partner that would meet his mother's approval and fulfill his own needs. He later accepted his homosexuality at a time when it was propitious to be discreet.

For many adults, there can be a significant period of learning how to relax, have more fun, and even to laugh easily. If laughter has been stifled over a long period of time, it can sound almost like uncontrollable hysterical jerks until it can eventually become more spontaneous and pleasant.

Inner conflicts between what you really are as a person and ingrained patterns from childhood do need some form of understanding before you can be creative and loving. It is often necessary to break away from home and parental influence in order to develop a larger perspective of what you can really be. Often the Saturn return is very dramatic as you try to overcome guilt in wanting to sever the proverbial umbilical cord. I have known people who have had to emphatically tell mother to "butt out", and then later to make up as friends, rather than as mother and child.

When the same sign appears on the tenth and eleventh houses, you may start your adult life by falling into the most convenient career pattern without any particular sense of direction or goal in mind. It is only through societal exposure, meeting others and viewing a variety of opportunities, that new possibilities begin to open up and long- range goals can be formulated. Sometimes, it is through having children and shedding a particular parental grip that life can take on a deeper personal meaning, which can result in career goals becoming more important.

Your business success may also be enhanced by joining organizations affiliated with your work, or for the betterment of your community such as your local Chamber of Commerce or a society designed for social improvement. It may be a fund-raising endeavor for a worthwhile cause. Whatever you chose will undoubtedly increase your networking skills and give you much satisfaction in releasing your love and humanitarian instincts.

You need to chose your friends carefully, preferably not within your immediate working environment. Those friends often turn out to be the very people who cause you the most grief by expecting favors that may jeopardize your own position. Also, if you accept a job as a favor from a friend, you may be the one expecting favors and end up being disappointed.

If you are disappointed with your progress and feel your goals are continually falling short of your expectations, be patient with yourself and go on a journey of self-support. It may help to realize that your parents have their own struggles and you need not be a victim. Emotional security is to be found within yourself. Once attained, you can begin to unfold your creative potential in order to make a worthwhile contribution to the flow of society. We are not all destined to make it into the

Figure 42

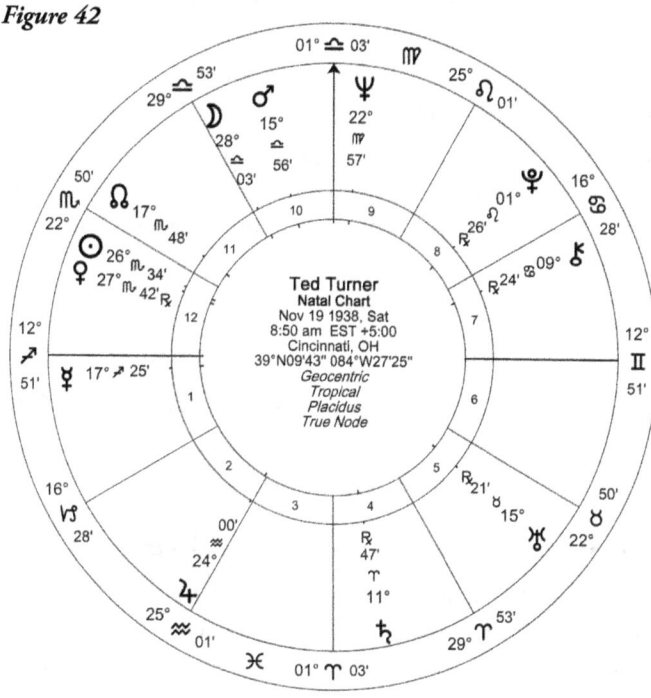

Ted Turner, Television Tycoon, Philanthropist

We do not know much about his early environment, but we do know he was kicked out of university for having girls in his dormitory. After his father committed suicide he went into the family billboard business. With Aries on the fourth/fifth houses it was imperative that he become his own person in spite of what must have been a stormy parental influence. His achievements in the television industry are legendary. In 1997 he donated one billion dollars to the United Nations, which is just one of many humanitarian contributions. With Pisces intercepted in his third, he has an uncanny intuition in providing communication links. His third marriage was to Jane Fonda in 1991. Ref: Biography.com; Gauquelin Data IV

Other Examples

Barbara Hutton, Heiress: Cancer fourth and fifth/Capricorn tenth and eleventh. Often referred to as "the poor little rich girl," her mother died when she was only four years old. Her early experience was one of abandonment and loneliness. To help overcome her lack of self-confidence she became exceptionally self-indulgent. She paid off seven husbands. Her latter life was spent in and out of hospitals.

The Duke of Windsor, Royalty: Gemini fourth and fifth/Sagittarius tenth and eleventh. He defied his parental influence and what his heritage was meant to be by abdicating from the British throne to marry the woman he loved. Thereafter he traveled extensively, with homes in various countries.

Willie Brandt, Politician: Cancer fourth and fifth/Capricorn tenth and eleventh. As a passionate anti-Nazi he fled Germany and joined the resistance movement in Norway. After the war, he returned to Germany and continued in politics as a member of the Bundestag (eleventh house), mayor of West Berlin, Chancellor and foreign minister. He resigned office when it was discovered that a close aide had been an East German spy. He was awarded the Nobel Peace Price in 1971. Rodden, in ABC, says "he was a hard drinker with spells of melancholy."

Whoopi Goldberg, Actress, Comedienne: Gemini fourth and fifth/Sagittarius tenth and eleventh. She grew up in a housing project in New York, was a school drop-out, and became a civil rights activist. In the mid-1970s she pursued her acting career much more diligently and further developed her comic persona.

Dean Martin, Singer, Actor, Comedian: Cancer fourth and fifth/Capricorn tenth and eleventh.

Billy Graham, Evangelist: Cancer fourth and fifth/Capricorn tenth and eleventh.

H.G. Wells, Writer, Historian: Gemini fourth and fifth/Sagittarius tenth and eleventh. Often predicted doom and gloom.

Herman Melville, Writer: Leo fourth and fifth/Aquarius tenth and eleventh.

Same Sign on Fifth and Sixth . . . Eleventh and Twelfth Houses

With the fifth and sixth houses being occupied by the same sign, your creativity, ability to love and enjoy life's pleasures are linked in some significant way with your ability to problem solve, function in your everyday working environment and take care of your health. Conversely, if you are overwhelmed by everyday problems, or you are in poor health it certainly has an effect upon your ability to enjoy life, love and the pursuit of happiness.

It is important that you find work with a creative flair that you love. Sometimes it takes a few years of searching to find your niche. I have a client who started out in what she called a boring clerical job with a boring wholesale fuel company. She felt she was stuck with it forever because she had no specific training. However, she had a deep interest in cultural history. About five years passed and the boredom lifted considerably when she fell in love and got married. As luck, or destiny, would have it, her husband was able to influence her getting a job with a museum helping to set up aboriginal displays. He got her the interview, but the excitement and glow in her face did the rest. She advanced her education, rose in the ranks at the museum and spent many fulfilling years doing the work she loved. She also had three healthy, happy children.

I had a client several years ago who had Taurus on his fifth and sixth houses. He said, "I am only a draftsman. It is dull and boring with no creative outlet. Besides, I have a son now and I never realized how much it would change my attitude towards life. I want him to be proud of his father. I want to be a role model of success for him. I want to go to university and become an architect."

I know several single mothers who have had employment difficulties due to taking care of their children. Some can only work part-time, which creates problems of survival on a limited income. Others lose valuable time at work when solving the seemingly endless daycare or health problems of their children. Still others find it easier to seek help from social services, at least while their

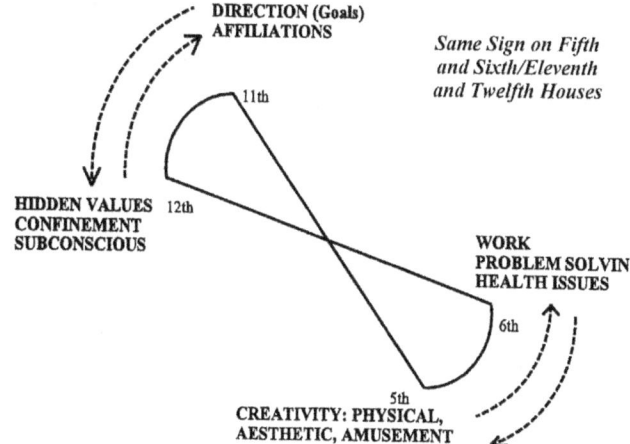

children are small. Social services provides funds for upgrading education, which in time helps them to be more self-sufficient and off welfare.

You may be one of the people whose love life interferes with your job. Maybe your lover lives in another part of the country and you are tempted to take time off work to see each other. This may also put a financial burden on your daily living expenses.

I have the chart of a friend who is an athlete, but he must also work to support his expenses. His training and trips out of town jeopardize his job. In fact, it has been directly responsible for him not receiving a promotion he felt he was in line for. Perhaps he needs to prioritize his goals. At the moment he is not succeeding in either area.

If you have the same sign on these two houses, you must not be tempted to take time off work on false pretenses for an afternoon of golf with a visiting relative, a quick trip out of town or spending a day with someone you love. The temptation increases every time you get away with it.

Handicapped people who cannot function comfortably or easily in a regular working environment, can often find fulfillment in some type of creative development. Henri Toulous-Lautrec, Figure 29, is a dramatic example of such a person. He was expected to fall in his father's footsteps as a banker, but due to his physical difficulties, he retired to the artist's community in Paris and found expression in his painting.

Adding the eleventh and twelfth houses, which, among other things the twelfth rules institutions such as hospitals, you may teach special needs children or work in a children's hospital. Dr. Tom Dooley, Figure 34, did not work exclusively with children, but he must have been deeply touched and influenced by the suffering and impairment he witnessed among them. The double occupancy of Aries/Libra, in part, prompted him to take action to help relieve the suffering of war-torn people. Registered Nurse, Figure 32, also does not work exclusively with children either, but as a nurse she is dedicated to relieving the suffering of others.

Other possibilities connected with having the same sign on the eleventh and twelfth houses indicate the need to set long-range goals that are realistic according to your talent and ability, supported by faith in yourself and beyond. You may doubt yourself and spend idle hours dreaming up impossible scenarios that are totally out of your realm of possibility. Of course, as previously mentioned, a whole chart works in synthesis. Our most prevalent characteristics are indicated in several different ways; thus, judgment of potential qualities indicated by all facets of the intercepted condition can be observed and supported or modified by other parts of the chart.

If you are dissatisfied with your work, you may indiscriminately gather a large group of friends to fill the void. These friends may lean unduly upon your kind nature, thus forestalling your own plans and goals. You need to ask yourself how far you are willing to extend yourself in order to satisfy a friend and if the friendship is worth the sacrifice.

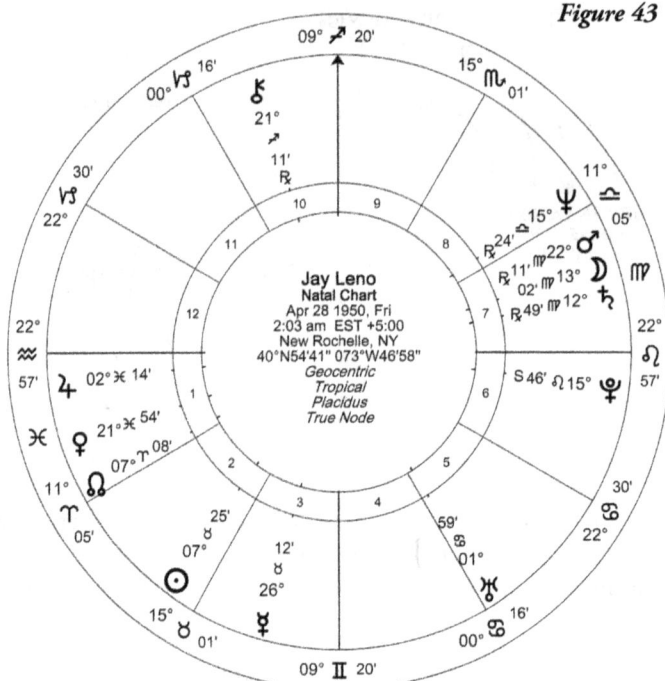

Figure 43

You may join an organization and do more than your share of voluntary executive or committee work. Have you ever noticed that the more you volunteer, the more you are asked to do? You may be a natural born "patsy" who does not know where to draw the line on how much is a fair contribution.

Jay Leno, Comedian, Talk Show Host

As reported by Biography.com, his fifth-grade teacher wrote on his report card that "if Jay spent as much time studying as he does trying to be a comedian, he'd be a big star." How prophetic! At college he earned a BA in speech therapy. From his chart and speech, one can understand why he was attracted to this study. I worked with him many years ago on a television production and found him to be warm and personable. He always wanted to help. His last contract with *The Tonight Show* in 1998 was for five years at $100 million. AA: BC to LMR

Lee Iacocca, Automobile Executive

With chart in hand, I found reading his autobiography, *Iacocca*, especially interesting. It was a bestseller, partly due to the publicity surrounding his activities, as well as the volume of press he was receiving. He made no secret about being fired as president of Ford Motor Company, but he turned his bitter disappointment and anger into triumph. He was hired as president and CEO

Figure 44

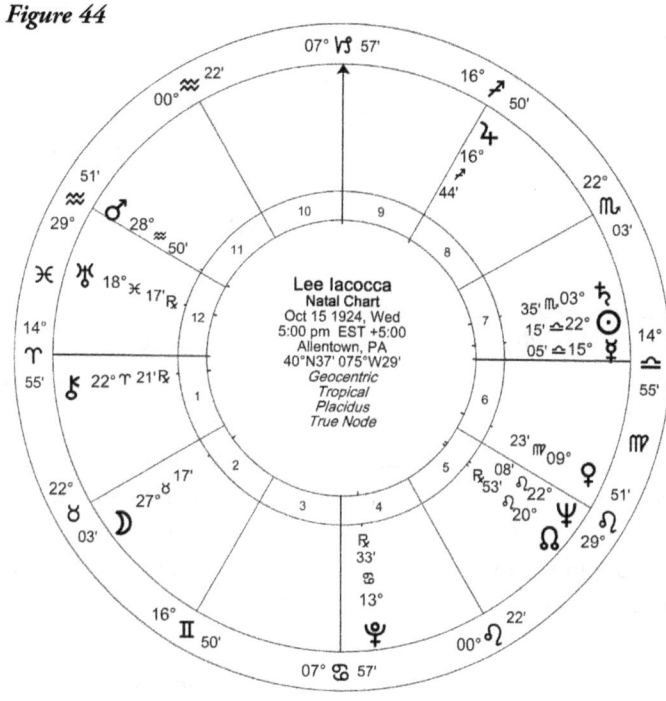

of the doomed Chrysler Corporation, and through his creative advertising, often using his own personality as spokesman in the ads (Leo on the fifth and sixth) he returned a failing company to profitability. He considers that a pretty good accomplishment for the son of immigrant parents. AA: BC: ADV

In my list of charts with these repeated signs, there is a noticeable abundance of actors/actresses and entertainers. This is to be expected. Their work is creative, and they can keep extending their goals due to the wisdom and experience they store in their twelfth house. Nervousness and apprehension never seem to leave them, but one successful performance can lead to many others; a poor one haunts them forever. I have shared green-room chatter with many of them and have been in the wing when they were ready to go on stage or in front of a camera and can attest to the large amount of last minute confidence-boosting many of them need.

Other Examples

Merle Haggard, Country Singer, Composer: Gemini fifth and sixth/Sagittarius eleventh and twelfth (intercepted signs are Leo/ Aquarius across seventh/first). Haggard had a difficult childhood. His carpenter father died when he was eleven. His mother was very strict, but it did not keep him out of reform schools or jail. He spent several years in San Quentin. Once on the right track, he released nearly seventy feature albums, 600 songs, 250 of which he wrote himself. That is an impressive amount. As of 1999 he has had "thirty-eight number-one songs," according to Biography.com.

Audrey Hepburn, Actress: Cancer fifth and sixth/Capricorn eleventh and twelfth (intercepted signs Virgo/Pisces across sixth/twelfth). She said she owed her life to the people who helped her when she was a child during the German occupation of her country. After she attained fame and fortune, she wanted to repay some of the kindness so she became a goodwill ambassador for UNICEF, comforting homeless, hungry, abandoned children.

Understanding Interceptions

Paul Newman, Actor, Director, Producer: Gemini fifth and sixth/Sagittarius eleventh and twelfth (Virgo/Pisces intercepted across eighth/second). He won an Oscar for Best Actor in *The Color of Money*. He was a notable race car driver, and his two marriages produced six children. He endorsed food products carrying his name and donated all the profits to a camp for children with terminal illnesses. He spoke out for social causes and was a delegate to the United Nations Disarmament Conference in 1978.

Hal Holbrook, Actor: Taurus fifth and sixth/Scorpio eleventh and twelfth. See Figure 30 for chart and brief biography.

Arthur Rimbaud, Poet: Pisces fifth and sixth/Virgo eleventh and twelfth. His career was short but notable. He published his first book when he was sixteen, after which he moved to Paris and lived a life of ill repute. When he was nineteen he wrote *A Season in Hell*. It was so poorly received that he gave up writing and traveled extensively throughout Europe and Africa.

Clint Eastwood, Actor, Director, Producer: Aries fifth and sixth/Libra eleventh and twelfth. I wonder how applicable his macho Dirty Harry character is to Aries being on his house of creativity. He worked at odd menial jobs until he was called into the army, after which he took a screen test in Hollywood and signed a contract. He did a series of "spaghetti westerns," which were popular and launched his motion picture career. He was married only twice but had at least seven children out of wedlock.

Sean Connery, Actor, Politician, UNICEF Spokesman: Gemini fifth and sixth/Sagittarius eleventh and twelfth.

Fred Astaire, Dancer, Actor: Taurus fifth and sixth/Scorpio eleventh and twelfth.

Dane Rudhyar, Astrologer, Author, Lecturer, Musician: Taurus fifth and sixth/Scorpio eleventh and twelfth.

Glen Campbell, Singer, Guitarist: Aries fifth and sixth/Libra eleventh and twelfth.

Robert Cummings, Actor: Taurus fifth and sixth/Scorpio eleventh and twelfth.

James Hoffa, Union Leader: Cancer fifth and sixth/Capricorn eleventh and twelfth.

Erwin Rommel, General: Gemini fifth and sixth/Sagittarius eleventh and twelfth.

Same Sign on Sixth and Seventh . . . Twelfth and First Houses

With the same sign occupying the sixth and seventh houses, your attitude towards duty, the way you handle your daily habits, your problem solving skills, as well as your health, are all connected with your ability to integrate with others, particularly your close partner. Conversely, the way you handle your relationships and the fulfillment derived from them, can affect the job you do, how you feel, and the complexity of problems you face that need a resolution.

When relationships are not satisfying, you can literally worry yourself into an illness. If pro-

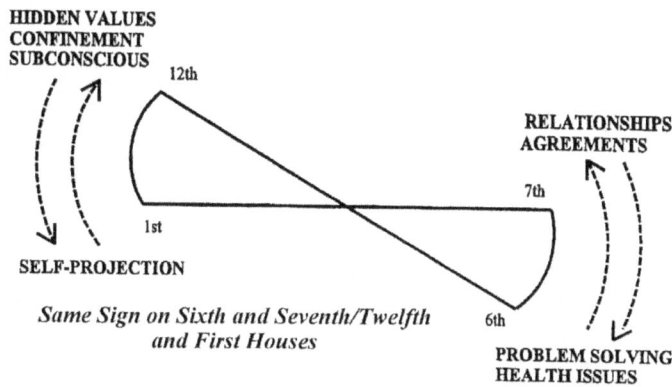

Same Sign on Sixth and Seventh/Twelfth and First Houses

longed, the illness can be quite serious and even chronic. Princess Diana's chart, Figure 26, with Gemini on the sixth and seventh houses is a good example of a prolonged relationship difficulty resulting in a serious illness. Its ruler Mercury is in her seventh house, indicating a perceived lack of satisfactory communication with her husband. She suffered from bulimia which is characterized by eating binges followed by induced vomiting and taking laxatives for purging the body of excess food. According to medical reports it is both physical and psychological, often started by a real or imagined male rejection. I have a current client with Pisces on the sixth and seventh houses who suffers from anorexia nervosa, which is a starvation disorder. She is very beautiful, excessively thin but feels fat, unattractive and unworthy of her husband's adoration. She grew up in a very large family and received little personal attention. In *The American Book of Charts* by Lois Rodden there is a chart that is just called Anorexia Nervosa, that also has Pisces on the sixth and seventh houses.

Please do not think that everyone who has the same sign on these two houses will react this dramatically. However, many students and clients have told me that they often experience an upset stomach or headache if they have an argument with their partner in the morning, but it usually only lasts for an hour or two. Such is the case with Student 5, Figure 27, with Taurus on the sixth and seventh houses. I have not seen her for several years but I recall her saying that the most stressful arguments were about money. Her husband did not want her to go to work. He wanted to prove he could provide for his family all by himself. Her job was to take care of their home and children.

With Gemini on these two houses you may suffer from allergies or rashes, due in part to relationship problems, particularly if Leo/Aquarius are intercepted and you are struggling with your level of self-confidence. A criticism or negative feedback can crush your ego. It is hard for you to realize that the other person may be the one at fault.

You may be so concerned about health issues, real or imagined, that you are constantly in search of a healing, or a new book on health and nutrition or a new exercise machine. I am certainly not suggesting that this is wrong unless you feel it is the only solution to a more complex situation. Illness brought on by relationship problems are often psychological in origin that manifest physically and should be examined from both points of view.

I have a client with Cancer on both of these two houses who feels she is the one who handles

Understanding Interceptions

ALL of the family problems from business concerns to family arguments without her partner sharing the load. They have a large integrated family and a complex business arrangement. Physically, female problems can manifest.

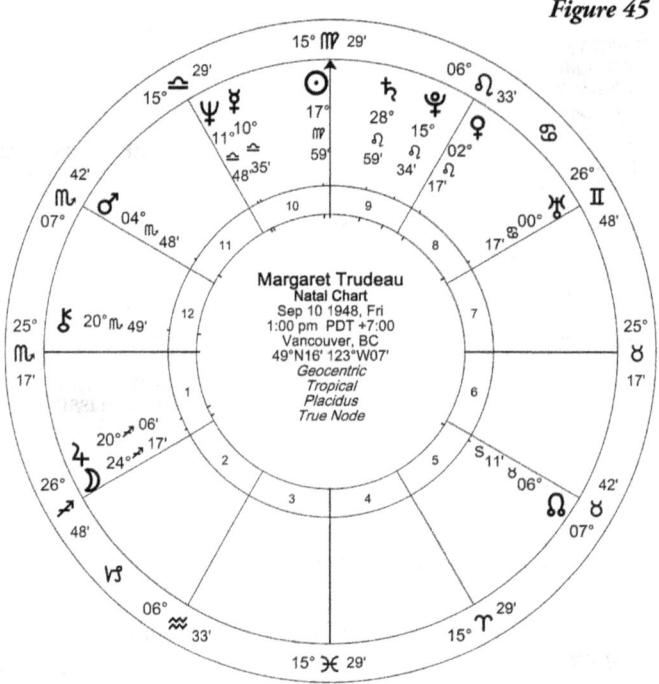

Figure 45

On the opposite side of the chart, with the same sign on the twelfth and first houses, it has often been written that "you are your own worst enemy." There is little doubt that you do need to build a stronger self-image and have more faith in yourself as a person. You cannot expect everyone to like or appreciate you, but if you do not like or appreciate yourself it is difficult for others to do so. It is not possible or necessary for everyone to like you. You need to have faith that you are a likeable, honorable, reliable person, who is striving to understand the complexities of life the same as everyone else. You need to have faith that you can in time shed a little light on some of the dark shadows lurking in the recess of your mind.

With the same sign on the twelfth and first, it is important that you bring your past forward into a conscious understanding in order to make your future brighter. That is how you will accumulate wisdom that you can also bring forward into conscious understanding to help you be a better problem solver and an inspiration to others. Some of you may improve your self-image by doing good works such as visiting people who are afflicted, infirm or elderly. You may be a block parent, a neighborhood watch volunteer, a foster parent, a big brother or sister. You may adopt a needy child in a destitute land. You may volunteer to do disaster relief. It helps you to feel needed and by comparison, you often realize you are better off than many others.

Refer to Figure 20, which is the chart of a client with Libra on the twelfth and first. This person told many lies to his wife. He said he did not want to worry her by telling her the truth about his business and particularly his financial problems. With Aries on his sixth and seventh, he felt he could handle everything himself. Eventually, when he was caught in a fraud real estate scheme, he had to face her, but equally as important, he had to face himself.

Figure 46

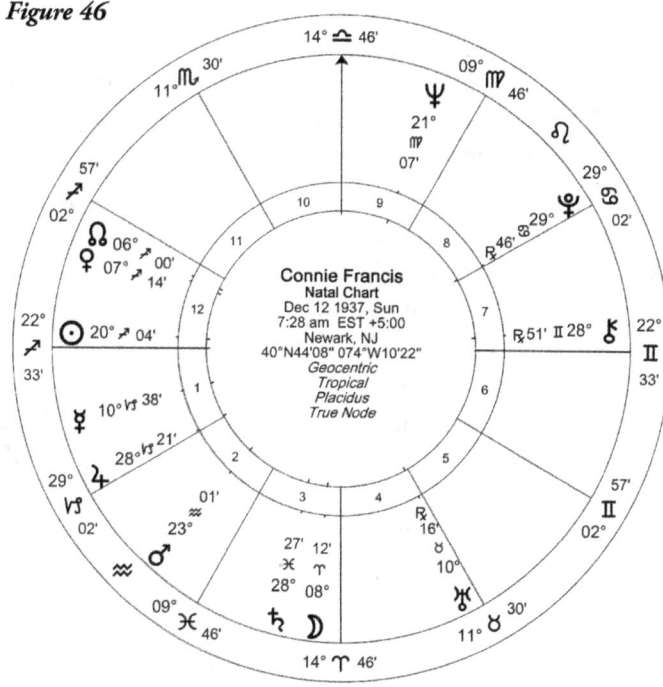

I once had a lady in one of my lectures with this position who said, "I often withdraw into myself because I am afraid people will see me as I really am."

Escapist tendencies may be strong in order to avoid facing oneself and the harsh realities of life. The most debilitating of these is drugs and alcohol. An occasional retreat can be very therapeutic for a rest or getting in touch with spiritual values, as long as it is not prolonged or permanent.

Margaret Trudeau, Former Wife of Pierre Trudeau

She has been dubbed "the most scandalous first lady in history," as revealed in her autobiography, *Margaret Trudeau Beyond Reason*. At twenty-two she married the fifty-year-old prime minister of Canada. As a flower child she struggled with the pressures of public life and the seemingly indifferent, logically minded attitude of her husband. Many of their arguments were about money (Taurus on sixth and seventh). She smoked marijuana, feuded with her security guards, broke protocol and was finally admitted to a psychiatric hospital for a rest. She said that the colder Pierre got the more hysterical she became. After six years they separated and she gave him custody of their children. They later became good friends. A: from mother

Connie Francis, Singer, Actress

This is a very dramatic example of a duplicated sixth and seventh/twelfth and first. She had countless hit songs including "Who's Sorry Now," "Everybody's Somebody's Fool" and "Don't Break the Heart That Loves You." Her notable movies include *Where the Boys Are* and *Follow the Boys*. She was dominated by her father, had four marriages that "included physical abuse and a nervous breakdown." She was brutally raped and robbed at knife point and was unable to sing for many years. She slowly recovered and began to sing again while continuing to battle depression. She has many dark shadows to overcome in order to project a positive self-image. Ref: Astro Data IV, Lois M. Rodden; AA: BC: ADIV

Understanding Interceptions

Other Examples

Sarah Ferguson (Fergie), Duchess of York, Royalty: Taurus sixth and seventh/Scorpio twelfth and first. Her marriage to Prince Andrew was plagued with public scandals and continual press scrutiny. They divorced after ten years. No doubt her extravagance, both in personality and finances, were partly to blame. They have two daughters.

Ivana Trump, Celebrity Divorcee: Taurus sixth and seventh/Scorpio twelfth and first. She is the former wife of billionaire Donald Trump. Their relationship was reputedly very stormy. After the divorce she published a self-help book on divorce in which she said "get yourself a great settlement-and before you do, take his wallet to the cleaners." She won a $20 million settlement at about the time he was tottering on bankruptcy.

Julie Andrews, Singer, Actress: Pisces sixth and seventh/Virgo twelfth and first. She had an unhappy childhood and did several years of therapy to overcome her deep-rooted problems. In *Profiles of Women*, Rodden quotes her from *People* magazine, "I loathed singing and resented my stepfather." Her first marriage ended in divorce but her marriage to Blake Edward, a director, endured until his death. She won an Oscar for *Mary Poppins*, and a nomination for *The Sound of Music*.

Lenny Bruce, Comedian: Gemini sixth and seventh/Sagittarius twelfth and first. He shocked the world with what is termed "blue comedy." He was also addicted to drugs.

Frank Sinatra, Singer, Actor: Aries sixth and seventh/Libra twelfth and first. He married his childhood sweetheart, Nancy Barbato. Ten years later he had a tempestuous relationship with Ava Gardner, and when she left him it nearly destroyed him. His marriage to Mia Farrow was brief. He married Barbara Marx in 1976 and that one lasted until his death in 1998.

Mario Lanza, Singer, Actor: Taurus sixth and seventh/Scorpio twelfth and first. He rose from obscurity to fame so fast that perhaps he could not catch up to himself. He died of a heart attack shortly after an eating binge.

Oscar Levant, Pianist, Composer, Actor, Author: Pisces sixth and seventh/Virgo twelfth and first. He was indeed a very talented but intense, haunted, neurotic man with many dark shadows lurking around the corners of his productive mind. He starred in the memorable film, *An American in Paris* and his books include *Memoirs of an Amnesiac*.

Jimmy Swaggart, Evangelist: Gemini sixth and seventh/Sagittarius twelfth and first (Figure 24). He certainly bad relationship problems, as evidenced by his affair with a prostitute in a sleezy motel.

H.R. Haldeman, Advertising Executive, Government Official: Pisces sixth and seventh/Virgo twelfth and first. He was convicted of perjury in the Watergate scandal and spent a year in prison. He wrote his version of the affair in a book entitled, *The Ends of Power*.

Pope Paul II: Aries sixth and seventh/Libra twelfth and first.

Danny De Vito, Actor: Gemini sixth and seventh/Sagittarius twelfth and first.

CHAPTER FIVE

Intercepted Planets

"God gave man an upright countenance to survey the heavens, and to look upward to the stars."—Ovid

THEME: INTENSIFICATION DUE TO INTERNALIZATION. *Must consider sign, house, ruler ship, as well as the rest of the chart for support or mitigation.*

It is certainly not uncommon to find a planet in an intercepted sign, more so in extreme northern or southern latitudes. It is important to note if the position is angular, succedent or cadent.

Angular demands more attention and more overt action from you than the other two positions. The need to find expression is more critical and any shortcomings felt seem to be more noticeable. I believe you would strive harder to find avenues to exemplify that particular planet for the first half of your life or until the period of inner understanding or development has occurred, even though it may not be in the customary fashion. There is much pressure on that planet.

An intercepted planet in a succedent position is less overt, but you would be more likely to apply the planetary necessity with a more urgent sense of application and greater caution as to outcome. The second house is concerned with security, the fifth house is concerned with creative expression, the eighth house is concerned with a deeper meaning of life and the eleventh house with success in intermingling with others.

An intercepted planet in a cadent position is likely to be even less overt than the succedent one but not any less important. There is greater need for internalization so that knowledge gained and ideas germinated can be carefully examined and then digested before being utilized. No one position is better than the other one. It is just a different way of utilizing the planet's energy.

Whatever house the intercepted planet is in, that planet also rules another one, unless it is in its own rulership. If it rules a non-intercepted sign, it will be stimulating the need of that other sign from an internal point of view until experience in an outer form is gained. You may wish to refer to Chapter One, where the basic urge of the twelve signs is outlined. The internalization magnifies the need to find a form of that planet's expression through the basic urge of that sign.

For example, Mars in Leo intercepted in the third house and ruling the eleventh house (Aries on the cusp of the eleventh) is intensified in gaining information that will help develop self-confidence through creative application and extend the long-range goals and aspirations.

Friendships will likely be sought within the immediate environment one is operating in, be it a school, college or neighborhood, but carefully selected within a particular comfort area. These people within the secluded group would help to inspire and motivate further learning and expansion.

It is not uncommon to find the Sun, Mercury and Venus intercepted in the same sign, simply because, from a geocentric position, Mercury can never be more than 28 degrees from the Sun, and Venus can never be more than 46 degrees from the Sun. A perfect example is the chart of Hal Holbrook, Figure 30, with all three planets intercepted in Aquarius in the second house. These are categorized as personality planets (along with the Moon and Mars) indicating an introvert. He did not find his niche in the acting profession until he became Mark Twain on stage, a feat which had never been tried before and set him apart in the history of entertainment as a unique performer. A comprehensive meaning of each planet in interception will unfold in the following pages.

F. Scott Fitzgerald, Figure 41, is another example of the Sun, Mercury and Venus being intercepted, this time in Libra in the eighth house. Both his life and his literary works reflect this struggle.

Some charts have even more intercepted planets indicating a complex inner nature. Such is the chart of Mario Lanza, Figure 33, who had five of the ten planets all intercepted in Virgo/Pisces across the sixth and twelfth houses respectively. There seemed to be so many facets within his nature that he was uncomfortable expressing overtly in the very public life he found himself propelled into without much preparation.

So you do not get the idea that having a planet(s) intercepted is a liability, I will present examples of those people who have experienced them both in a positive and negative fashion. Jay Leno, Figure 43, is an exceedingly successful talk show host in a highly competitive market where few hosts survive, let alone make it to the top. He too has five planets intercepted (angular). There is no doubt that he had many inner fears, and probably still does, but that he was driven from a deep inner need to be successful in his chosen profession. There is a very private side to his life that is kept carefully concealed from the press.

Queen Elizabeth II of England, has two sets of intercepted signs, containing five planets in all. These are Moon, Neptune in Leo intercepted in the seventh; Mars, Jupiter in Aquarius; and Mercury intercepted in Aries in the second. She is indeed a very private person and does not show any emotion in public. Her speeches are given in the same withholding manner. Lady Diana accused her of being cold and unyielding.

The examples chosen in the following pages required careful selection because the struggle with intercepted planets is very personal. This kind of information is often difficult, if not impossible, to obtain for celebrities.

Sun Intercepted

The Sun is the center of the universe and hence the glue or influence that holds the solar system together. Therefore, it is the center of our own being, the core of our existence in this personality embodiment and gives the rest of the chart meaning or holds it together. The Sun is not what we are as much as what we are striving to become. If you were a perfect Taurus, or Cancer, or Capricorn, you would not have to strive to become one.

If your Sun is intercepted, you seem to require more time for inner development before being confident and comfortable projecting outward. You may seem shy, insecure and lacking in self-confidence particularly as a child and young adult. I do not feel that each of our developmental characteristics need to reach the same plateau at the same age. However, parents, teachers, psychologists and much of society seem to think this should be so. If our developmental stages differ significantly, we may be labeled backward, shy, slow, etc. One child may be more precocious and another one more self-contained. One should not be right and the other one wrong. You will see by examples given that success is not necessarily governed by these yardsticks, otherwise the young shy, skinny, awkward Bill Gates with his Sun, Venus, Saturn in Scorpio, intercepted in his fifth, would not be the great success he is today.

If your Sun is intercepted, particularly in a cadent position, and particularly more so in the twelfth house, you will go through a profound period of inner search and development. Earlier in this book I mentioned a man with an intercepted Sun in Pisces in his twelfth house who is multi-talented but was very shy as a young man. As he grew up he found a fitting avenue to utilize his creative urge without being a performer. His own creativity gave him sensitivity to the talents of others and he became a television and motion picture producer/director. In this venue he had a great deal of self-confidence working behind-the-scenes. In his early forties he was finally able to appear on camera himself and do a considerable amount of public speaking. However, even in his maturity he often prefers to remain a very private person.

With your Sun intercepted, you will likely find it difficult to graciously accept praise or even a simple compliment. This reflects to where you have the signs of Leo/Aquarius posited. Leo is your creative need, and its polarity to Aquarius is where you hope to have your creative selfhood accepted. If you are able to gain support and appreciation from others, it will eventually help you to express your individuality more overtly. Criticism is taken very personally and penetrates very deeply.

It will likely take you longer than many of your friends to determine your purpose, your goal and the direction of your life. Your early employment may seem pointless and unsatisfactory but in the interim you are growing inwardly in understanding yourself. Your father may have expected you to fall into the family business, or may have had certain expectations of you, and may be disappointed in your progress. This can foster guilt and a sense of failure. I have counseled many young people with this position and I ask them to be patient with themselves. The Saturn return period can be very profound and often brings a stronger sense of purpose and a direction that you can put your energy into. By this time your Sun will have progressed into a new sign, giving you an opportunity to integrate new ideas into your purpose and a new sense of urgency to forge ahead.

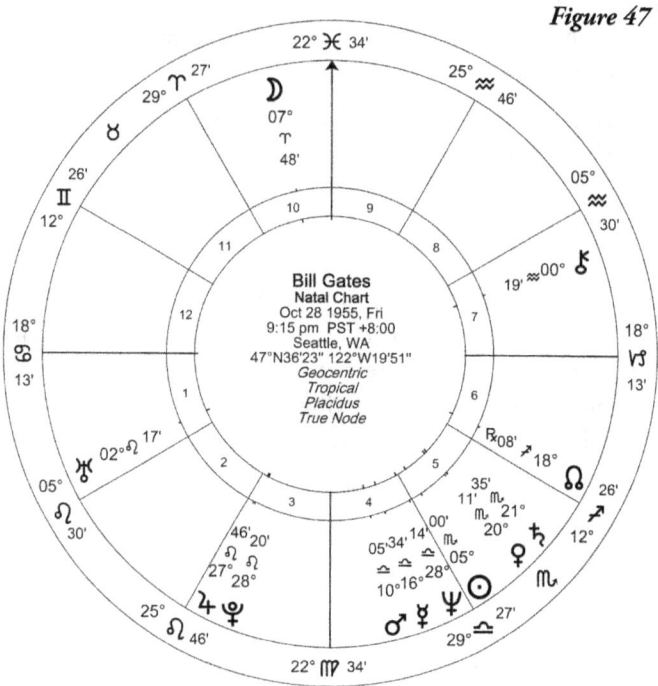

Figure 47

Your Sun may start in an unintercepted sign and move into one during the first thirty years of your life. This does not mean that you will suddenly go from being an extrovert to an introvert. The natal stamp remains but you will grow in understanding and effectiveness. My natal Sun progressed from Aquarius in the eleventh house into my twelfth intercepted in Pisces, at about age twenty-two where it remained for about thirty years. It has now progressed into Aries and into my first house. I never ceased my public life during those thirty years, but began a deep, meaningful search for the purpose of life in general, not just my own. This eventually led me to astrology. In spite of everything else I have done, I consider this to be the most profound part of my life. I feel privileged to have been given this opportunity which would not have developed in the same way if I did not have the interception by progression.

Bill Gates, Entrepreneur, Philanthropist

Bill Gates was a shy, skinny awkward young man, not showing any leadership skills, and was "an unlikely successor to his over-achieving parents." He went to Harvard to study law but left before graduating to try his hand at the computer software business. He became a billionaire at age thirty-

Figure 48

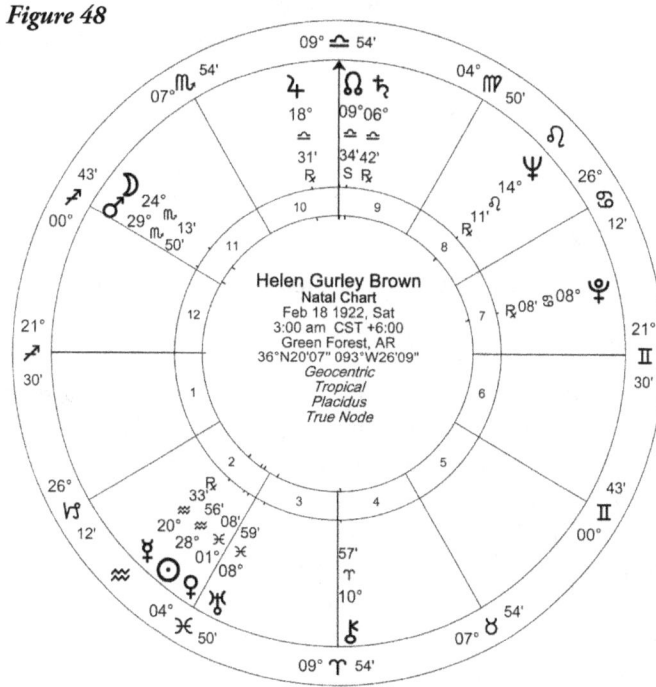

one. He was thirty-nine before he built his dream home, married and started his family. In 1994 he set up a charitable foundation of $17 billion. Ref: Biography.com. DN#59: from biography *Hard Drive: Bill Gates and the Making of the Microsoft Empire* by James Wallace and Jim Erickson. DN #61: 10:00 PM from him to Cindy Rempel.

Helen Gurley Brown, Author, Editor

Helen Gurley Brown grew up during the Depression. Her father died when she was ten years old. As a child she was unattractive and shy. Rodden in *Profiles of Women* (Ref: *Current Biography* 1969) quotes Brown as saying, "I have been mildly terrified from the day I was born and still am." She started office work and rose through the ranks to become editor-in-chief of *Cosmopolitan* magazine. She grew into a very glamorous, successful enterprising woman. She wrote *Sex and the Single Girl*, which was a best-seller. Ref: PW

Other Examples

Linda Ronstadt, Singer: Sun and Saturn intercepted in Cancer/seventh. Her early career indicated that she seemed to struggle with her image as she presented herself in many different ways. Eventually she bought a Malibu home and it seemed to help her with a sense of security, both internally and externally. With the help of her analyst, she overcame her drug dependency. In PW, Rodden suggests her Sun conjunct Saturn indicates "painful timidity and insecurity." I believe the interception made it even more acute.

H.G. Wells, Author: Sun and Mercury intercepted in Virgo/seventh. He started out as an apprentice to a draper, a teacher, a private tutor and then a student of biology, before becoming a journalist and a very prolific author. His most notable fantasy novels include *War of the Worlds* and *The Time Machine*. He also wrote *The Outline of History*, in two volumes. During the latter part of his life he became increasingly more pessimistic about the future of mankind.

Ava Gardner, Actress: Sun and Mercury intercepted in Capricorn/sixth, Pluto in Cancer/twelfth. Both her career and personal life depicted a restless nature, as if she was in a constant struggle to find her own personal identity. Her marriages to Mickey Rooney, Artie Shaw and Frank Sinatra are legendary. At forty-five she went into voluntary retirement in Spain, only occasionally being enticed to do another movie.

David Berkowitz, Serial Killer: Sun, Mercury, Mars, Jupiter intercepted in Gemini/eighth.

Peter Ustinov, Actor: Sun and Mercury intercepted in Aries/tenth.

Jacques Yves Cousteau, Oceanographer: Sun and Pluto intercepted in Gemini/ninth.

Moon Intercepted

The Moon represents our emotional nature. It is symbolic of our home, our early nurturing and our capacity to nurture others as we mature. It is the storehouse of memories from our earliest experiences, whether or not they are in our conscious memory bank. If you were endlessly left wet, hungry and crying, you might not remember the incidents but there is little doubt that those impressions would be carried forward into adulthood. You no doubt accumulated impressions received during growth in your mother's womb, whether she was happy, sad, indifferent or even abused. Certainly her understanding of how to take care of herself is reflected in the new person that is growing inside of her. I am also inclined to believe that emotional impressions may be carried forward from a previous personality embodiment, or reincarnation.

We need to fully realize that the Moon has no light of its own. It shines only by reflected light from the Sun. It is reactive. If we are resonating well with our Sun, it is much easier to develop a healthy emotional life. The more we are struggling with our Sun's creative development and self-confidence, the less brightly our Moon is likely to shine meaning we are likely to experience more emotional discontentment and challenges. With a highly sensitive Moon, we are likely to respond more impulsively to the actions of others rather than retaining the power of our own Sun and being able to initiate our own action. Certainly the signs and aspects will also make a difference.

If your Moon is intercepted at birth, you will likely keep your feelings shielded inside which intensifies them. There is a feeling of being exposed and vulnerable to hurt, ridicule and misuse. If you cry in front of someone you will likely feel embarrassed and childish. It is important to understand that hurt is a part of life. Even a well placed, brightly reflecting Moon experiences hurt. The more self-absorbed you are with your emotions, the more you will appear uncaring and unloving to others. The less you are able to give of yourself, the less you will receive and the more you perpetuate the feeling within yourself that you are unpopular, unloved and even rejected.

In many cases, there are mother issues that need to be resolved or at least understood. As a child you probably required a great deal more attention and affection than you received. I have clients who grew up with working mothers who were away a great deal of time, were often tired from a hectic day, or busy taking care of family chores. I have two clients with this position who grew up in very large Catholic families where chores were always more important than bedtime stories, hugging, or supplying the emotional requirements needed by children facing their daily concerns. I know others who were abandoned by their mother and brought up by either a grandmother or in foster homes. Abandonment is often a big issue with this position.

Princess Diana, Figure 26, had the Moon intercepted. Her mother left when she was quite young. When Diana married into the Royal Family, she felt Queen Elizabeth did not give her the help and support she needed and that her husband did not understand her emotional needs, which were probably quite extensive. She turned to others, including the public, in the hope that someone would understand the loneliness and despair she felt. She thought her outcry would help them. She certainly made sure her own children were loved. Much of her charity work was with sick and neglected children. One of her last charitable deeds was to visit Bosnia to focus on clearing landmines that were maiming hundreds of innocent children.

It is important to come to terms with these mother issues at sometime in your adult life. It may come through the trials and tribulations of your own parenthood. Sometimes therapy is required. Other times your own inner nature will help you to realize that everyone, including your mother, has their own issues that they are dealing with, in varying degrees of severity. Clarity rarely comes prior to the Saturn return and often much later because it is a gradual process of unfoldment. Some women with this interception may gravitate to working with women's issues, either medically or with programs benefitting single mothers or abused women, as a way of using and defraying their own emotional intensity.

The Moon by house in any chart shows where you are likely to experience the greatest amount of change. The house where you have Cancer is where you are seeking to find security which is difficult until you begin to realize why you react the way you do. In an intercepted condition, changes can be difficult, even traumatic.

The maturation process is helped by the movement of the Secondary Progressed Moon as it visits each sign approximately every 28 years, spending about two-and-a-half years in each, allowing for developmental understanding and stabilization. Mother issues most often come to the fore as it is progressing through your fourth house, aspecting its ruler, or planets contained therein.

If your Moon is not intercepted in your birth chart but you have a pair of intercepted signs, the secondary Moon will go into each one for a period of about two and a half years. This is quite different from having it there natally. It does not mean that you will suddenly become sullen, aloof and self-protective, but it does mean that you will internalize your feelings more than at any other time. It can provide opportunity for introspection and the deepening of your emotional life. It is an opportunity to discover a great deal about your emotional matrix through the affairs unfolding in that house.

Following the transit of the Moon as it stimulates various parts of your chart can be time consuming and fanatical, and it is certainly not recommended. I had to scold a student once who did this.

She turned on her computer and checked the transits every morning before she even brushed her teeth. However, if you are a highly reactive person, you should at least check the New and Full Moons each month to see if either one is stimulating your intercepted Moon, or anything else in your chart. The most potent effect occurs within the first three to five days after the lunation. A favorable New Moon aspect, particularly a conjunction, can begin a new phase of understanding for you. A Full Moon can bring a matter to fruition and help clear the air.

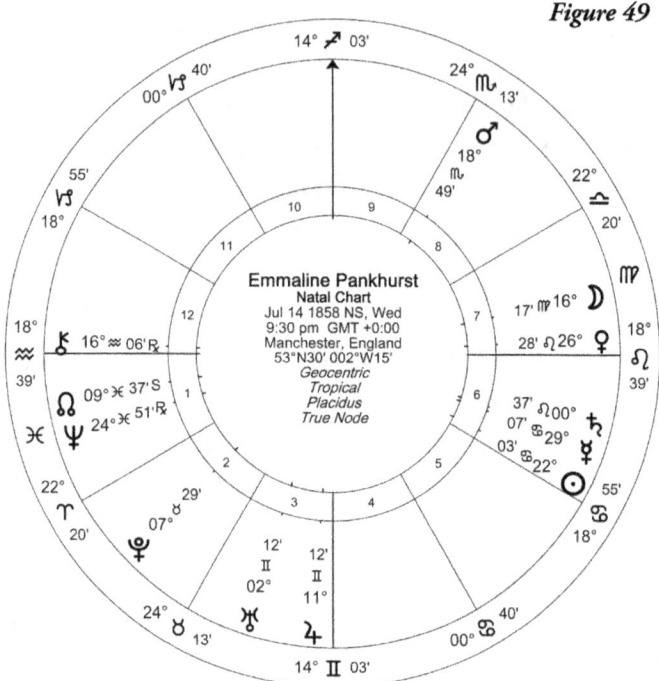

Figure 49

You might also wish to observe the transiting Sun as it conjuncts and opposes your intercepted Moon. In a way this is like a New or Full Moon This, of course, only occurs once a year for each of the two aspects and would not clutter up your calendar. At the conjunction you may find it rewarding to spend a few hours contemplating your feelings and allow the light of the Sun to brighten your Moon.

Emmaline Pankhurst, Suffragette

Her marriage to Richard Pankhurst, a radical Manchester barrister who was already championing women's rights, was a perfect match for her intercepted Moon trine Pluto, and her Sun/Mercury in Cancer, conjunct Saturn in Leo. Together they founded the Women's Franchise League. She fought militantly and passionately for women's rights, both peacefully and violently, often landing in jail and going on hunger strikes. During the First World War she put her efforts into "the industrialized mobilization of women." Ref: Biography.com/PW/F&WE; Lyndoe in AA, Jan. 1970

Montgomery Clift, Film and Stage Actor

He was a stage actor in New York for ten years before starring in his first picture, Red River, which made him an instant star. He loved the stage but found movies exhausting. He earned four Oscar nominations. He dissipated himself through drugs, alcohol and indiscriminate homosexual relationships, and died at forty-six. He was so emotionally insecure that he would not appear on

Figure 50

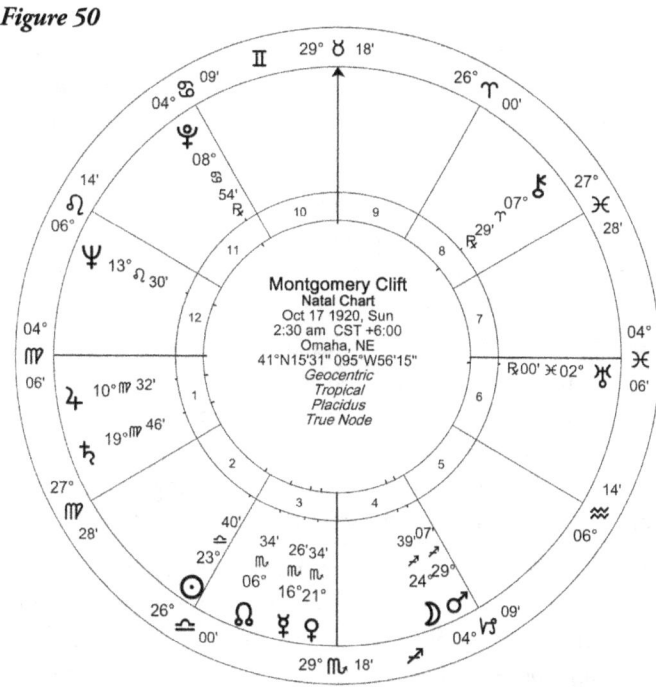

a set without his coach. His most notable films include, *A Place in the Sun* and *From Here to Eternity*. Ref: *Montgomery Clift, A Biography* by Patricia Bosworth, 1978; A: CL from BC

Other Examples

Merle Haggard, Singer, Guitarist, Composer: Moon intercepted in Aquarius/first. His Father died when he was eleven and he was brought up by a very strict, religious mother, which must have created deep emotional problems, judging from his time spent in reform schools and San Quentin. In time, he sorted out his problems and became a notable country singer. He was elected to the Songwriter's Hall of Fame in 1977 and the Country Music Hall of Fame in 1994. In my two-day professional association with him I found him to be aloof and impersonal.

King Edward VIII, Duke of Windsor, Royalty: Moon intercepted in Pisces/first. His need to be with the one women he felt understood him was so strong that he abdicated from the British throne to marry her, which changed his title to the Duke of Windsor. Later in life, his loyalty to his homeland during the Second World War has been questioned.

Steven Spielberg, Author, Director, Producer: Moon, Jupiter, Venus intercepted in Scorpio/fifth. The intensity of his fifth house of creativity is shown so vividly in the body of work he has done. He explored basic human fears in Jaws, a childlike sense of fantasy in *Close Encounters of the Third Kind* and *E.T.* He gave us the daredevil adventures of Indiana Jones in *Raiders of the Lost Ark* and *The Temple of Doom*. He returned to fantasy in *Jurassic Park* and *Hook*. He then won an Academy Award for *Schindler's List*, a film he had wanted to do for a very long time about a man who risked his own life to save countless Jews from the gestapo during the Second World War. In 1998 he gave us another Academy Award winner, *Saving Private Ryan*. His family life is very important to him. He has seven children.

Jules Verne, Writer, Attorney: Moon, Jupiter intercepted in Scorpio/sixth. He delighted us with *20,000 Leagues Under the Sea*, and *Around the World in 80 Days*.

Mercury Intercepted

Mercury is the smallest planet in our solar system but that does not diminish its importance. It is the planet of communication and hence the gathering and disseminating of information. It is our reasoning ability and the awareness of our surroundings in whatever we do. Thought precedes action, however fleeting it may be.

Mercury rules our conscious mind but is not that limited due to its association with Hermes, the Winged Messenger in Greek mythology who was given the privilege of traveling the whole sphere of the gods from the top of Mount Olympus to the depths of Hades, as well as being able to enter the domain of earth. In fact, it is he who guides the souls of the dead to their final dwelling place. In his farflung travels, he is forever gathering and disseminating information. In other words, we are receiving data from more than only our earthly source. Erin Sullivan, in her Chapter on Mercury in *Planets: The Astrological Tools*, edited by Joan McEvers, calls Mercury the "translator of all sensory data, assimilating them into the consciousness. . . ." She further states that "it is through Mercury that we not only absorb but also disseminate all of our perceptions." These are important thoughts and will be wended into our understanding of an intercepted Mercury.

On a regular basis, our conscious mind is very occupied with immediate tasks and perceptions as we go about our daily activities. At night, when we still our conscious mind and drift off to sleep, we can receive perceptions from the realm of the unconscious. I am sure you have gone to bed with a problem and awakened the next morning with a solution. We all have a vast storehouse of knowledge and understanding gleaned over the years, some of which is stored in our unconscious, and it comes to the fore when we are looking for a solution or solving a puzzle. We may feel we are getting a flash of insight or an inspiration. There is also a transmission from our soul experience feeding into our current consciousness otherwise our evolutionary journey would only encompass this single lifetime and somehow that seems somewhat futile. All of this is related through Mercury, the planet of information, and from time to time we are provided with opportunity to still our conscious mind and go inward for additional insight. When our conscious mind is quiet, the little messenger is still busy flitting from one realm to another, sometimes playfully and sometimes seriously. No wonder he needs wings!

If you have an intercepted Mercury, you keep many of your thoughts to yourself. The more a thought is kept inside, the more intensified it becomes which can make it complex and profound, or confusing, contradictory and frivolous. You may have an idea in your conscious mind, be it simple or complex, and due to that one idea the unconscious mind is busy feeding in all sorts of other information, not all of which is relative, but it does give you a choice. After all, Mercury is also a trickster due to its dualistic and polymorphic nature. You are quite comfortable with this process within yourself, but all of this intensity may make it difficult for you to feel you have anything significant to say, so you probably do not say anything.

The sign and aspects of Mercury will help determine how practical and experimental or useless and foolish your ideas are. Saturn can provide a stabilizing influence. Uranus can add a note of originality and cleverness. You will need some process of discrimination or selectivity to keep from cluttering your mind with too much superficial or diversified information, Mercury rules Gemini, which stimulates curiosity, but it also rules Virgo through which you learn selectivity and discrimination. Observe what planets, if any, you have in those signs and their aspects.

If your Mercury is intercepted, it is certainly not an indication that you are stupid. In fact you may be the smart one but lack confidence in expressing yourself until circumstances force you to do so. You may be afraid of being ridiculed. Perhaps your parents kept saying "don't be so stupid." Perhaps you grew up with a bully in your neighborhood who called you stupid and you took it to heart. Perhaps your responses in the classroom were often corrected. Perhaps your formal education was interrupted and incomplete. For whatever reason, you may feel you have nothing significant to say. You may feel that others do not understand you because they ignore your comments or look at you strangely. One of my students said she did not like talking, particularly when there was a lot of people around, because she did not like the sound of her own voice.

Your need to feel clever enough to overcome your own doubts is often so strong that you may be a perpetual student gathering information from a great variety of sources. You may read a lot of books. You may take a great variety of courses. You may spend a lot of time alone allowing your mind the freedom you cannot give it when you are with others. In a group discussion, you probably listen more than you contribute. The reverse may also be true. You may feel so inadequate that you quit trying to learn anything new. Even if you do, some form of perception is taking place.

Various speech impediments can occur when an intercepted Mercury is combined with other factors. Mercury with Saturn can add organizational ability or build a bigger barrier. Mercury to Neptune may be inspirational or have difficulty separating logic from illusion. A natal Mercury retrograde and intercepted is even more internalized. Mercury retrograde needs to digest and sort information internally before forming a conclusion and sending it outward.

The purpose of an intercepted Mercury in your life is to help you understand and perceive at a very deep level. It gives a greater necessity to your contemplation and sense of curiosity. Everyone receives this opportunity from time to time by various progressions and transits, but this is your Mercury motif at least until after your Saturn Return when you have had an opportunity to develop more confidence in projecting your ideas overtly.

Sometime during the first thirty years of life, your Mercury will likely progress out of interception and into a new sign offering greater scope and additional expressive needs. However, by retrogradation it may stay even longer than normal. If it is not intercepted at birth, it may progress in. This does not mean that you will lose your ability to articulate or express yourself easily, but it will stimulate a greater depth of perception. My own Mercury in Aquarius progressed into intercepted Pisces when I was five years old. It retrograded back into its natal sign, went forward again into the intercepted sign and will progress out of this interception in a couple of years. That progressed interception has encompassed a great deal of my life, including the years I was a television broadcaster, so it did not inhibit my ability to communicate. I believe it has stimulated a profound search for truth and understanding, the depth of which I am sure could not have occurred without the long progressed interception. Everything in our chart is designed with an evolutionary purpose in mind. We can learn by expanding consciousness, or experiencing pain, and often both.

You may not experience either of the above-mentioned progressed conditions, but if you have a pair of intercepted signs not containing your Mercury, the transit of Mercury will occupy each of those signs for approximately one month each year, except for its period of retrogradation. This is a wonderful opportunity to turn inward and allow messages to come from a variety of sources as Hermes flits freely carrying messages throughout its unlimited domain.

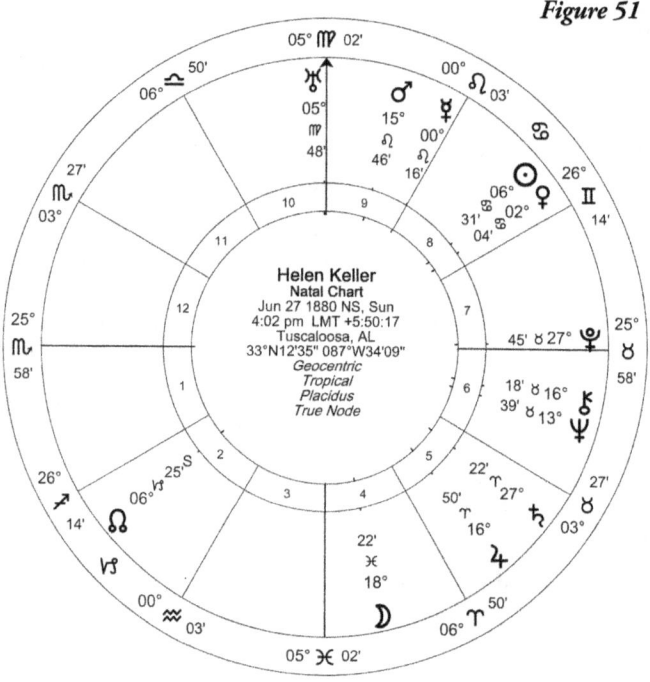

Figure 51

A great range of possibilities is open to all of us to utilize and express ourselves through our Mercury. We are not stuck in only one mold. Mercury is, after all, a shape-shifter.

Please refer to the chart and brief biography of Erik Von Daniken, Figure 39. Note that he has both Sun and Mercury in Aries intercepted in his twelfth house. His Sun is square Pluto, and Mercury is opposing intercepted Mars. He has studied unexplainable markings and ruins all over the world and looked for a logical explanation for their existence. His mind is fertile and unfettered by formal archaeological and scientific thought. He heeds the inspiration flowing through him and forms his own conscious evaluation. In spite of much criticism, loss of social and economic prestige, he has forged ahead. In 1972, shortly after his explosive books were published, I had the opportunity to converse with him for many hours and found him to be intensely passionate about his beliefs. This is a form of expression born out of an intercepted Mercury trying to dig deep for whatever truth emerges. Once again, twenty-seven years later, I recently saw a documentary on television of him on location, expounding on his theories. At least some of his explanations may one day be accepted by the scientific community.

Figure 52

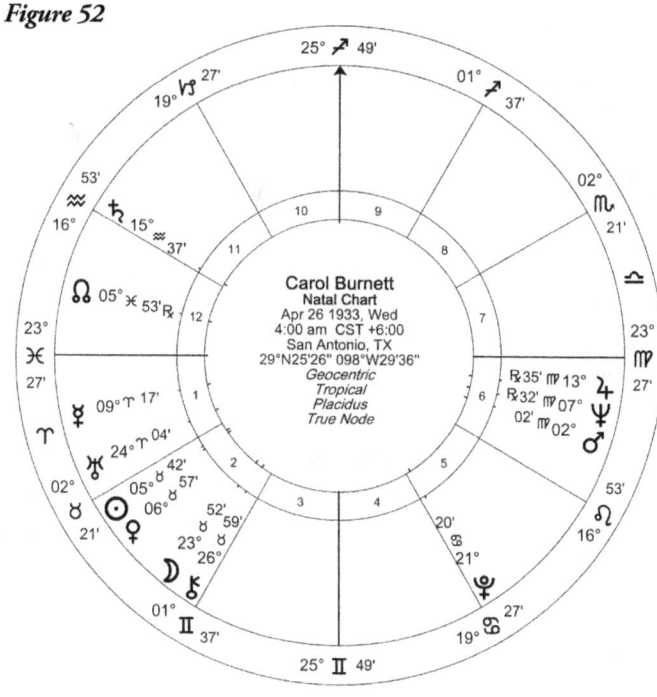

Helen Keller, Educator, Author, Lecturer

Helen Keller was an extremely remarkable person to have achieved so much for someone so severely handicapped. At nineteen months old she became blind and deaf. In desperation that she might become institutionalized as an insane person, her parents hired a teacher named Ann Sullivan who became her companion until death. Keller communicated through lipreading, braille and finger-spelling using a manual alphabet. She graduated from Radcliffe College and lectured worldwide on her experiences, as well as on social and political issues. She was a suffragette and a fundraiser for the American Foundation for the Blind. Ref: *World Book*/PW; Biography.com; *Astrological Quarterly*, PW

Carol Burnett, Comedienne, Actress

Carol Burnett had much to contemplate from childhood. Both of her parents were alcoholics, and she was raised by her grandmother. Both of her parents died when she was in her twenties. She studied journalism but loved theatre. She was not a stand-up comic but her skits were hilarious. It was not her lines, although clever, but her ability to create so many characters through her mobile face, physical antics and vivid reactions that made her comic-variety television show so popular. It ran consecutively from 1967 to 1979 when she canceled it herself. (A special note about this birth data: From PW, Lockhart from BC. Gallo quotes her personally at 4:15 AM CST. Both charts indicate a Mercury/Uranus Aries, intercepted in first. However, the 4:15 charts shifts the into her first house.)

Other Examples

Note that the people listed below are deeply contemplative, with an ability to focus intently.

Sir Peter Ustinov, Actor, Playwright, Producer: Mercury and Sun intercepted Aries/tenth. Although he was a stage and motion picture actor, he preferred to live a more secluded life in Switzerland. He was a prolific playwright who traveled extensively, spoke many languages, became known as a satirical comedian and was a great storyteller.

Sir Arthur Conan Doyle, Author, Father of Forensic Medicine: Mercury and Pluto intercepted Taurus/twelfth (also Venus Aries/twelfth, Sun, Mercury Mars in Gemini/twelfth). He created the character Sherlock Holmes, who is depicted as being deductive and super-observant, offset by the questioning but good-natured Dr. Watson, indicating Doyle's intensified Mercury. Doyle converted to spiritualism later in his life.

Betty Ford, First Lady: Mercury intercepted in Aries/ninth. The second wife of former President Gerald Ford, she was soft-spoken but not afraid to voice her opinion on such issues as women's right and abortion. She spoke courageously about her own battle with breast cancer, as well as her addiction to alcohol and drugs. She was instrumental in helping establish a clinic, which bears her name, for the treatment of addictions.

Glenda Jackson, Actress, Politician: Mercury intercepted in Gemini/twelfth. On stage and in film she often portrayed complex women. In 1992 she became a Labor MP, and devotes most of her time to politics. In 1997 she was appointed transport minister. Mercury rules transportation. Through her Mercury she is capable of great depth of thought.

Woody Allen, Figure 16: Mercury, Jupiter, Sun intercepted in Sagittarius/fourth.

Hal Holbrook, Figure 30: Mercury, Venus, Sun intercepted.

Venus Intercepted

Geocentrically speaking, Venus can never be more than forty-eight degrees from the Sun; therefore, it is often posited in the same sign as your Sun but never more than two signs away on either side. You have already been observing that some people have Sun, Venus and Mercury intercepted together.

Venus is often called the "lesser benefic" compared to the more grandiose display of Jupiter. That should not suggest that its role in the chart is lesser, because the scope of its interpretation is of vital importance in achieving harmony with others and our environment, as well as experiencing love and appreciation. Venus indicates what you value, be it something tangible or a person. How you value yourself is in relationship to what you expect and receive.

In a nutshell, Venus represents love. The sign it occupies in your chart indicates that you love expressing yourself according to that sign and you appreciate what it represents. Here are a few examples.

- Venus in Aries has a love and appreciation of self.
- Venus in Taurus loves possessing what their pay cheque can buy.
- Venus in Gemini loves exploring new ideas.
- Venus in Cancer loves home and family.

The house Venus occupies indicates where you play it out. Venus in Cancer in the second house indicates the love of buying items to beautify your home. Venus in Virgo in the tenth indicates the love of having a good reputation for being a good worker. With even a beginners knowledge of astrology, you would know that focus is also indicated where Taurus and Libra are located, both requiring Venus's influence to find fulfillment.

If you have Venus intercepted, it indicates that you will focus and identify internally how you can best express yourself and what gives you the greatest sense of pleasure and satisfaction before you seek it overtly. You need to find value in yourself. You need to examine and explore your various talents and personal resources so you can find a substantial form of expression that will give you a reason to believe in your own self-worth. It isn't enough that others tell you how worthwhile you are; you do not trust their sincerity until you trust and believe in yourself at a deep internal level.

In the meantime, as various aspects play out their theme and various transits move around your chart, you will try various activities, explore relationships cautiously, only to withdraw for periods of evaluation. You are seeking to define what and who brings you pleasure. Refer to Student 3, Figure 19, and review her story. With Venus intercepted in Cancer in her tenth, ruling her second and ninth, she had to explore her feelings very deeply, discover the resources within her that she could develop, and then find a way to develop them. She eventually decided not to blame society any more for her illegitimacy, foster parentage or her lack of opportunity but undertook it as her own adult responsibility. She upgraded her education, found a career she could love and clients she could appreciate and nurture, was finally able to support herself, and then began expanding her understanding of life through metaphysical studies.

If you have Venus intercepted you need love and appreciation very much but often feel unworthy of someone else's respect. Hence you may withhold the giving of your love until the other person proves they truly love you. You may fear being hurt or rejected. You may find it difficult to realize that in loving you always run the risk of being hurt, but when the other person is receptive, the relationship is magical. As Dr. Joseph Zinker in *Creative Process in Gestalt Therapy* states, when we are truly loved, we feel "beautiful, perfect, graceful, profound and wise." He further states that "our deepest, most profound stirrings of self-appreciation, self-love, and self-knowledge surface." You cannot be part of someone else's life or be part of a cooperative loving spirit until you learn to share.

The previously mentioned Student 3, Figure 19, had experienced so much hurt in her life that she was unwilling to share herself in a personal relationship. At sixty years old she had still not married nor found any of her blood relatives. However, she did find much fulfillment in many other kinds of relationships. She personalized her clients and she had many friends who enjoyed being invited to her home for an exchange of ideas and delicious morsels of food. This is a very vivid example and would not, of course, apply equally to every chart with an intercepted Venus.

It is often an indication of marrying later in life as in the case of Bill Gates, Figure 47, with Sun, Venus and Saturn in Scorpio, intercepted in his fifth. Venus rules his intercepted eleventh. However, it does not negate happiness.

There are reasons why someone would have difficulty trusting in intimate situations. Your parents may have been cold and austere or away a lot (or abandoned you), as in the case of Hal Holbrook, Figure 30. Surroundings may have been austere and unattractive, as in a boarding school. You may be unduly possessive due to growing up in a large family, sharing a bedroom with several siblings and having no privacy. A client with this position in Cancer square Saturn has memories of frequently being hungry. She is now glutinous, fearing that the next meal will be long in coming.

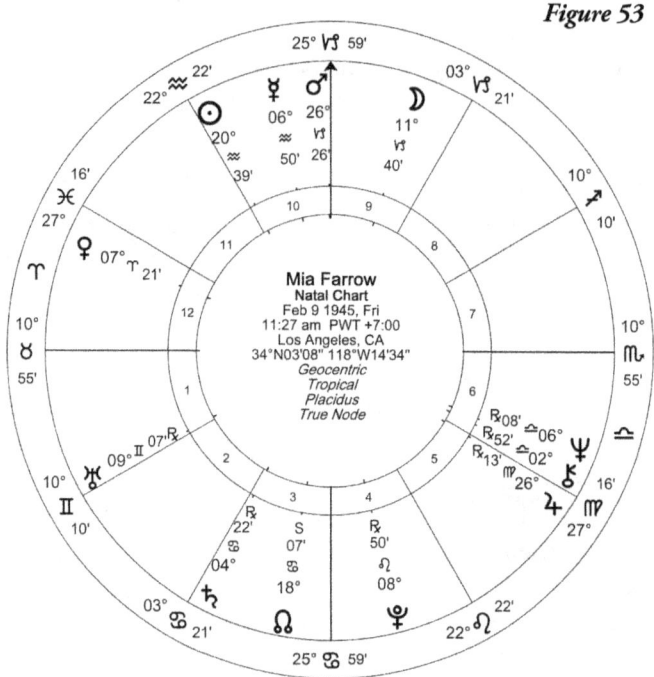

Figure 53

The natal aspects can indicate a path of release and revelation. None of these indications is chiseled in stone. We have an opportunity to grow in our realization that responses can be tempered. Although we came here to gather experience for our soul's growth, we did not enter this personality embodiment to become someone we are not; but it does encompass being the best of what we can be. In all probability your intercepted Venus will progress out of its sign and into another one unless it retrogrades. That is one way we can incorporate new means of expression. My Venus has progressed through three signs and will soon go into the fourth. It started in Capricorn (not intercepted) and went through Aquarius, and for the past twenty-four years has been intercepted in Pisces, where I feel I have had a wonderful opportunity to be more sensitive in a healing way to other people's needs. It has helped me to become a more sensitive astrologer and a better counselor.

Transits moving around your chart will also stimulate your need to overtly express your Venus through other people and outer experiences. Some of these experiences may be exceptionally vivid through some of the strongest planetary contacts and some of them exceptionally memorable for the happiness they bring. Life is a mixture of circumstances.

Mia Farrow, Actress

Mia Farrow's affairs have livened up gossip columns on many occasions. First there was her affair with Frank Sinatra, followed by a short marriage. He was more than twice her age. She had twins from Andre Previn, after which they married. Her relationship with Woody Allen ended

Figure 54

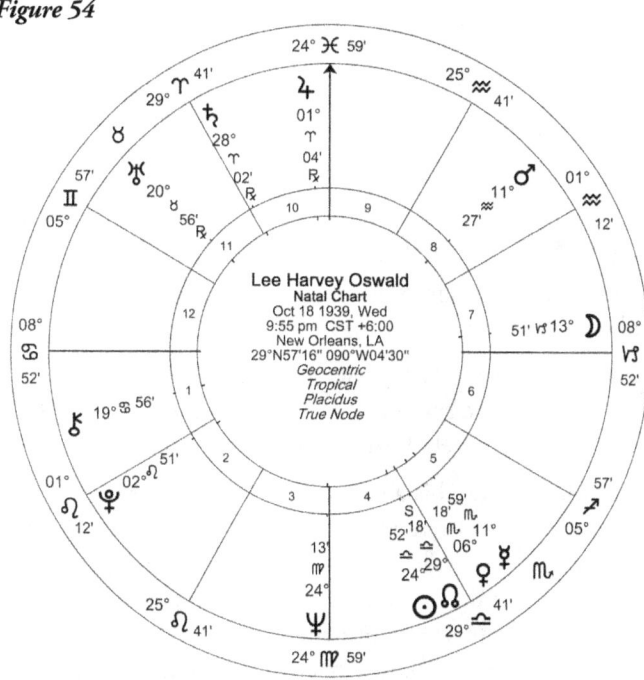

in scandal when he began an affair with one of her adopted children. Then she accused him of molesting one of their mutually adopted daughters. As an actress, some of her most notable films include *Rosemary's Baby*, *The Great Gatsby*, *Crimes and Misdemeanors*, *Alice* and *Husbands and Wives*. Ref: PW; Biography.com; DN#37, BC

Lee Harvey Oswald, Alleged Assassin

Alleged assassin of John F. Kennedy on November 22, 1963. He was a former United States Marine and lived from 1959 to 1962 in Russia. He was arrested a few hours after the assassination of President John F. Kennedy on a charge of killing a policeman. He was charged the following day with the assassination of the president. Before he could come to trial he was shot by nightclub owner Jack Ruby, while millions of people watched on television. The Warren Commission held him responsible, but the conspiracy theory still exists. Ref: Biography.com; A: from mother

Other Examples

Barbra Streisand, Singer, Actress: Venus intercepted in Pisces/twelfth. In some respects she is a very private person, but she pours a great deal of sensitivity into selling a song in a way that reaches one's heartstrings. She has had several stormy marriages and is now married to actor James Brolin.

George Sand, Author: Venus intercepted in Leo/sixth. She left her husband and children to live in Paris as a vagabond, bohemian writer. She had several notable lovers, including Chopin and de Musset. She wrote more than 100 books, as well as plays and letters.

Lawrence Welk, Bandleader: Venus intercepted in Aries/first and Mars Libra/seventh. Biography.com calls his music "sweet-sounding 'champagne' music." When hosting his television shows, he seemed almost possessed with presenting young, beautiful performers. Everything always seemed so proper.

Hal Holbrook, Figure 30

Mario Lanza, Figure 33

Lee Iacocca, Figure 44

Bill Gates, Figure 47

Lisa Minnelli, Figure 9

Steven Spielberg

Mars Intercepted

Mars is a hot, dry, fiery planet that glows red in the night sky daring us to move outward into new adventures. It is the first planet beyond earth and hence takes us beyond ourselves.

The first five planets in our hierarchal system (Sun, Moon, Mercury, Venus, Mars) are symbolic of our personality, the next two (Jupiter, Saturn) are symbolic of our societal thrust and the last three (Uranus, Neptune, Pluto) symbolize a higher level of existence or experience.

Mars has often been called The War Lord. Its symbol is a sword and shield that equips us to go into battle as we initiate action to fulfill our desires. There is another, even more significant battle going on within our psyche, and that is the battle to evolve beyond our primal animalistic nature. Therefore, Mars can be aggressive, combative, and destructive, or it can be initiatory, courageous and motivational. For most of us in a civilized society, we are utilizing our Mars to fulfill our goals, not only for personal accomplishment, but to be a contributing member in the flow of society. So, as we work towards our own achievements we can also help to motivate others so that we can all be carried on the stream of evolution together. I therefore perceive Mars to be pivotal in connecting our temporary personality to universal principles.

If you have Mars intercepted, its sign is extremely important. It is quicker to take action in Aries even in an intercepted condition than a Mars in Taurus might be. Of course, we always look at aspects as well as where its ruling sign is posited.

When intercepted, the drive and motivation becomes intensified. It may be kept inside, seemingly quiet, but that is not usually the case. It may be building up steam. You know what happens when you enclose a boiler without a safety valve. When sufficient energy has been built up, it blows. Any Mars that is under stress needs to be released regularly into a worthwhile project. It cannot be contained. If you are in a non-physical environment much of the time, you need to find an energetic outlet. It may be a hobby upon which you can focus your time and energy. You may like gardening. A sport would be even more beneficial, but not everyone is athletic. Join a gym or take frequent walks. I do not think you should try to control Mars for any length of time. You must use it or it will use you in anger, frustration, accidents and even violence.

An intercepted Mars in Aries can make you very restless and you need regular periods of exercise and activity. In Gemini, when it builds up you may either tell someone off or get into an accident. If you tell someone off, hopefully it is someone who will forgive you and not your boss who could fire you on the spot. Mars in Capricorn always needs to be working towards some goal or project, where a sense of accomplishment can be recognized. A Mars in Pisces can really build up steam.

I know a man with Mars intercepted in Pisces in the twelfth house who uses his in several interesting ways. His career is highly creative and he works behind the scenes with little visible credit. He realizes that his inner frustration can accumulate until he feels like he is going to blow up. Even his skin begins to itch or feel like it is crawling. He has numerous hobbies that he alternates between and he enjoys many sports activities. When the stress builds up, his most therapy is going to the mountains. In the summer he will challenge himself to climb one (or two) that are more than 10,000 feet and have an element of danger. In the winter he is a downhill skier. In the city he will never go for a walk, but in the mountains he loves to don a backpack and head up the trail. After a period of heavy physical activity, he feels more creative until it builds again. He also does hands-on healing, particularly to relieve muscle strain. He has found healthy ways to experience his Mars interception.

I have a random list of twenty-five notables with an intercepted Mars. Six are award-winning or record-breaking athletes. I realize that this is not a formal research result, but it does make a point that an intercepted Mars need not be destructive. It can provide intense focus.

Helen Keller, Figure 51, had both Mercury and Mars in Leo intercepted in her ninth house. She was not an athlete but in order to overcome such a severe handicap she needed a great amount of inner focus, courage and determination. Her teacher, Ann Sullivan, had to motivate her, but that would not have been possible if Keller did not have that inner drive and need to succeed.

I cannot stress enough the necessity of finding a constructive outlet for an intercepted Mars. It is the natural ruler of Aries, and Aries is where we have a need to initiate action in the direction our Sun is pointing us. Mars is the activator. You need to start something in order to have something happen unless you want to wait until something happens to you. If you are also using it as the ruler of Scorpio, you will realize that your Mars energy needs adjustment and transformation in order to utilize its energy constructively and combine it more appropriately with the needs of others.

Since Mars rules our basic animal instincts, it is also our sexual energy. With an intercepted position, there can be suppression and difficulty in experiencing fulfillment. There will likely be periods of activity and periods of internalization, depending on how the chart is progressing and what transits are stimulating it at any given time. With healthy physical activity in other areas of life, sexual energy seems more gratifying.

Examine all the conditions connected with your Mars to determine its potential, and then incorporate the whole chart for additional input.

Tonya Harding, Figure Skater

Her early background fostered hostility and resentment within her basic nature. She grew up with a succession of seven of her mother's men moving in and out of her life. Her skating was a saving grace and allowed her to vent much of her anger and frustration. Her marriage to Gillooly was volatile and abusive. She was a fighter. Four men, including Gillooly, were convicted of an attack on her rival Nancy Kerrigan just prior to the Olympic Games in Lillehammer, Norway, in 1994. Harding pleaded guilty to hindering the investigation. Ref: F & WE 1994 Yearbook; personal knowledge from news of the time; DN#46

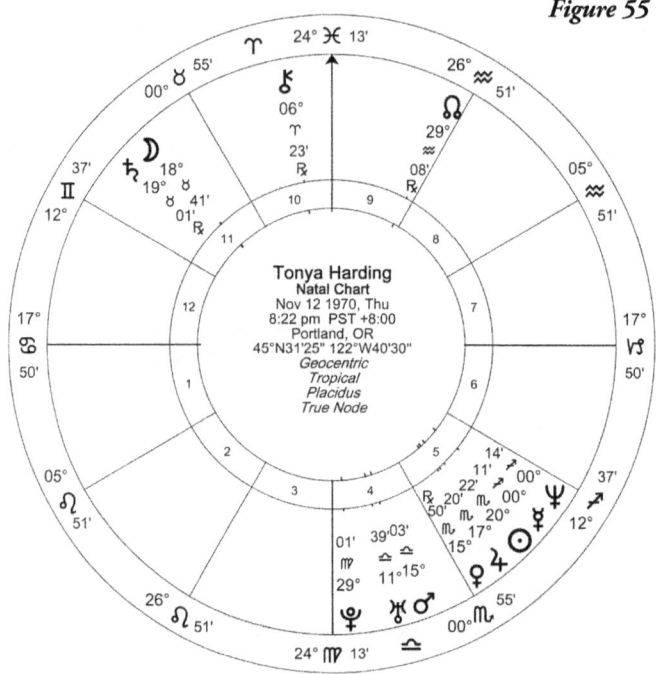

Figure 55

Vincent Price, Actor, Writer

Vincent Price once said, "I love playing a villain." This was a great way to use his intercepted Mars in Pisces! He starred mostly in horror movies such as *House of Wax*, *The Fall of the House of Usher* and *The Fly*. He had a low-pitched expressive voice and a curious expression, that lent itself well to such films. His last role was Edward Scissorhands in 1991. During his later life he became interested in cooking. He and his second wife Mary Grant wrote *A Treasury of Great Recipes*. ABC: March quotes MacKenzie in AA: Sept/76, "from him by letter.". Ref: ABC; Biography.com; ABC

Other Examples

Adolph Eichmann: Mars intercepted in Taurus/twelfth. He was a prime organizer of Germany's anti-Semitic activities during World War II. After the war he was captured, tried and executed.

Herb Elliott, Runner: Both Mars and Saturn intercepted in Aries/fifth. Olympic Gold Medal winner in 1960. His time was unbeaten for seven years. He ran the sub-four-minute mile seventeen times and his record has never been beaten. According to Biography.com, he was "noted for the rigor and severity of his training schedule."

Pancho Gonzales, Tennis Player: Mars intercepted in Pisces/eleventh. "He was the dominant player during the 1950s. At age forty he played in the longest ever match at Wimbledon" claiming victory (Biobraphy.com). After he retired from competition, he became the tennis pro at Caesar's Palace in Las Vegas.

Figure 56

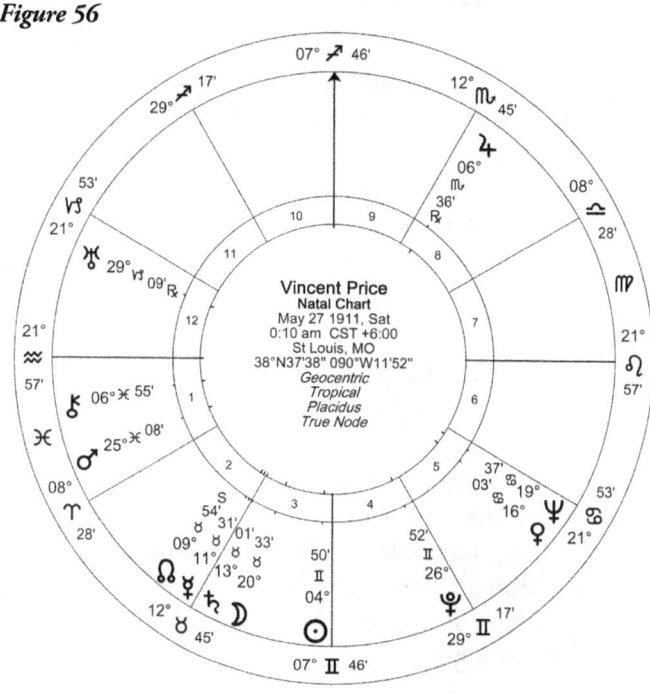

Chris Evert, Tennis Player: Mars intercepted in Pisces/fourth. She has won 157 professional singles titles, and has often been called "Ice Maiden" due to her coolness under pressure.

Uri Geller, Telekenic: Mars intercepted in Capricorn/third. His intercepted Mars exalted in Capricorn in his third house does more than anything else in his chart to explain the intense focus necessary to bend spoons through the power of his mind. This demonstration was shown on television.

Polly Bergen, Actress, Singer, Businesswoman: Mars intercepted in Taurus/eleventh. A multi-talented lady who needs to keep reinventing herself through new goals and aspirations. Rodden in PW says she was "a hillbilly singer, a light opera and pop singer, television panelist and actress, writer, and a Manhattan businesswoman."

Jupiter Intercepted

Jupiter is the largest planet in our solar system and has more satellites than any other planet. Therefore, it is often said that Jupiter does everything in a big way. Jupiter is often referred to as the "greater benefic," Venus being the "lesser benefic."

Jupiter expands, not only in its general influence, but also in consciousness. It is one of the societal planets. As we mix with other people gathering information through Mercury the Messenger, then Jupiter, through our higher mind, gives us the capacity to gain wisdom in order to develop a philosophy upon which to build our life. Alan Oken calls Jupiter "The Light of Wisdom." We accomplish this wisdom according to the attributes of the sign it is in and through the house it occupies.

On a mundane level, Jupiter can indicate good fortune and benefit through material gain. Its optimistic nature attracts enterprising people who are moving forward and upward. If its aspects are difficult and discipline is lacking, it can signify waste through over-expansion, over-expenditure and self-indulgence. A well placed Jupiter gains expansion and cultural understanding through physical travel, but an ill-starred Jupiter simply wanders with no real purpose in mind. This wandering influence can be either physical or mental.

If you have an intercepted Jupiter, the natural sense of optimism and expansion are internalized. Much inner preparation may be necessary before trust in oneself is developed. Student 4, Figure 21, is an example of someone with Jupiter intercepted in the tenth house who is afraid to reach for the brass ring in case he cannot reach it. He has the education and qualifications, but fear of expansion holds him back. In time he will learn to trust himself. He has studied a broad range of metaphysical subjects, including astrology, in an effort to find the answers that are buried deeply within him. Jupiter rules his fourth house, which is not only his physical home but his own internal home or dwelling place.

Insecurity can prompt self-indulgence because the principle of expansion is working on some level. Refer to the chart of Princess Diana, Figure 26, with Jupiter in Aquarius, intercepted, in her second house. She was extravagant in her expenditures. However, she no doubt grew in consciousness in giving of herself through the charity work she did. I am sure this work helped to boost her confidence in spite of her failing marriage, Royal criticism and the continual press attention examining every nook and cranny of her life. Note that Jupiter rules her Ascendant. By the way, it is also retrograde, further indicating its internal functioning. However, it also gave her courage to openly explore ideas that others were afraid to tackle because she firmly believed there was a social need to do so and that she had a right to speak up. She literally walked mine fields.

Mario Lanza, Figure 33, is another example of a self-indulgent personality. He died of a heart attack after an eating binge. He was propelled rather quickly into a singing career and he suffered greatly from a lack of confidence. That is hard for an on-looker to understand because he was truly gifted and very handsome. Some of you may recall Rosemary Clooney, a talented, popular singer who starred with Bing Crosby and Danny Kaye in *White Christmas*. The movie is still shown during the Christmas season. Over the years she has gained a tremendous amount of weight. She has an intercepted Jupiter in her first house. I have worked on television productions with her and she has always been warm and friendly but is continually waiting "for the other shoe to drop."

Many people with Jupiter intercepted feel unlucky. They feel others get all the breaks, and they only get what is left over. Every time someone at work gets a promotion they think to themselves, "There it is again. I never get a break." Yet they will secretly go out and buy lottery tickets thinking that maybe they will get lucky. Their approach to their work is often somewhat timid. They may be reluctant to offer suggestions because they feel others are smarter and more qualified.

With this interception you may feel that you do not have enough knowledge and education to be considered witty and smart. You may accumulate more degrees, take more courses and read incessantly because you feel something significant is eluding you. You may feel that if only you had more education a promotion might just be around the corner. That is not always true. If you are writing an essay, your research will likely be voluminous or even excessive. The good news is that all that studying, research and reading does contribute to your wisdom and understanding. In time

Figure 57

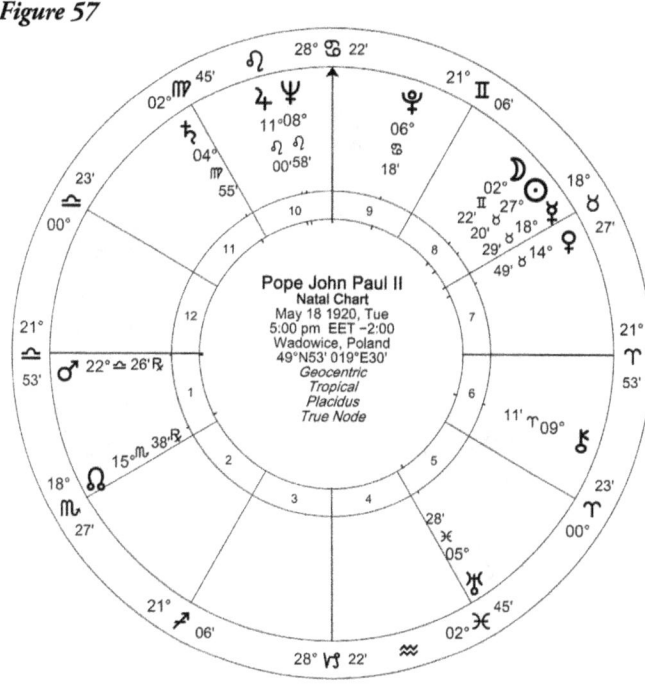

you can indeed be an authority on any chosen subject.

Many authors have an intercepted Jupiter because they can expound on their ideas in the privacy of their own study. However, an unfavorable comment or critique is very hurtful and may cause a period of withdrawal. Lord Byron had this experience. His Jupiter was intercepted and retrograde in Gemini in his twelfth house. At age nineteen his collection of poems was badly reviewed, after which he took off on a grand tour visiting many countries. It was five years before he published again. Nevertheless he is considered to be one of the great English romantic poets.

Ernest Hemingway's story is quite different, but he too was a wanderer. He never stayed in one place very long, seemingly always in need of a new adventure. He went big-game hunting in Africa, deep sea fishing off the coast of Florida, attended the bull fights in Spain and covered the Spanish Civil War as a journalist. He had Jupiter in Scorpio intercepted in his third house. He gave us some memorable stories, some of which were made into motion pictures such as *For Whom the Bell Tolls* and *The Old Man and the Sea*. He finally became so restless that he could not complete anything new. Depression and paranoia overcame him and he committed suicide.

With Jupiter intercepted, if you are not a mental explorer, you may do so physically. Aimless travel is indicative of a restless spirit that may not know what it is seeking. It may be in search of the ultimate adventure, whether it be to an exotic land or a dangerous sojourn up the Amazon River. It may be visiting an Ashram in India or looking for the proverbial Holy Grail. It is like an itch that never gets scratched. Much understanding and wisdom can develop, but this understanding and wisdom needs to be recognized as a source of achievement and usefulness.

Pope John Paul II

The intensity of an internalized Jupiter intercepted in the tenth house, ruling the third, particularly coupled with its conjunction to Neptune, is a fitting position for a Pope. According to Biography.com, "he was noted for his energy and analytical ability." He visited many foreign countries and preached to tremendously huge audiences. He spoke about economic justice, the right of the Church in Communists countries, and was unwavering on moral issues. Ref: Biography.com. DN#60: *Seattle Times*, May 19,1996, submitted by Michael Munkasey, quoting from the Pope himself to a newspaper reporter, on the day of his birthday celebration.

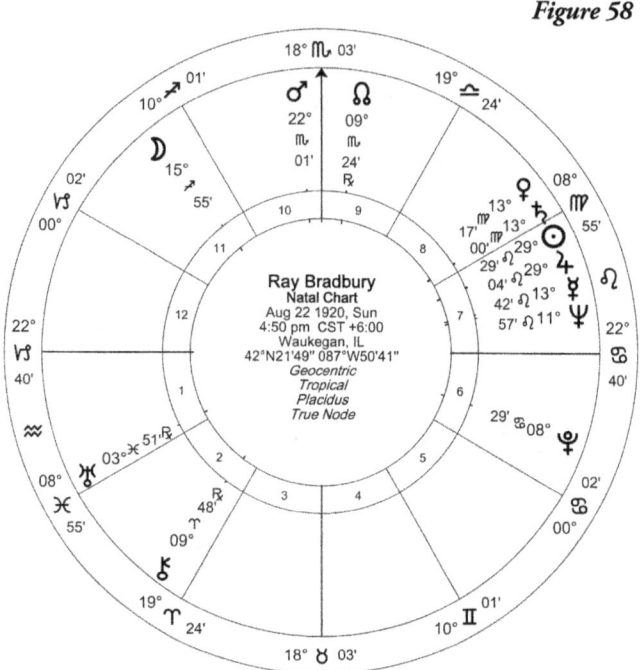

Figure 58

Ray Bradbury, Author

Ray Bradbury is best known as a science fiction writer, but he also wrote other novels, dramas, essays and verse. His works have sold more than forty million copies in twenty countries. Some of his most notable works include *The Martian Chronicles, The Illustrated Man, Fahrenheit, The Pendulum* and *A Memory of Murder*. I once heard him say on The Tonight Show that he was terrified to travel personally, even by car to get to the studio, but air travel was by far the worst. AA: ADIV. Ref: Biography.com; AA: ADIV

Other Examples

Jules Verne, Author: Jupiter/Moon intercepted in Scorpio/sixth. He was educated in law before writing. His writings exaggerate and seem to depict the possibilities of scientific advancement. His most notable works include, *Journey to the Center of the Earth, Twenty Thousand Leagues Under the Sea* and *Around the World in Eighty Days*, all of which were made into blockbuster motion pictures.

Ursula Bloom, Novelist, Playwright: Jupiter intercepted in Aries/tenth. She had very little formal education but in spite of that she published her first story when she was only seven years old. She wrote more than 500 books, mostly historical romances.

Louise Bogan Poet, Editor: Jupiter/Mercury/Mars intercepted in Virgo/sixth. She was poetry critic and editor for the New Yorker for most of her life. She received many poetry awards.

Gabriel "Coco" Chanel, Fashion Designer: Jupiter intercepted in Cancer/seventh. She was orphaned and raised by her aunts who taught her how to sew. She first became a hat designer, fashioned costume jewelry and began opening her boutiques. She changed women's fashion including the wearing of pants and "the little black dress." In 1921 she launched Chanel No. 5 perfume, which is still fashionable at the turn of the millennium.

Charley Pride, Singer: Jupiter intercepted in Libra/sixth. He was born poor and rose to country music fame. He was the first African-American to break into the Grand Ole Opry.

Ivana Trump: Jupiter intercepted in Capricorn/second.

Liza Minnelli, Figure 9: Jupiter intercepted and retrograde in Libra/sixth.

Saturn Intercepted

Saturn has been called "The Wise Old Teacher," "Father Time," "The Taskmaster," and even "The Reaper."

Whatever keywords we use to describe Saturn's function in our chart, its influence does call for self-discipline, responsibility, organization and structure, thereby setting boundaries for appropriate action to strengthen character. As Alan Oken says, in *Alan Oken's Complete Astrology*, The Classic Trilogy, ". . . for Man to successfully function both as a universal and as a social being, he must abide by certain terrestrial and heavenly laws which govern his behavior."

Sometimes our ego gets in the way and we expect inappropriate returns. We may not understand our Sun's purpose; our emotional responses may need development; our opinions may be biased; and, our desire nature may be selfish. If our expectations are unreasonable according to the structure we have built, then we will surely be disappointed. We will then experience the limitations, frustrations and delays, which are often associated with Saturn. We may feel that the world is unjust and that we have been dealt an unfair hand.

If we abide by universal principles, build our life upon a solid foundation, in time we will experience earthly fulfillment that will endure the onslaught of negative forces. We can build a strong character or a weak one. The choice is ours. Saturn is our teacher. It is often said that Saturn gives us what we deserve. If we deserve to be brought to our knees, we will. If we deserve success, we will also get that but not before we have earned it. Along the way our endurance will surely be tested.

If we understand and abide by Saturn's laws, we will experience enlightenment through the remaining three outer planets: Uranus, Neptune and Pluto. Otherwise we will experience upsetting conditions, chaos and perhaps severe losses requiring us to start back at square one and build a new foundation. Of course, we all experience chaos and losses from time to time; it is one way we learn.

Where Saturn is posited in your natal chart will indicate where you will be learning the principal of responsibility and duty. For example: In the first house you will be learning to trust yourself and project with confidence. In the second house you will be learning about values and handling your own resources. In the seventh house you will be learning about relationships. In the eleventh house the lesson is in developing your long-range goals with patience.

If your Saturn is intercepted at birth, it is certainly not a case of being unable to accept responsibility. In fact, the reverse may be true. Your sense of responsibility may be so strong that you overemphasize it to the point of taking the joy out of life. It will likely take time before you understand what responsibility you should be taking and how you should go about accomplishing it. In releasing some of this stress, you will eventually be able to integrate greater diversification in your life, such as relating to others more easily, taking time off for social activities, and, in general, having more fun. If you are fortunate, your work will provide some of that for you. If not, work will be a chore.

Jay Leno, Figure 43, is a workaholic who loves what he does, but he does reserve a little spare time for his hobby of collecting antique cars. Otherwise we have no way of knowing how balanced his life is or what effect it is having on his family life. He has been married since 1980 to the same lady, Mavis Nicholson. This is the longevity part of Saturn. His Saturn interception is in Virgo in his seventh house, ruling his eleventh and twelfth. He also has Jupiter and Venus intercepted in Pisces in his first house. He appears to be very outgoing and jovial but underneath that part of his personality is a very serious, hard-working, ambitious, ever-planning introvert. Many comedians are that way due to their sensitivity and inner intensity. One cannot be "turned on" all the time. Comedy takes serious contemplation.

On the longevity side of Saturn, refer to the chart of Bill Gates, Figure 47, with Saturn intercepted in his fifth house. He did not marry the love of his life until he was thirty-nine years old. I do not know how long they knew each other, but she was a marketing executive within his corporation. Remember that for several years he was shy and awkward while gaining the personal confidence to command his own authority. In the meantime, his creative, mathematical genius was the focal point of his Saturn intensity. This is a reminder that an interception creates *intensity due to internalization.*

With Saturn intercepted, you may drive relentlessly for success and never be satisfied with any level of achievement. Each milestone creates another one. If you diversify your life, you may be able to keep going indefinitely gaining momentum with each challenge, but if you never learn how to relax you could experience periods of exhaustion. Look to the sign your Saturn is posited to determine an area of physical vulnerability.

On the other hand, it may take you time to realize that you must assume the responsibility for your own maturity, structure worthwhile projects, and be a contributing part of the societal flow in your own career endeavor. There may be tragic and depressing issues to deal with from childhood, like Student 3, Figure 19, who had Saturn intercepted in her fourth house. Children normally look to their parents or guardians as authority figures and role models of adulthood. Student 3 never had a role model. She never knew her parents and bounced from one foster home to another. One day she realized that she could no longer blame society for her problems and decided it was her responsibility to change her life. The responsibility of restructuring her education and attitude was immense, but she felt a powerful sense of accomplishment when she finally did it.

Figure 59

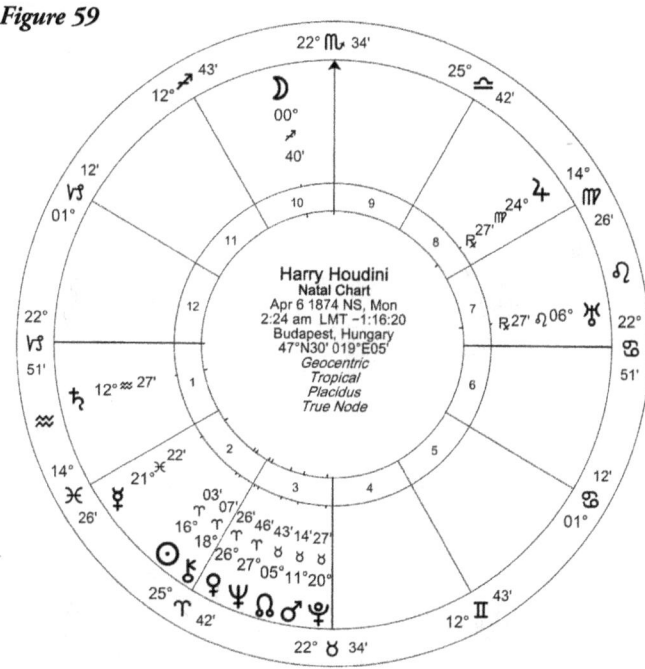

You may wish to review the chart and biography of Patty Hearst, Figure 37, with her Saturn intercepted in Scorpio in her third house.

With an intercepted Saturn that has challenging aspects, you may have a fated attitude that life has dealt you a "bad hand." In time you may realize you can take charge of your own life, and will do so with the same intensity that you harbored resentment.

In most charts, Saturn will not progress out of interception by secondary progression unless it is in the last part of the sign, and only if it will not retrograde before it goes into the next sign.

Harry Houdini, Magician, Escape Artist

Houdini's father was a rabbi who moved from Budapest to Wisconsin when his son (born Erich Weiss) was an infant. He changed his surname "after that of a French magician, Jean Houdin." He showed amazing skill at escaping from handcuffs, locked trunks, padlocked chains, underwater containers, jail cells and assorted other bonds. These were feats requiring an acute sense of timing and self-discipline which are the Saturn qualities emphasized in his personality. He exposed tricks of fraudulent mediums but encouraged attempts to contact him through a medium after his death. Ref.: F .& WE; P/C: SS

Annie Besant, Social Reformer, Theosophist, Lecturer

With great intensity, Annie Besant put her heart and soul into everything she did. She was well educated and became an intense social reformer. She fought for intellectual freedom, labor reform and women's rights. She was arrested for alleged immorality when she published birth control information. She undertook theosophy with the same intensity and moved to India where she became the president of the Theosophical Society. She founded the Central Hindu College at Benares, was president of the India National Congress, and organized the India Home Rule League. Ref. F&WE. Birth Data: PW: "Alan Leo, who knew her personally, and rectified the time from a given time of 5:00 to 5:45 PM."

Understanding Interceptions

Other Examples

Mick Jagger, Singer, Musician: Saturn and Uranus intercepted in Gemini/eleventh. He attended the London School of Economics, but left to form The Rolling Stones rock group. Their behavior was unconventional, their lifestyles uninhibited, all of which appealed to the teenagers of the 1960s. Decades later, The Rolling Stones are still popular.

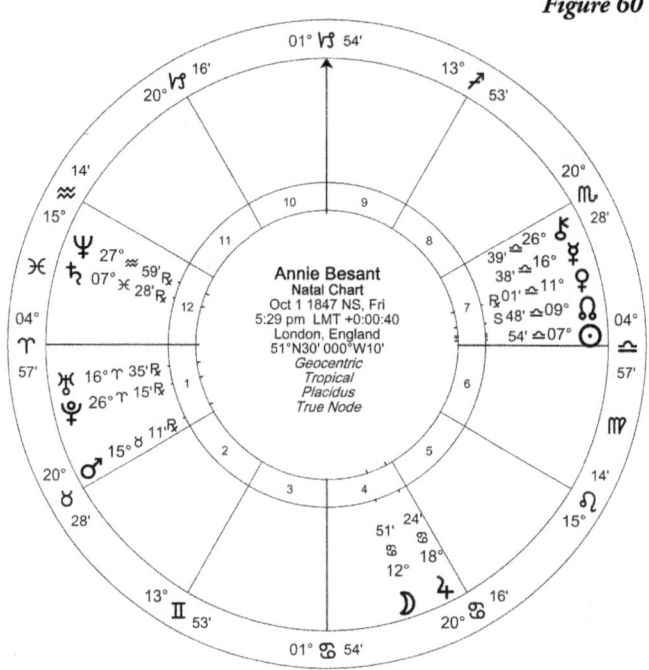

Figure 60

Joseph Lyle Mendez, Murderer, Saturn intercepted in Aries/twelfth—and **Erik Galen Mendez, Murderer**—Saturn intercepted in Taurus/ninth: The Mendez brothers were sentenced to life in prison for shooting their parents. Their father was an overachiever and reportedly "pushed his boys mercilessly to be winners and champions." Their father was reportedly worth millions.

Fitzjof Capra, Physicist, Author: Saturn intercepted in Aries/twelfth. Researcher of theoretical high energy physics. His book, *The Tao of Physics*, "suggestively bridges the gap between ancient religious teachings and modern physics and deals with the greater social and cultural implications of modern science" (Rodden, ADIV). That certainly sounds like an intense Saturn.

Russell (Wayne) Baker, Journalist, Author: Saturn intercepted in Scorpio/sixth. Longtime writer for *The New York Times*, mostly humorous observations on politics and life. He won the Pulitzer Prize for Commentary in 1979 and again in 1983.

Merv Griffin, Figure 12

Mario Lanza, Figure 33

Patty Hearst, Figure 37

Uranus Intercepted

Uranus is indeed a strange planet creating everything from flashes of insight and ingenious ideas, to disruption and even chaos. Its action is sudden and unexpected, catching one completely by surprise. The physical characteristics of Uranus are unusual, most notably being the tilt of its axis at about ninety-eight degrees to the plane of its orbit. Its northern and southern hemispheres alternate between darkness and sunlight for many years at a time. Sometimes the pole appears to be at the center of the disk from the vantage point of earth and at other times the planet shows us its equator. These unusual features are captured in its meaning.

Uranus creates chaotic change. It can break ties, disrupt circumstances and create havoc in our lives if we resist change. On the other hand, it can free our individuality and hence our unique creativity from the expectations other influences place upon us during our growing-up period. In this way we can discover and release that special gift that each and every one of us has within us to contribute to the societal flow, however great or small and subtle it may be. Saturn creates necessary boundaries of social conduct and acceptability, but Uranus beckons us into new realms of experience, encouraging new insights and possibilities, sometimes peacefully, sometimes rebelliously. Uranus is sometimes referred to as "The Awakener," particularly from an evolutionary viewpoint.

Its duration in a sign is seven years creating a generation of people who will, consciously or unconsciously shake up society's present state of evolution connected with that sign. For example, when it was in Cancer, the concept of home and family began to change as women sought new freedom from the stereotype homemaker; in Virgo we began to change the way data was collected, organized, sorted and categorized; in Libra the concept of marriage was shaken from its foundation and the divorce rate increased dramatically: in Capricorn big business, governments and international borders changed dramatically.

If you have Uranus intercepted, it does not mean that you cannot release your special gift, develop your individuality or experience revelation and insight. However, some form of inner development and understanding is often required in order to be able to accept and trust these facets of yourself with confidence and comfort. You may tend to couch yourself in familiarity according to your up-bringing until greater understanding of your individuality demands release. A great number of notable people have Uranus intercepted, which is understandable when you consider its duration in a sign. However, Neptune is in a sign twice as long and my list is much shorter. Whatever the reason, Uranus is much more vivid in its expression and Neptune is more subtle.

Internalization creates intensification and Uranus can only be contained for so long before it needs an outlet thereby giving the world that individualized creativity that opens new ways and creates new patterns. It may also indicate a revolutionary person who shakes up the establishment.

The period of internalization varies but it usually begins its emerging struggle sometime after the first Saturn Return at about age twenty-eight to twenty-nine. There are always exceptions. For example, David Frost exhibited his genius as a skilled communicator and objective interviewer when he was in his early twenties, and continued forging ahead (Figure 62). His whole chart indicates ease and potential lifelong success. Note the stellium in the tenth with Jupiter conjunct the Midheaven as one corner of a grand trine in water signs. His Uranus also forms a trine with both Mars and Neptune. Adding to his drive are five cardinal planets, seven planets on the eastern side of his chart, and a square between Sun/Mercury to Mars.

With Uranus intercepted, when you are young you will likely feel unusual, awkward, different, like a square peg in a round hole. This can cause you to pull your creative needs and impulses inside. You cannot deny them because they will literally scream at you for some form of expression and outlet. When Carol Burnett discovered that she could make people laugh, her whole life changed (Figure 52). With her first house placement of both Uranus and Mercury, she discovered a talent in mimicking many different types of characters by exaggerating body language and facial expressions. She was a good singer but that is not the path she chose to take. She is an unique, one-of-a kind talent.

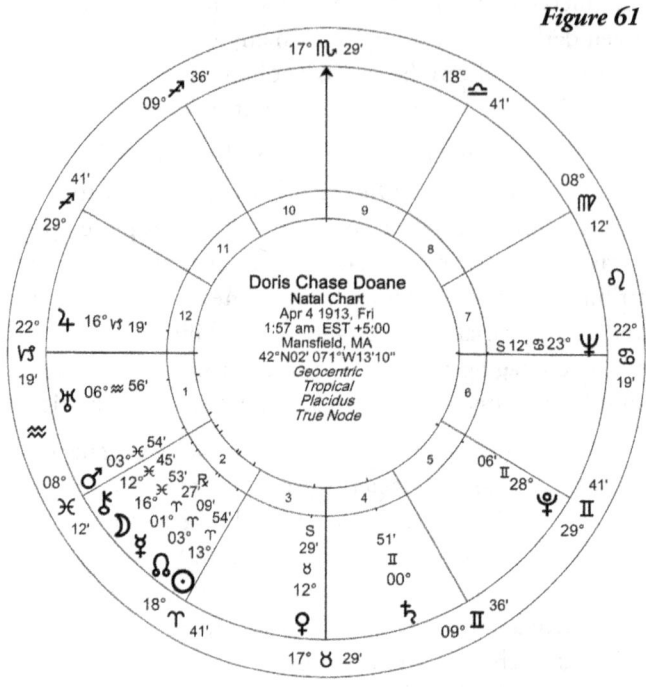

Figure 61

Your inspiration may not come in the usual Uranus flashes, but seep into your mind more slowly to give you an opportunity to examine and digest it before getting too excited about how you can use it. You may be suspicious of the origin of such inspiration and wonder if your mind is slipping. I have known other people who do get flashes of insight but will intentionally slow down the impact until they have had an opportunity to examine the worth of the idea.

You may also be the kind of person with an Uranus intercepted that is so uncertain about your own unusual ideas and attitudes that you join a group with similar ideas and interests, only to merge your own identity with that of the whole group. Some of you may eventually get so fed up with the general experience of accepted society that you may join a commune, or live a rustic existence for awhile. I have a client whom I have known since she was a teenager and she is now nearly forty who has two sets of interceptions encompassing four planets, including Uranus intercepted in Leo in her sixth house, as well as Sun and Venus intercepted in Aries in her first house. She is well educated but struggles continually with her identity. A couple of years ago she developed a new relationship and moved onto an island off the West Coast to live a rustic rural life as a vegetarian. Her mother is very concerned and feels she is wasting her potential, which is a commercial point-of-view. Uranus, of course, is only one part of the whole chart but each piece fits together as supporting evidence of a main theme.

Figure 62

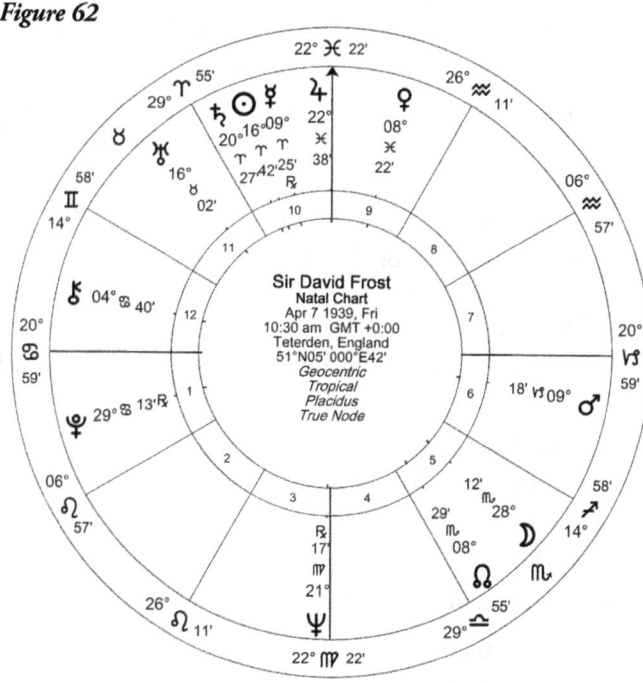

I have had many people with Uranus intercepted tell me that they feel out of phase with time, particularly when young. Others know their path is unusual and are willing to risk being different because their calling is unavoidable. These are the path-finders preparing the way for others to follow. Some of you may have been closet-astrologers, only to realize that it is now getting easier to admit you are dedicated to such an unusual study.

Doris Chase Doane, Astrologer, Author, Lecturer

Doris Chase Doane was one of the most distinguished astrologers of the twentieth century. She started studying the subject in her early twenties in order to disprove it. She gave us the first time changes books covering the world, as well as a legacy of at least twenty-four books and hundreds of articles. She was president of Professional Astrologers, Inc., founder of the Astrological Faculty, and was president of the American Federation of Astrologers for many years. We salute her for the Uranus gift she gave us. It was indeed a calling. Ref: Interview with LRM; PW

Sir David Frost, Broadcaster, Businessman

This is a good example of a person with an intercepted Uranus who started his remarkable career as a very young man. You must look at the whole chart. At twenty-two he presented an "innovative, satirical and irreverent late-night show" on the BBC and has since hosted many programs in both the United States and Britain, as well as interviewed many world leaders. He is articulate, probing, objective and tasteful thereby gaining the trust of both interviewee and audience. He is considered a genius in his field. Note the grand water trine. He has received many international awards and honors, including Knighthood in 1993. ABC (from him). Ref: Biography.com

Other Examples

People with Uranus intercepted are often path-finders in their chosen field, capable of opening the door for others to follow.

Bette Davis, Actress: Uranus intercepted in Capricorn-second/Neptune in Cancer/eighth. She was a unique talent. She began her career in her early twenties, often playing highly dramatic, daring roles. She fought studio executives and underwent numerous suspensions in order to exercise her individuality. She starred in no fewer than eighty-two films, received ten Oscar nominations, and won two. She also received a Life Achievement Award from the American Film Institute. She had four marriages.

Jack Paar, Talk Show Host: Uranus intercepted in Aries, first/Neptune in Leo/seventh. Talk shows have changed greatly over the years and have become big business. Jack Paar was a pioneer in this field. He started as a radio announcer in his teens, joined the US Army as an entertainer, had a few minor movie roles and then hosted *The Tonight Show* on NBC which became *The Jack Paar Show*. He was known for feuding both on and off camera. In his mid-fifties he retired because he did not want to do it any more.

Hedda Hopper, Hollywood Gossip Columnist: Uranus intercepted in Virgo/seventh. She was another very unique, individualistic person. She came from a large family and ran away from home. She had little formal education, fractured the language in her reporting, but was read far and wide because of her unique journalistic approach.

Otto Oscar Binder, Science Fiction Author: Uranus intercepted in Capricorn/third.

Robert Albert Bloch, Author: Uranus intercepted in Aquarius/third. The writer of weird fiction, his novel *Psycho* became an Alfred Hitchcock horror movie.

Of charts already printed in this book, you may wish to refer to Carol Burnett, Princess Diana, Dr. Tom Dooley, Bill Cosby, Margaret Trudeau and Lee Iacocca.

Neptune Intercepted

Neptune is often referred to as the shadow planet, the planet of illusion, delusion, dreams and escapism. But it is much more than that. It is a transcendental planet. When Spirit penetrates consciousness, we experience genuine inspiration, a joy in giving selflessly and an uplifting sense of spirituality. Its highest manifestation is universal love; its lowest is escapism in its many forms from drugs and alcohol to hallucinations and even suicide.

Many people with a pronounced Neptune influence in their natal chart are healers of mind and/or body. A healer is concerned with the comfort and well-being of others by easing their physical and/or emotional burdens. Other Neptunian people are inspired, creative people who delight us with music, dance, poetry, beautiful paintings and even motion pictures. Sensitive entertainers give us a brief interlude from our everyday concerns to a world of fantasy, beauty and wonderment. Then there are the mystics who help us become attuned to a meaning of life that exists beyond the nuts and bolts of reality, and take us into penetrating the realm of universal principles.

Where Neptune is in your chart you are expected to learn compassion and give love selflessly. It is not uncommon for someone with Neptunian issues that surface in adulthood who, as a child grow-

Figure 63

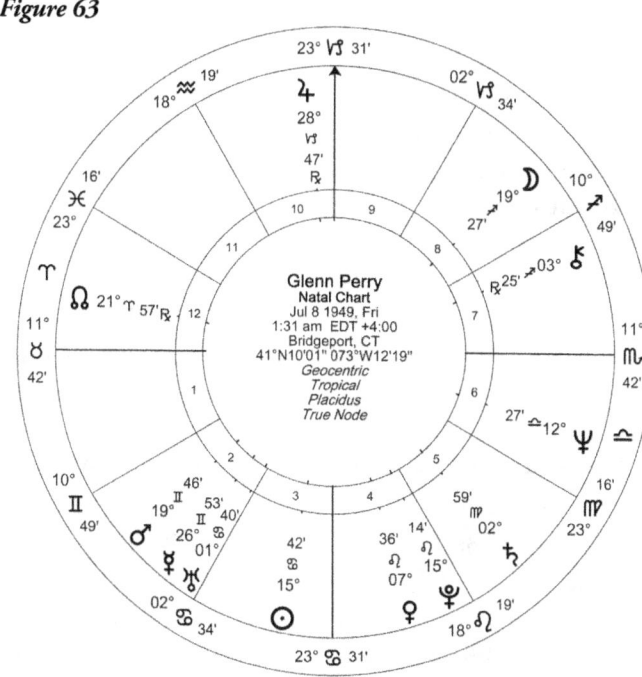

ing up, had to care for a parent who was ill, who was an alcoholic or emotionally dependent in some way, thus denying or suppressing certain of his/her needs. The child may take the blame and feel that if he/she could do more, the situation would change. A sense of guilt often carries into adult life.

If Neptune is intercepted, these issues are often dramatic, and the path to understanding, spirituality, and genuine compassion, can become very significant as adulthood unfolds. The theme surfaces in many ways.

Glenn Perry, Clinical Psychologist, Astrologer, Author, Lecturer

This is clearly exemplified in the chart of eminent astrologer/psychologist Glenn Perry, Ph.D., Figure 63. I had the pleasure recently of attending a full-day workshop conducted by Dr. Perry entitled, "Essential Principles of Psychological Astrology," in which he unfolded his own chart and talked about his journey of healing, understanding and compassion.

When I asked him if I could use his chart as an example of a Neptune needing overt expression and finding a path of healing, he said, "How do you separate your interception from my Sun square Neptune?" I replied that indeed I do not. Whenever something is very prominent in our psychological needs and drives, it is shown in more than one way in our chart but understanding an interception can add additional nuances including a very powerful inner drive to find an outlet for a complex inner need.

Dr. Perry went on to explain that the stress and pain his mother carried was acted out in the family, making it difficult to depend on her love. When he grew up he began a long journey to outwardly express "the stuff that was fermenting inside of me for years until I eventually got into the helping professions and began my own journey of healing." His process covered the study of metaphysics, astrology and psychology, and I am sure much more.

Dr. Perry is a clinical psychologist, working as a marriage therapist, which I believe he does with great sensitivity, compassion, creativity and intuition. Note that Neptune is in Libra in his sixth house of work, which disposits Venus in Leo in his fourth house, and rules his Ascendant and co-rules his sixth house. I see the Aries intercepted in his twelfth house as an intense inner need to exert his own initiative to heal himself, and then in turn to help others heal. He may not have done this with the same passion and drive if the position in his chart did not acquire additional intensity by being internalized. He also explained that when he was growing up his life was so enmeshed with that of his father that he was not always sure where one left off and the other began. With Aries intercepted in the twelfth, he had to initiate action to shed light on his personal doubts and establish his own identity. The story of his journey is a great inspiration and it touched me deeply.

The Moon is also a powerful influence in this chart. Note that it rules Cancer, which occupies both the third and fourth houses, tying those together (refer to Chapter Four). It is also at 27S14 declination, which is beyond the boundaries of the ecliptic and therefore experiences a larger than usual scope of sensitivity and feeling. This is all so perfect for a compassionate therapist who understands being wounded.

I know a very gifted artist with an intercepted Neptune, but as a young man he had trouble assessing the beauty of his own work. His work was unduly criticized when he was a child. When his paintings were exhibited, he had trouble selling them, perhaps because he still did not believe they were good enough. As a maturing person, he still has pangs of doubt about his own creativity.

I have a couple of clients with Neptune intercepted whose lines of reality and the dream state are frequently blurred. One in particular has her Neptune intercepted and retrograde. She said that, often when she wakes up in the morning and goes about her morning chores of brushing her teeth and combing her hair, she is not sure if she is still in a dream or actually awake until she forces her conscious mind to focus on reality, or even pinches herself to see if it hurts. I mentioned this a couple of years ago in a lecture I was giving. The room was full. I saw several heads bobbing affirmatively up and down. Naturally, signs, aspects, and the connection of everything in the chart determines how significant this is.

I have also had several clients with none of the above manifestations, but who attest to the fact that it took several years of testing, doubting and re-testing before they could accept their intuition as genuine. Once accepted, their intuition began to accelerate.

Others I have known have tried to accelerate or induce psychic experiences or spiritual ecstasy through altered states of consciousness by means of drugs; or, sitting for long periods of time in a meditative state; or, moving to a geographic location that is deemed spiritual. With this interception there seems to be a very deep longing for something that is difficult to identify.

Neptune intercepted can also indicate a truly spiritual being. Refer to the chart of Pope John Paul II, Figure 57, who has both Jupiter and Neptune intercepted in the tenth house exemplifying his religious/spiritual calling.

Figure 64

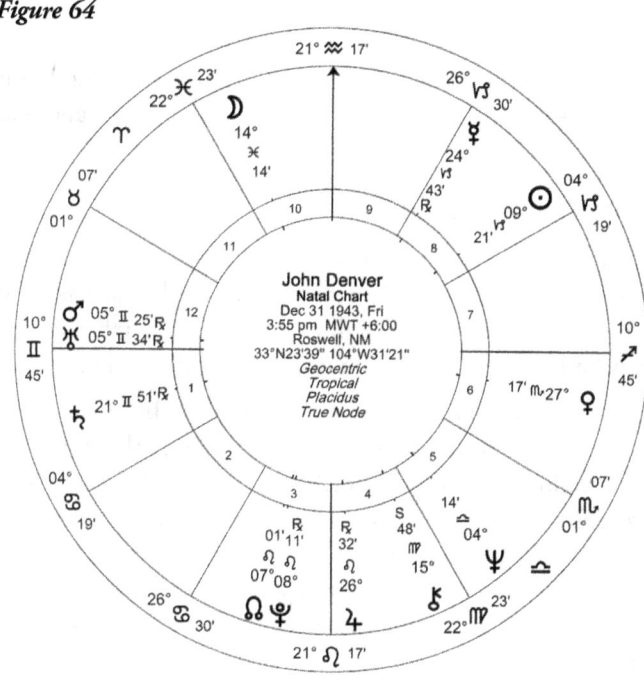

John Denver, Singer, Songwriter, Actor

I know nothing about John Denver's early life, nor what doubts and insecurities he experienced with his Sun square intercepted Neptune, but he was certainly beloved by many for his unique music extolling both the outdoors and the simple pleasures of life. He recorded fourteen gold and eight platinum records. He became a tireless environmental advocate and co-founded the Windstar Foundation in 1976. As a UNICEF spokesman, he also had a commitment to end hunger and poverty, especially for children. He died in a plane crash. CSH quotes BC. Ref: DN#68; Biography.com

Other Examples

Madonna, Singer, Songwriter, Actress: Neptune intercepted in Scorpio/third. Often referred to as "Queen of Punk." She is an unusual artist with an outlandish, even vulgar stage presentation but has nevertheless sold millions of records. Her reputation has suffered from time to time. Some critics believed she was morally unfit to play the role of the beloved Eva Peron. She has often been referred to as a marketing genius who intuits what will sell.

Evangeline Adams, Astrologer: Neptune intercepted in Aries/first. I would surmise from her Neptune interception in her first house as well as her Pisces Rising, that she was able to blend her astrological skill with a strong sense of intuition. When she was accused of being a fortune-teller, she read the chart of an unknown person, who was the judge's son, and the case was dismissed.

Loraine Hansberry, Author: Neptune intercepted in Virgo/ninth. She wrote *A Raisin in the Sun*, which is the story of a black family trying to escape from the ghetto. She died prematurely of cancer, but in her short life she was a significant spokesperson for African-Americans in their trials and aspirations.

Leslie Caron, Dancer, Film Star: Neptune intercepted in Virgo/seventh (Neptune rules both film and feet). Her most notable films include *An American in Paris, Lili* and *Gigi*. I know of three marriages between 1951 and 1964.

Lenny Bruce, Comedian: Neptune intercepted in Leo/eighth. His humor was called outrageous and obscene. He was denounced for blasphemy in Australia and banned from performing in England. He was arrested for obscenity in 1964 in New York. He became increasingly paranoid and died of a drug overdose.

Pluto Intercepted

The power of Pluto is so complex that one cannot do it justice in a couple of paragraphs. Its distance from planet Earth is very great, its orbit eccentric, its features are largely anomalous and its density and size are probably much greater than expected, all of which can be reflected in its symbology. Its many layers have often been referred to that of an onion being peeled back.

It is the planet of transformation. From an evolutionary point of view it symbolizes a journey connecting man to his destiny or true purpose in life, a process which necessitates that some parts of the ego encased in this temporary embodiment must die in order for a significant evolution to occur. Pluto therefore rules death and rebirth or renewal. This change or evolution is not always evident on the surface. The fermentation or germination may be going on for a long time before a noticeable change takes place, and then either an eruption occurs spewing out unconscious residue, or new sprouts of consciousness begin breaking through the surface in a gradual evolutionary advancement. Often times it is both effects.

Pluto's changes are always massive, whether it is removing some aspect of our life that is not working, healing wounds or even shifting land masses. In a general sense, Pluto digs as deep as necessary with an unparalleled intensity to get to the root of any issue in order to restore our own individual strength and power. This power can be joined with others to increase capacity for everyone involved. This is evident with large financial enterprises. It is also evident from a personal point of view in the sex act when the power and life force of two lovers combines to release the energy that creates new life.

Pluto is also about owning your own power and exerting your own life force. If you do, you can use this power effectively and wisely to fulfill your own personal mission, as well as sensing deep within your psyche that you can contribute to a particular type of societal advancement and improvement. An intercepted Pluto will build these premises over a long period before understanding the direction it had been taking all along. So many of these people have said, "What is my purpose? What am I here to do besides my everyday activities?" They sense that life exists on several different levels.

If Pluto's intensity is not used constructively, it may be wielded abusively. You may vent this abuse on a personal relationship or manipulate business and money to satisfy an insatiable greed. Conversely, if you give your power to an abusive mate, you literally invite that person to abuse you. This powerlessness often comes from abusive parents under the guise of discipline and love. In order to become whole, and assume your own power, a remarkable transformation must take place.

Figure 65

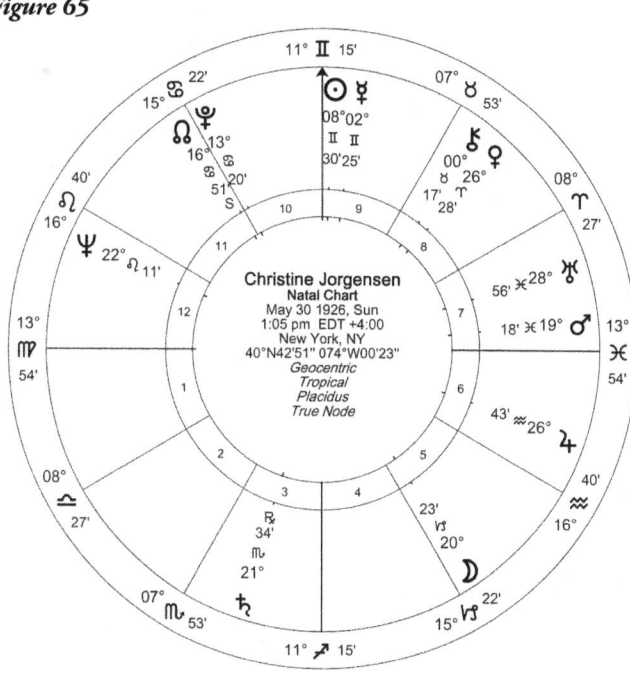

In observing an intercepted Pluto in a chart, you must first determine if the Pluto is capable of wholeness and is being used relatively wisely, or if it is dysfunctional and how it is being manifested. You cannot assume a scenario without a dialogue with the person whose chart you are viewing. Sometimes people will not divulge the whole story until they are desperate, trying to overcome or transform their situation.

A dysfunctional Pluto that is intercepted will often go through long periods of denial due to its internalized effect. In this regard, refer to Figure 24, which is the chart of evangelist Jimmy Swaggart, who has an intercepted Pluto in Cancer in his seventh house, but note that Pluto is also conjunct his Moon, apexing a T-Square with Mars, Uranus and Venus, as well as being part of a water grand trine. It is certainly a pivotal planet in his chart.

Jimmy Swaggart was a passionate, charismatic preacher. He preached fervently against adultery, sexual deviations and particularly "demon lust," while keeping his own deviant habits hidden and masked by piety. When he was caught and publicly humiliated, he wept equally as fervently and passionately in front of the camera claiming he was possessed by demons and seeking forgiveness. His intercepted Pluto gained intensity by being internalized, then surfaced explosively.

In comparison, look at the chart of Christine Jorgensen, Figure 65, where Pluto is NOT intercepted but planets involving sexual difficulties are in a similar pattern. Venus is apex a T-Square with Moon and Pluto. You will recall that this was the world's first sex change. She shared his/her joys and sorrows with the world, as well as disclosed details of the operation. Note that the chart contains a grand water trine encompassing Pluto, as does Jimmy Swaggart's chart, although in this case Pluto is in the tenth house. Data speculative: PW.

Please do not think that all Pluto intercepted positions create sexual difficulties. The point here is that whatever else Pluto is indicating in a chart, the interception adds intensity due to being internalized.

Understanding Interceptions

Let us now concentrate on a relatively functional Pluto that is intercepted. In a general sense, Pluto's position can give you a sense of overall destiny or purpose in this lifetime but when intercepted this awareness does not come until a lot of experience and maturity has been attained through struggle and often a crisis or two in that area of the chart, which is not usually until at least fifty years of age. In the meantime there is much deep probing into your subconscious during and after every crisis or major turning point when the deepest meaning is perceived. Pluto works slowly, more so in interception. If your intercepted Pluto is also retrograde, you may

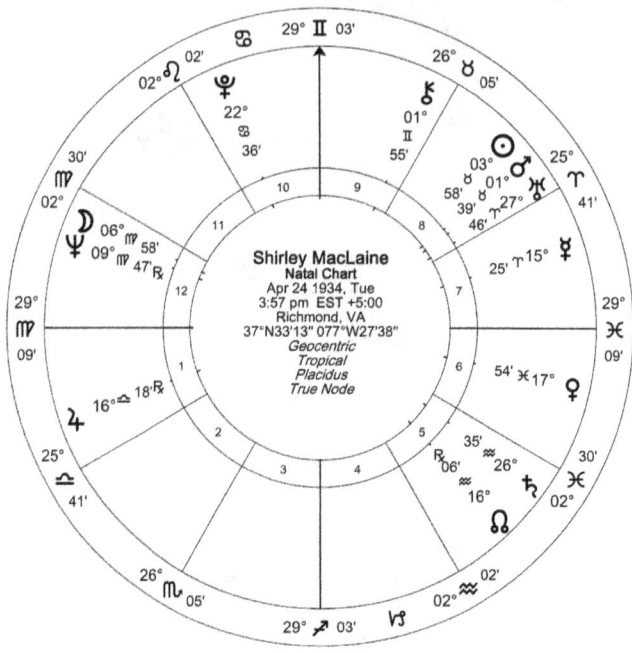

Figure 66

never fully understand the overall purpose of your life or what you really came here to do. Perhaps the quest is more important than the discovery. It reminds one of the Indiana Jones movie, *The Last Crusade,* in which he was searching for the jewel encrusted goblet that Christ used at the Last Supper. When the cave containing the trophy was finally reached, and the right one chosen, it tumbled into a deep fissure that was opening up in the rock, the cave began collapsing, and the seekers had to run for their lives, empty handed.

I am in close contact with a lady with an intercepted Pluto in her ninth house who many years ago as a young woman became a student of mine. A ninth house Pluto is the position of a searcher of truth, looking for a universal connectedness, but intercepted, I believe the struggle and process is even more profound than if not intercepted. I used to wonder why she was interested in astrology because she seemed so attuned to the pragmatic issues of life. I enjoyed her presence in class because she challenged every bit of information with a deep, even unconscious need to understand. It was as if she was saying, "make me believe there is something to this stuff. I dare you. I challenge you." I believe this helped to make me a more purposeful and responsible teacher. She learned well, developed her own philosophy and understanding of astrology according to her own individuality, and over the years became a significant spokesperson of astrology. Astrology has probably become the foundation of her philosophy but not her career because she continues to be a very successful business woman in a male-dominated sphere. I asked her to summarize how she felt her intercepted ninth house Pluto in Leo opposite her Sun works. In a nutshell this is what she said: "It gives me power behind the scenes. I live and work in an industry where women do not belong. It is male-dominated. If my Pluto was not intercepted I would not accept that. I would force it and they would see me as a contender. However, I do control everything in a different way. I am like an iron fist in a velvet glove. I never challenge their male dominance but they know not to mess with me. When a problem arises they come to me for the answers because they know I can deal with it. I challenge myself and when I am ready, I challenge them in a subtle way. I never challenge anything until I have challenged myself internally. I do it gently but with power and confidence through my grand air trine. It does not come off as a confrontation but a challenge for you to explore. It is not about ego, it is about doing it right. My ego is one of knowledge and knowing but I make sure first."

I know of one ninth house crisis that she had to face. She came to Canada with her parents at age six, which was naturally a culture shock. She had to learn a new language, adjust to a new culture and start school, all at the same time. She has successfully blended both cultures into her life.

This lady is now in her fifties, and I believe that when she retires from active business, which will not be in the immediate future, she will find some way of making a contribution to astrology from her own personal penetrating perspective.

An intercepted Pluto does not give up its secrets easily. I know I will continue to learn more about it as time marches on.

Shirley MacLaine, Actress, Dancer, Author

Between 1955 and 1997 her most notable films were *Some Came Running, The Apartment, Irma La Douce, Sweet Charity, Can Can, Ocean's Eleven, Terms of Endearment,* for which she won an Academy Award for Best Actress, and *Steel Magnolias*. With great courage and conviction, she wrote several best-selling books about her spiritual journey and belief in reincarnation, in spite of considerable ridicule by the press. These include *Don't Fall Off the Mountain, You Can Get There From Here, Out on a Limb, Dancing in the Light,* etc. BC: PW. Ref: Biography.com

Other Examples

Albert Einstein, Physicist: Pluto intercepted in Taurus/eleventh. Among other discoveries, he developed the general theory of relativity, which replaced Newtonian mechanics as the cornerstone of physics. In 1921 he received the Nobel Prize for his ideas on photons and the photoelectric cell. He urged the United States to develop an atomic bomb, which he did not help to construct. He spent the rest of his life promoting peace. Pluto was indeed powerful in his chart.

Madame Helen Petrovna Blavatsky, Theosophist: Pluto intercepted in Aries/tenth. Her birth time is questionable. She founded the Theosophical Society in New York City and later carried on her work in India. Annie Besant was one of her followers. Her works include *Isis Unveiled* and *The Secret Doctrine*. The depth of her work and the bravery she presented it with is reflected by her intercepted Pluto and its position.

Anne Frank, Diarist: Pluto intercepted in Cancer/twelfth. A concentration camp victim, she hid with her family for two years until they were betrayed. Her diary, which was later published by her father, was dramatized and filmed. She became a symbol of suffering under the heel of Hitler.

Catherine the Great, Czarina of Russia: Pluto intercepted in Libra/seventh. She made Russia into a great European power. She was tyrannical, ambitious, cruel and manipulative yet she encouraged science and art in order to enhance national culture. Shortly after she took over the throne from her weak husband, he was assassinated. This is truly a good example of the inner intensity of a need to control.

Jacques Ives Cousteau, Oceanographer: Pluto intercepted in Gemini/ninth.

CHAPTER SIX

Effect of Interceptions on Quadruplicities and Triplicities

"The strongest principle of growth lies in the human choice."—George Eliot

WHEN A CHART CONTAINS INTERCEPTIONS, both the quadruplicities and triplicities are thrown out of their natural position. The interpretation provides significant dynamics that may not be otherwise perceived. In some charts this influence is more subtle, while in others it can aid in the understanding of developmental needs.

The houses that are square to each other may not contain signs of the same quadruplicity thereby creating either sextiles or trines where natural developmental tension would be helpful in providing growth potential.

The houses that are trine to each other may not contain the same element, which means the natural flow of beneficial influence is interrupted and rendered less helpful without significant effort. This is not necessarily "bad" but adjustments may be necessary in the process of expectations and social integration.

Quadruplicities

- Cardinal: Aries, Cancer, Libra, Capricorn
- Fixed: Taurus, Leo, Scorpio, Aquarius
- Mutable: Gemini, Virgo, Sagittarius, Pisces

Figure 67 shows the cusps taken from Figure 11, Student 2. We observe that on the angular houses of one/four/seven/ten, instead of the same quadruplicity on each we have fixed, cardinal, fixed, cardinal, respectively, due to the fixed signs that are intercepted.

On the succedent houses of two/five/eight/eleven, we observe that all four bear signs of the same mutable quadruplicity.

On the cadent houses of three/six/nine/twelve, instead of the same quadruplicity on each we have mutable, cardinal, mutable, cardinal, respectively, due to the signs that appear on two cusps.

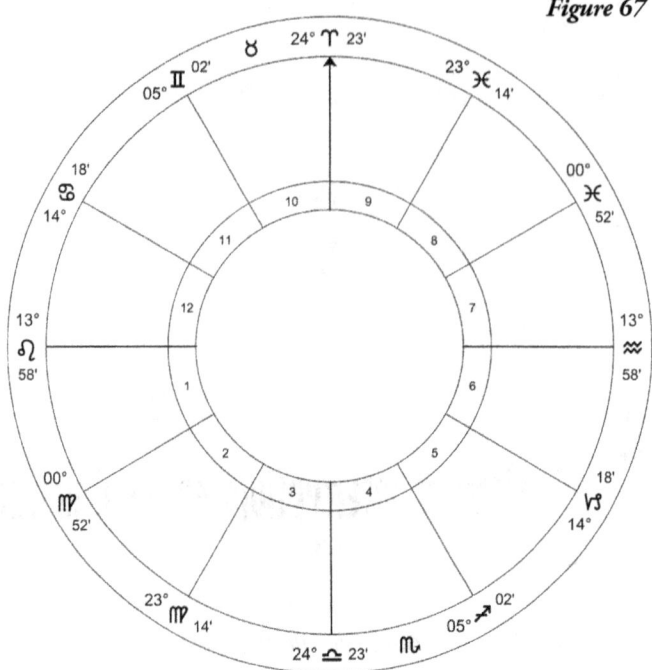

Figure 67

This same pattern does not exist on all charts. In Figure 68 we see a pair of intercepted signs across houses six/twelve, which retains cardinal on the four angles of one/four/seven/ten, but the succedent houses have fixed, cardinal, fixed, cardinal respectively, due to the repeated signs. Cadent houses contain mutable, fixed, mutable, fixed, respectively, due to the intercepted signs.

Angular Squares

With no interceptions, we unconsciously utilize the natural squares between the angles to excite action pertaining to need. We will use the Natural Wheel, Figure 69 (see chart on page 146), as a useful reference for this study.

The first house is the focal point of self-projection. It is in square to the fourth house of home, parental influence and domesticity where we develop a sense of emotional perspective. As a child, under reasonable conditions our parents provide the necessary care and attention; however, our every whim is not met and we do not always get our own way. There are other household considerations and personalities to deal with. When dealing with unpleasant circumstances, we build some type of protective armor around our emotions. The degree to which we do this depends upon the severity of the situations.

Under reasonable conditions, our first experience with tension may begin in a small way but

Figure 68

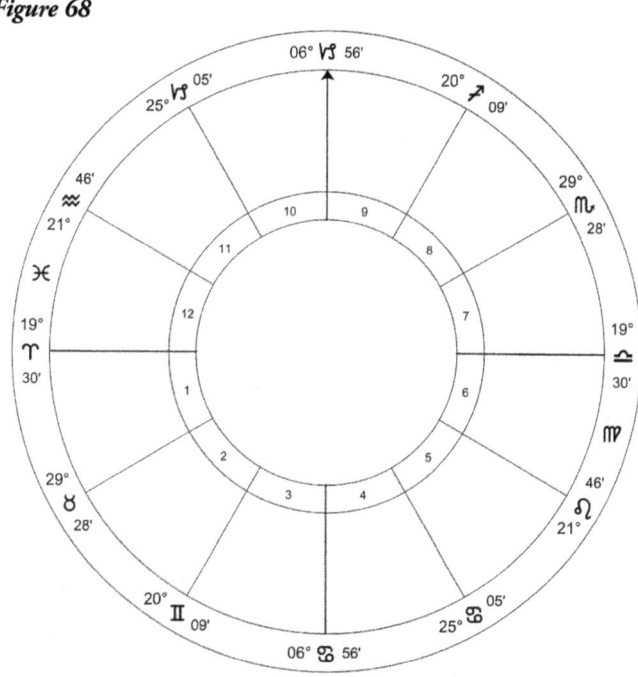

gradually gets exercised to the point where we exert ourselves more and more. Eventually we desire to get away from parental domination, make our own decisions, stay out as late as we wish, and form our own associations without the scrutinizing eyes and criticism of our parents or guardians. Without this natural square, our need to go out on our own may not be as acute. In fact, home may be the most attractive place to be. It is easier and less costly than striking out on our own. Also, our barriers against emotional stress may be securely in place permitting us to remain at home longer, which may be the case if the square does not exist.

Assuming that we have been nurtured sufficiently, we begin the process of setting up our own domestic environment, which usually means coupling with a partner. The natural square between the fourth and seventh houses indicates that it is never easy learning how to live in harmony with our partner. Tensions arise, compromises are required, adjustments are made, and growth in selfhood continues.

If our own chart does not contain this natural square because of an intercepted pair of signs, we may be overly willing to please, or avoid confrontations in order to achieve harmony. In this scenario our selfhood may develop more slowly, particularly if one of the intercepted signs is Aries, and/or Mars.

The next square, between the seventh and tenth houses indicates that further growth will occur as we are learning how to harmonize in a larger social context, with those who do not love us personally and are less willing to meet us halfway. External forces can cause us to shrink internally due to personal insecurities and conditioned responses or they can help us meet the challenges presented through our career and societal activities. Signs positions, rulerships and planetary combinations all contribute to this dynamic.

The square between the first and tenth houses indicates the challenge in fulfilling personal ambition. We learn that we cannot act or respond according to our personal impulses, which implies further growth in the process of integration with others. Without sufficient effort, progress may be much slower than usual. Without this natural square we may expect too much resulting in lack of achievement and disillusionment.

Succedent Squares

Without interceptions, there would be a natural square between succedent houses, stimulating growth potential.

As we begin projecting our selfhood outward, we start the process of developing our talents and abilities and turning them into tangible rewards. Thus the second house is the springboard of self-worth and self-appreciation. The natural square between the second and fifth houses indicates how our self-worth relates to en-

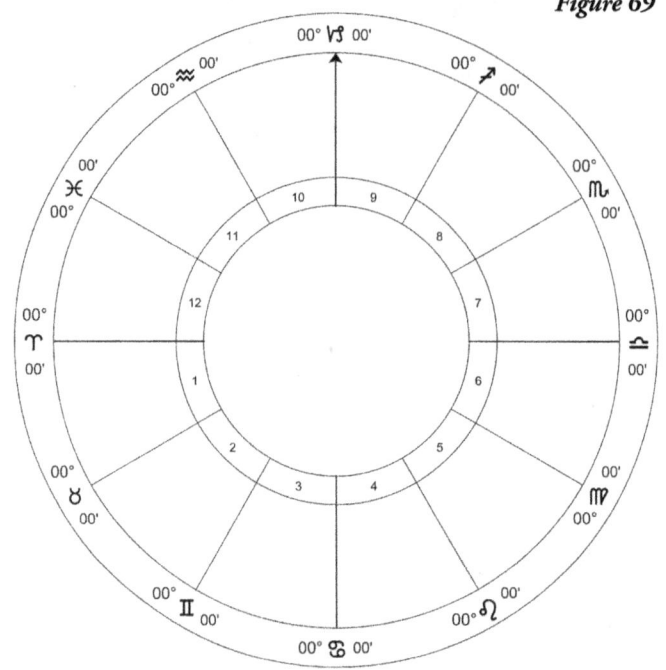

Figure 69

joying life, finding romance, creating offspring and being a creative individual in every sense of the word.

With a developing sense of self-worth, we are ready to undertake these challenges. The more we exert our creativity and the more we are willing to try new ventures, the more our self-worth increases. It is an unending excitement of challenges and rewards. With an intercepted condition, the sign that is square the second house cusp may be in the sixth, offering clues as to the kind of personal problems that need to be solved before being able to meet the challenge of creative/procreative development.

The natural square between the fifth and eighth houses indicates the challenges and adjustments necessary in order to mesh more closely with someone else, both physically and spiritually. This is how we discover the kind of changes we need to make in our own self-expression in order to integrate more successfully. With a trine here, we may be too self-sufficient and independent, relying too much on ourselves due to our own insecurities, making it more difficult to integrate. Sexual gratification is also contingent upon our ability to integrate successfully. The squared sign may be intercepted offering clues to development.

The next succedent square is between the eighth and eleventh houses, never losing sight of the second house of self-worth. As we develop a sense of personal viability, seek romance and begin a personal transformation process, we find greater fulfillment and satisfaction through friends and associates. This begins our networking chain that can assist us in fulfilling our goals and aspirations. If one of these houses is out of the developmental tension position by reason of an interception, we need to look further into the kind of internal awareness we need to develop in order to take the next step in our growth pattern. Please do not consider this an abnormal condition. Many people have intercepted conditions in their chart. It is merely another indication of individuality.

The natural square between the second and eleventh is also highly significant. If we find ourselves socially unacceptable, we can look inward to determine how we value ourselves. If this evaluation is low, the natural tension may prompt further development in our ability to increase resources, which in turn can influence both our goals as well as acceptance through others. It all goes back to us. We cannot expect results without effort. We must be able to accept ourselves before others can, and we must be willing to take the next step in our growth pattern. In this case, if the natural square does not exist between these two houses, look to where the squaring sign is and see what clues unfold. If it is to the tenth house instead of the eleventh, as you continually upgrade your skills to elevate your career, so does your self-worth increase and aspirations begin to unfold. This is certainly not an impairment but a personalized path to success.

Cadent Squares

The third house is where we exert our curiosity, gain new ideas and find better ways of solving our sixth house problems, as well as being able to do our work more efficiently and effectively. The square sign may be intercepted in the sixth putting an extra burden on problem-solving necessities. More education, information and communication may be necessary in order to upgrade these skills. In childhood, our curiosity may have been stifled, or emotional barriers erected for the purpose of self preservation. The internalization of the interception simply raises the level of need. Internal insecurities and emotional protectiveness, stemming from early environmental conditioning may need to be unraveled before confidence and skill in problem solving is developed.

As the tension to learn (third) and do our job more efficiently develops (sixth), we then must struggle with the acceptance of different beliefs, morals, ethics and attitudes (ninth). We find at every turn in the road that we cannot have everything our own way. Interaction produces growth in tolerance and understanding, or it can foster hatred and bigotry. We realize that the world is a melting pot of ideas, concepts and beliefs. However, without the square between these two cusps, we may have to access this growth through an intercepted sign or another house containing a repeated sign. Refer to Chapters Three and Four, which deal with these structures.

The square between the ninth and twelfth houses challenges us to formulate our beliefs from all the experiences of our life, from everything we have listened to and studied, in order to discover a concept of spirituality in a world fraught with contradictions, trials and oppositions. The limitations we experience in society and relationships help us to realize our own self-imposed limitations and the experience gained leads us to personal growth and a deeper understanding of the whole process of life. The twelfth house is where we find the deepest level of understanding from the pain and suffering we have endured, or where we try to escape from the realities that brought the pain.

Whatever transpires through the twelfth house can further stimulate our third house sense of curiosity, and the cycle begins all over again, each time elevating our understanding and effectiveness to another level like a never-ending upward spiral.

Each of us will grow according to our own tempo and individual needs as indicated in our natal charts. Our paths of experience are different and so are our paths of growth.

Remember also, that the interceptions change by progressions, giving us opportunities to try many different approaches. The natal signature will be the main path of unfoldment, but we should also be aware of the more subtle paths that can provide us with an expanding view and additional choices. Astrology is rich in interpretation which makes it rich in indicating alternatives.

Triplicities

Each group of signs in a particular element expresses itself in like fashion.
- Fire: With inspiration, enthusiasm and energy
- Earth: In a practical, earthly, physical way
- Air: Through mental activity and interrelating
- Water: These are emotionally expressive and reflective

The houses are also grouped in patterns of three and are called trinities. These are as follows:
- First/Fifth/Ninth: Trinity of Life
- Second/Sixth/Tenth: Trinity of Substance
- Third/Seventh/Eleventh: Trinity of Associations (or Relationships)
- Fourth/Eighth/Twelfth: Trinity of Psychism (sometimes also called Trinity of Endings or Trinity of Emotionalism; may also be referred to as terminal houses)

When there are no interceptions in a chart, the Houses of Trinity are occupied by signs of the same element, resulting in a natural path of ease and development.

When interceptions occur, the houses of trinity are altered and development of these areas will follow their own individualistic path, often through the house following or preceding the intercepted one.

Trinity of Life: First/Fifth/Ninth

First House: The first house is symbolic of our physical self. It is also how we reach outward into the environment to discover who we are and to build a personal image.
- Fire Sign: We will do so enthusiastically and spontaneously
- Earth Sign: We will do so with patience

- Air Sign: We will do so through our intellect, through relationships and through our reasoning ability
- Water Sign: We will do so through sensations, feelings and intuition

Fifth House: This is where we release our potential as we express ourselves through various creative and procreative urges and activities, and seek the pleasures of our heart.

Ninth House: This is where we extend our understanding of life through our own experience as well as incorporating into our understanding the beliefs of other religions and cultures, all of which form the societal mix. The first and fifth houses are subjective in nature in terms of being below the horizon, but the ninth is objective in terms of being above the horizon.

With a pair of intercepted signs, these houses of triplicity may or may not bear a sign of the same element.

Refer to Figure 68. Here we see fire/water/fire on houses one/five/nine. The Aries Ascendant reaches out enthusiastically and energetically to create a self-image. Leo is on the cusp of the sixth house (rather than the fifth in the natural triplicity) indicating that certain problems must be solved within the self in order to tap into the personal creative resources. With Cancer repeated on the fourth and fifth, early parental training was strict, following the pattern of the mother's desire rather than the individual expressive urges and needs of the child. This pattern needed to be broken in order to externalize selfhood. Mother tried to seep into every nook and cranny of her daughter's life from marriage to motherhood. Each time the daughter stood up for her own rights and feelings, she had to overcome the guilt of offending her mother whose basic fault was in over-protecting and extending her nurturing influence too far. After marriage, the mother thought the daughter was not physically strong enough to bear a child (sixth house) so even the delight of pregnancy had a shadow cast across it. Mother was the sole parent trying to be both mother and father.

The enthusiasm of the fire element picks up again on the ninth cusp, indicating an enthusiastic and expansive search for the meaning of life to assist in self-realization, but she had to first wean from mother's influence in order for individuation to occur. Understanding this through the chart was very helpful. It became a lesson for both mother and daughter as mother had to learn how to let go through the encouragement and insistence of her daughter.

We will look at one more example, Figure 70, Client. Here we see the origin of selfhood on the tenth (Aries) where fulfillment is an extension of self in societal terms. Leo is on the Ascendant indicating the need to present herself enthusiastically, energetically and dramatically in order to develop something concrete that she would be proud of (Leo repeated on second). There was some reticence or shyness in her early life due to emotional insecurity as seen by the Cancer/Capricorn interception across the twelfth and sixth houses.

Gemini on the twelfth shows some fear of communicating freely and expounding on her ideas for fear of losing face (Leo 1st), until some sense of emotional security is established. In this case it began when she fell in love, married and had two children.

Her approach to love is intense (Scorpio fifth) due to emotional insecurity and her need to shine and be appreciated (Leo Ascendant). Jealousy and possessiveness need to be overcome as she gradually becomes more confident. We talked at length about her attitude towards her children in allowing them reasonable latitude in expressing themselves. Fear of failure tends to be strong in many areas of her life, including her role as mother.

Water continues its theme through to the ninth house, where a main part of the philosophical framework of her life is learning to have faith in her ability to express herself creatively, enthusiastically and dramatically through her Leo Ascendant.

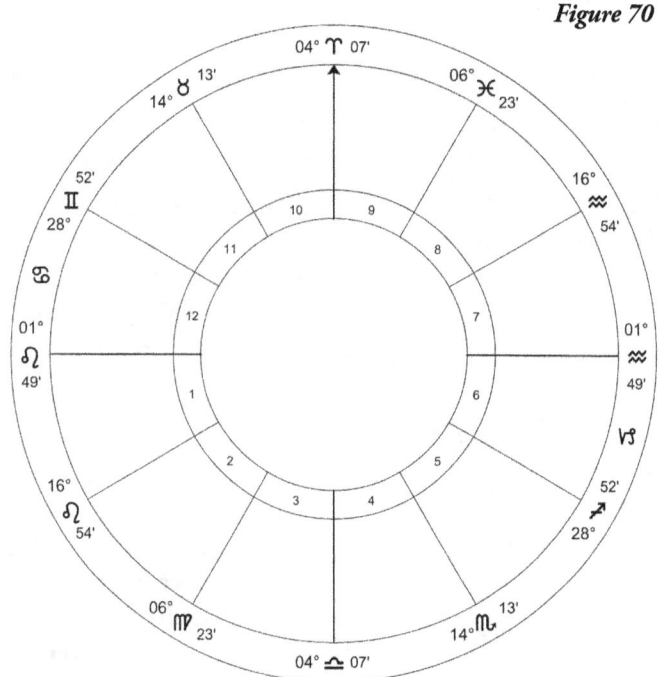

Figure 70

Trinity of Substance-Second/Sixth/Tenth

Second House: The second house is applicable to our earning capacity and the possessions we gain from our own effort as we seek financial security and comfort in this earthly environment.

Sixth House: The sixth house is applicable to how we do our job, take care of ourselves and solve everyday problems as we project our ego outward.

Tenth House: The tenth house is applicable to projecting ourself in order to gain respect, prestige and fulfill our ambition in the world at large. This is the area of our professional and societal image and reputation.

Since a triplicity is an underlying trine by sign, it can help us express an innate sense of creativity and confidence connected with those houses. Of course, their rulers by position and aspects, as well as planets in those houses, are much stronger but the triplicity provides an undertone for outer activities. If all three of these houses of substance do not contain the same sign, the house where the maverick sign is located can offer additional clues to our internal balance.

Figure 68 shows an earth/fire(earth intercepted)/earth respectively on houses two/six/ten. There is an earthly, practical approach to matters pertaining to income and career development, but the sixth is more complex. A great deal of effort will likely go into doing the job right with Virgo intercepted, but receiving credit and attention for creative input is equally as important and sometimes more so with Leo on the cusp. Discrimination is required in how this is to be accomplished. Confidence in competency needs to be developed through experience before the career can begin to provide a sense of achievement. The Trinity of Substance cannot follow the regular earth pattern due to the additional creative need of the sixth house. The job is approached with energy and enthusiasm but care must be taken to maintain a common sense approach to good health, otherwise burn-out and excessive fatigue results, which can affect the level of achievement through the tenth house.

Figure 70 has fire signs throughout this trinity with an earth sign intercepted in the sixth, and it is easy to see through just the cusps alone, that this person needs a professional outlet, in spite of her marriage and motherhood. Volunteer work in her community sufficed until her children went to school and then she began gradually easing herself into different part-time jobs, looking for a job that could develop into a career where her enthusiasm and creativity could be expressed.

Trinity of Associations: Third/Seventh/Eleventh

Third House: The third house is often referred to as the house of communication. It is where we learn to adapt to our immediate environment, first through association with brothers and/or sisters, then through neighborhood contacts, and early school experiences. This stimulates a sense of curiosity, communication and learning as we synthesize the power of our conscious mind with our ability to form sense impressions.

Seventh House: Dane Rudyar says this is where we have an "interchange of vital energies and ideas." It is an extension of self in a committed relationship with someone who also has a self, hence lessons in the essentials of cooperation and compromise.

Eleventh House: Relationships are now extended towards a circle of acquaintances, group affiliations and friends who contribute to our sense of social acceptance, thereby giving us the hopefulness and drive to achieve our goals and aspirations through the combined cooperation of many. In turn, by being a supportive, cooperative friend, we also contribute to the development of their goals and aspirations.

If we have a pair of intercepted signs, which may or may not contain planets, I would examine those first and look for ways to assist in their development. A valuable clue can often be found where the repeated signs occur, and through the triplicities that are out of their natural positions.

Refer once again to Figure 68. Here we observe an air/air/earth combination on houses three/seven/eleven respectively, indicating a natural sense of curiosity, Gemini on the third, and a good communicative sense in a committed personal relationship, Libra seventh; however, the eleventh of associations tends to be business orientated with Capricorn on the cusp, rather than seeking friends for personal pleasure. A fear of rejection in casual relationships had to be overcome which traces back to Cancer on the fourth and fifth houses. As previously pointed out, the mother created very strict guidelines of conduct and imposed strong disciplinary measures when these were not met. The child grew up with a constant concern of disapproval.

Continuing with our interpretation of Figure 70, Client, we observe houses three/seven/eleven have earth, air, and earth signs respectively on their cusps. This lady has a clear, analytical mind and enjoys serious conversation. She tends to be somewhat critical of her more lighthearted brother who enjoys teasing her, which she takes as a put-down. Her husband is a serious, successful businessman and seems to be his own person. With Capricorn intercepted in her sixth, rather than occupying the seventh house cusp, she worries and frets over every business move he makes for fear he experiences a setback but she doesn't like to say anything to him. He talks freely with her about his business dealings and is unaware of how seriously it affects her. She needs his admiration and respect, with Leo on her first and second, and will not confide her misgivings to him. With Taurus on her eleventh cusp, she has cultivated a circle of loyal friends over many years. They enjoy seeking her advice, and she enjoys giving it which takes us back to her third house.

Trinity of Psychism or Endings: Fourth/Eighth/Twelfth

These are difficult houses to capsulize, because they are concerned with the three most mysterious areas of life. Their meaning can be described from both a physical, one lifetime point-of-view, as well as from a metaphysical, soul-growth perspective. Since the purpose of this text is to help you understand your personal dynamics better, and in some way to help you live your life with less anxiety, I will focus on the practical, physical interpretation. That is the part I see operating most prevalently in my clients' and students' lives.

Fourth House: The fourth House is the focal point of our domestic activities. Its doorway is the springboard from which we venture out into the world on a daily basis, and the one we enter as we seek refuge from the darkness and chill when night falls. It is our inner home as well, or the place where we seek our own inner emotional security. It relates to the end of each phase of life as well as the ultimate end of this earthly existence.

Eighth House: Nicholas deVore in *Encyclopedia of Astrology* states that this is where we get "release from personal limitations through interchange." That is an all-encompassing phrase to describe this complex house.

As our viewpoint enlarges to encompass a partner, new considerations require that the selfish desires of our own ego need to die so that a new life can be born. In this way we can come into the essence of the beauty and power gained through sharing, like a brilliant rainbow after a violent storm. As new life emerges, a deeper understanding of the concepts of life and death is understood.

Twelfth House: This is often referred to as the house of limitations and self-undoing, and I believe this is so if we do not try to ferret out the secret fears and irrational longings that keep us chained to the past. It is also the house of ultimate understanding and initiation into a higher level of consciousness. This requires faith in dealing with twelfth house dilemmas, and faith in the evolutionary process of the soul. This house calls for compassion, inspiration and understanding.

Refer to Figure 68, where we will finish the house cusp analysis. Note that on houses four/eight/twelve, there is water, water, air (water intercepted). There was a two-fold struggle unfolding through this complex situation. First, with an Aquarian Sun and this sign on the cusp of the twelfth, her own individuality needed to shine through the clouds created by a dominant mother. She could be stuck with it or grow from it. With Pisces intercepted, she had strong pangs of guilt, which needed to be overcome and turned into love and understanding. Second, with a strong religious background, the need to find inner peace through spiritual understanding led her into the pursuit of knowledge. Faith could not be accepted upon religious premises alone, but had to make sense intellectually. She found this through the study of astrology. She concluded that the symphony of planetary influences is so grand that it must be divine.

CHAPTER SEVEN

Other Applications

"You must be the change you wish to see in the world."—Mohandis Gandhi

THE CONCEPT OF INTERCEPTIONS CAN be applied to any chart you erect, including relocation, horary, electional, judgment of events, and mundane. The interpretation must follow guidelines for the particular type of chart being erected, which will likely be quite different than applying it to a personal chart. The reader is challenged to consider the possibility that interceptions should not be ignored in any type of chart being examined.

I have no significant experience with interceptions in determining medical problems, but I would suggest that since interceptions increase the intensity of either the sign or planet contained therein, that it should be noted carefully as a potential problem area, but only if accompanied by very strong aspects. It would be difficult to prove that an interception added to a medical condition but it is a thought I would not ignore.

Since the study which evolved into this book was primarily on the psychological dynamics of individuals, we will only look briefly at a couple of other applications.

Horary

Horary astrology is the birth of a question which is paramount in a person's mind at a given moment in order to gain a perspective on some pressing situation or reach a decision. Marc Edmund Jones in *Horary Astrology* calls it a "minor focus in time relative to one problem." He further states that "there is not the essential critical presence of a living continuum provided in the delineation of a native's life." Delineation follows a rigid set of rules. The person asking the question and the matter being inquired about are the most important parts of the chart; therefore, their rulers are called significators. The Moon is considered a co-significator. These are the only factors important in ascertaining the answer.

Jones is of the opinion that "nothing in the horary chart is to be considered, except as it is pertinent to the immediate question." A simple "yes or no" question is always the easiest to answer but further considerations surrounding the matter can also be included. However, Ivy Goldstein Jacobson, another noted authority on horary astrology, says that you can read the whole if you so desire but it is not necessary.

It is assumed that the reader has at least a basic understanding of this branch of astrology so no further explanation is being offered here. If not, there are numerous texts and courses available. Some of these are listed in the bibliography at the back of this book.

Of a significator in interception, Ivy Goldstein Jacobson states that it means "interference and someone or something hemmed in," and that is often the case. In examining a significator's ruler, she notes where it is, whether it is "direct or retrograde, besieged, intercepted-or-free, well placed by sign . . . afflicted by aspects, and so on." She further states that if the querent's significator is in the first house, afflicted and intercepted, there is interference and the person "is sometimes refused a voice in the case."

My own experience indicates that an intercepted significator does not in itself deny a positive outcome, but it does seem to indicate a delay of some kind operating behind the scenes of which the querent has no way of knowing or understanding.

The Story of Ashes

I am only going to present two example horary charts, both with intercepted signs and planets. Since both of these involve a very precious cat we had called Ashes, I will give you a little background so you understand how significant these questions were. He was called Ashes because of his colors, which ranged from a white underbelly and under his great bushy tail, to a dark ash color on top. He was a belangese angora with curved white hair flowing out of his ears and large bright turquoise eyes that seemed to look right into your soul. He was so intelligent and people orientated that he deserved to be referred to as a "fur person." He was much loved and admired.

Ashes grew up in an apartment and when I got him his basic habits were firmly entrenched. He was not an outdoor cat but soon discovered the joys of the backyard. We have a six foot fence around the back of the property, which he could not jump because we were told he had been badly injured by a car when he was about a year old. We plugged areas of the fence where he might wiggle his body through so we could let him out each afternoon. He loved to sleep on a small platform, which was secured on a branch in a large apple tree just outside of my kitchen window. This worked for several years and then one day the inevitable happened. He sneaked out of the front door

Figure 71

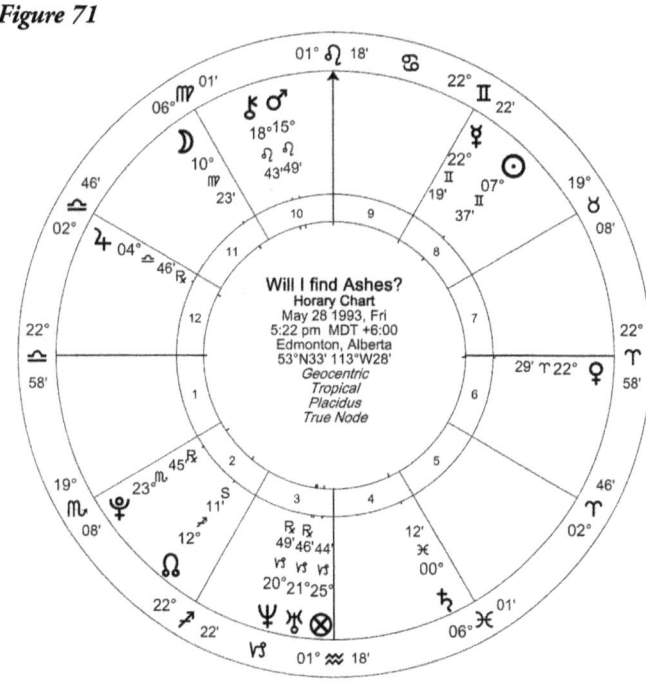

and was on his way to the greatest adventure of his lifetime. We were concerned that he would not be able to find his way home or someone would pick him up. He was both friendly and very beautiful.

He went missing at 10:00 P.M. on Thursday evening, May 27, 1993.

We searched throughout the whole night. By morning we thought he would be hungry and thirsty and find his way home, but this was not so. After a couple of hours rest, we searched the whole next day. We were getting discouraged and very tired. I was suffering from a deteriorating hip condition and was limping with a cane. I tried driving around the neighborhood in my car but could not easily talk to people along the way. By this time I was convinced that someone had taken him into his/her home and was feeding him.

I was being helped by my aging mother who would not give up. My son said he would come over and help, and I kept wondering why he did not show up. Each time I phoned he said he was coming. My husband had to work so he was not much help.

I decided it was definitely time to set up a Horary Chart. See Figure 71, Will I Find Ashes?

Querent is me: First house Libra, ruled by Venus in Aries, the sign of its detriment, in the sixth house. This house signified the discomfort I was experiencing with such an excessive amount of walking. I did not like the Ascendant being via combust way which renders it powerless.

Quesited is Ashes: sixth of pets, ruled by Mars. Mars is angular meaning that he was in the vicinity but with no applying aspect to bring the querent and quesited together my heart sank, but I was undaunted. Due to its tenth house position, I quickly did up a bunch of flyers, included a picture, provided a description and offered a reward. We put these up in local grocery stores, various community bulletin boards and handed them out to everyone we saw.

Moon as co-significator: The aspect previous to the question is listed first in brackets. The rest of the aspects that the Moon forms until it leaves the sign of Virgo, are listed in order. By the way, Vir-

Understanding Interceptions

go also rules pets. (Moon square Sun), Moon square Nodes, trine Neptune, trine Uranus, quincunx Venus, sextile Pluto, trine Fortuna.

The last aspect gave me hope. It was to Fortuna in the third house of near neighborhood, its dispositor is in the fourth house of home, but it is intercepted indicating a further delay.

Then I noticed that the horary Ascendant was conjunct my son's natal Ascendant, and I felt he would be the one to find Ashes. All day Saturday he kept saying he was coming over, but he did not show up. By midnight we were all frantic and very weary. I was very disappointed in my son.

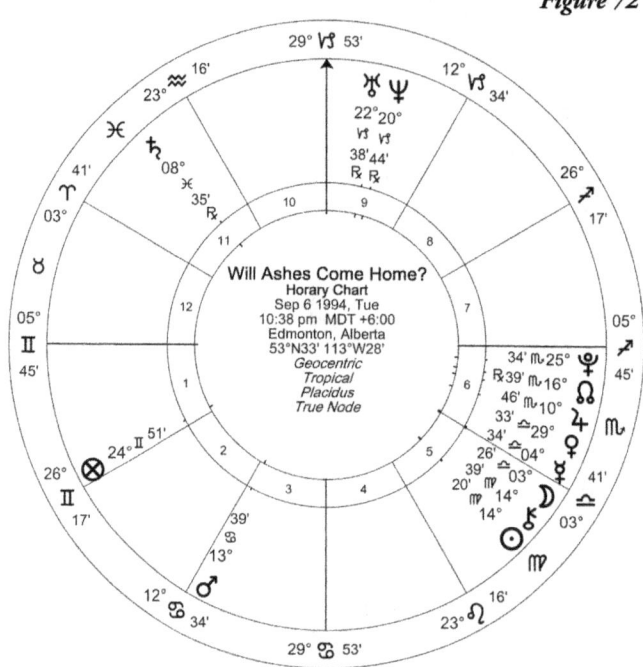

Figure 72

We were sitting having a cup of coffee, wondering what to do next, when in he came carrying a bedraggled Ashes. The poor animal's tongue was sticking to the roof of his mouth from dehydration and his foot pads were sore and bleeding. He had moved around a great deal and tried hard to get home but construction during the day in the area would have frightened him and all he could do was run and hide.

My son then told his story. He has four planets in Leo in his tenth house and was entertaining three girls with their tarot card readings. About 11:00 P.M. he just got up and left without any apparent reason. He said it was just a feeling he had. He drove to our place, and as he was turning the last corner he got out of the car and stood on the street corner. Ashes came toward him from under some bushes. In spite of all that had transpired, it was a happy ending and we were all reunited.

But there would be another such incident involving the escape of Ashes and another horary question where interception played a significant role. This time he dug a hole in the soft dirt under the fence and wiggled out. We searched for a couple of hours and then I decided to do a horary question. Figure 72. When I realized he would soon be coming home all by himself I decided to go to bed. Perhaps he would be sitting at the door in the morning waiting to be let in for breakfast.

About 2:00 A.M., my aging Pisces mother who was living with us at the time, bolted upright in bed because she had just received a message from Ashes. She knew he was at the back door and there he was.

Figure 73

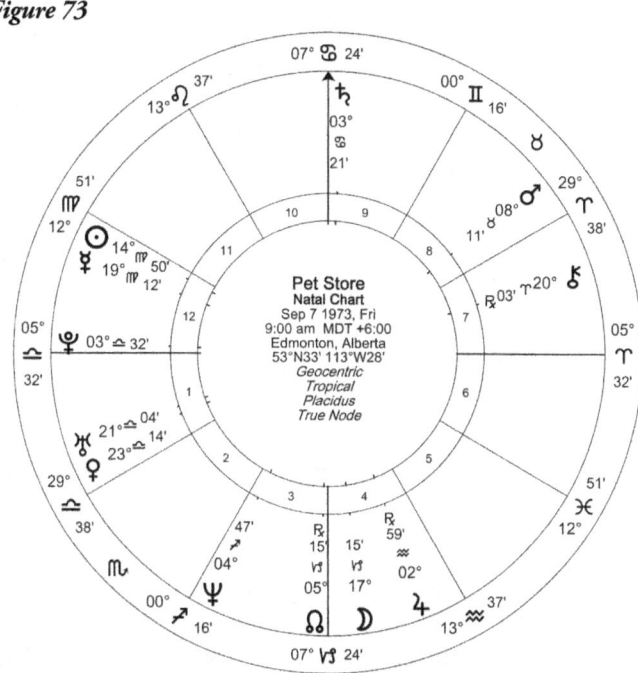

The question was, "Will Ashes come Home?" He is a sixth house matter, and his ruler is Venus at 29 Libra 33, but not quite into the intercepted sign. The Moon as co-significator, ruling the fourth house of home, was in the sign on the sixth house and just about to enter. It would conjunct the ruler Venus before leaving its present sign. The Moon also rules the third house so we knew he was in the near neighborhood.

In Horary Questions 1 and 2, Figures 71 and 72, the interception was involved in some significant way, in each case providing additional insight into the answer.

Electional and Event Charts

In setting up a business, you will likely want to keep any planets or signs to do with its growth and success out of an intercepted position, unless you do not mind later development and have the appropriate resources. In some situations a long term policy may be an advantage. Such is not the case in the following chart which is the opening of a neighborhood pet store upon which a family's survival depended.

Electional Chart, Opening of a Neighborhood Pet Store

This pet store was a mom and pop run business which relied on the couple's two children to help out after school and evenings. The children hated working there and their attitude was plainly visible. The business had no working capital and quickly ran into financial problems. In order to secure a bank loan to give them inventory capital, the wife took another full-time job, thus straining the family further. The father was a poor business man. He did not stand behind his products and did not seem to understand how important a little public relations would have been for a neighborhood business. For instance, I purchased a bird cage, which was packed in a cardboard box. When I got it home it was damaged and he refused to exchange it or reduce its price. In fact he was rude to me. I owned both a bird and a cat and was obviously someone with an income source.

Understanding Interceptions

The business limped along for about two or three years and finally went bankrupt. Note that the interception is Taurus/Scorpio across houses two/eight, with Mars in Taurus and no good applying aspects to increase the business. It is also in a sign of its detriment, ruling the seventh of public. The Moon is in its detriment in Capricorn in the fourth with only one applying aspect to Mercury which rules the twelfth of problems. Venus in Libra, ruling the Ascendant is in dignity but there are no helpful aspects. It was only a matter of time before the business would fold.

There are different types of event charts. I will refer mostly to trip charts because I have much experience with them. I fly a great deal but those times are harder to manipulate than motor trips. First of all you would check your own chart with progressions and transits to make sure this was not an accident-prone period. If all looks reasonable, you would then set up the trip chart for departure time. I use trip charts a great deal for motor tirps because my husband and I drive every winter over mountain roads through Montana, Idaho and Utah as we journey from Canada to Arizona. We return in the spring when driving conditions also can be dangerous in the mountain regions. We will not leave without a trip chart. We sit with car keys in hand, ready to walk out the door at the precise moment.

In planning a trip chart, you would not want to place any of the significators of the chart in an intercepted sign. However, you may be trying to "bury" a difficult planet in a cadent houses, in which case you could also accept it being intercepted. Do not consider the following brief explanation of trip charts a full outline but refer to a book entitled *Electional Astrology* by Vivian E. Robson.

- The start of the journey is the Ascendant.
- The place where you are going is the seventh.
- The circumstances of the journey to get there is the tenth.
- The circumstances of the return journey is the fourth.

The aspects to the rulers of these angles, for obvious reasons, should be as unimpaired as possible. You would certainly not want the rulers of the angles, nor the Sun or Moon to be intercepted. The Sun is the driver or pilot and the Moon is the passenger's. Mercury rules short journeys by car and Uranus rules travel by airplane. Interceptions in themselves do not cause accidents but, as previously stated, they do cause delays, as seen by the following example.

My Son's Motor Trip from Edmonton, Alberta to Victoria, British Columbia

My son asked me to do a trip chart for this journey but unfortunately he was not able to go at the suggested time. When he was finally ready to leave, I told him to look at his watch and give me the time.

The interception is across the first and seventh angles. He was late getting away and late arriving at his destination. The purpose of the trip was to start a new job. He was hired as general manager of a golf and sporting goods wholesale outlet. With the Moon intercepted in the seventh, he became ill on the trip, causing delays. He was still ill when he arrived and asked to start the job a

Figure 74

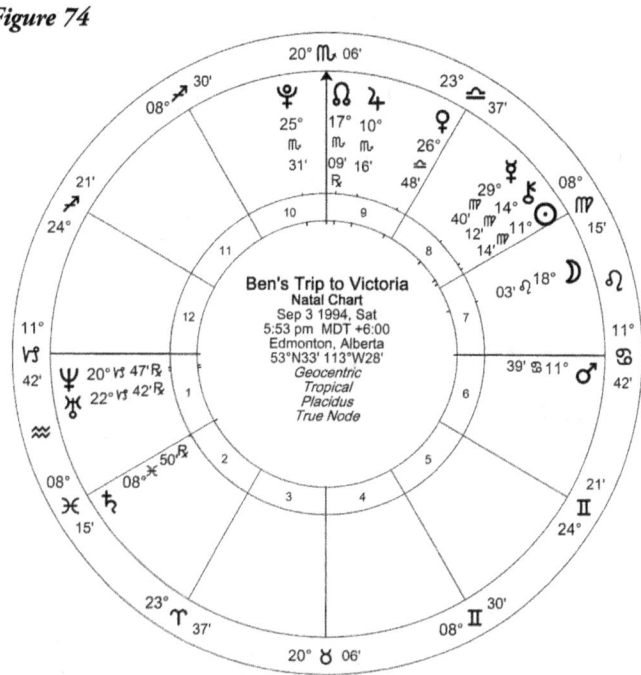

day later due to his illness. The owner of the business was an ex-army officer and a taskmaster. He reneged on his salary promise and rode my Leo son mercilessly until he resigned after a couple of months.

This next story will not be accompanied by a chart but the telling of it will suffice. A friend of mind belonged to an organization with whom she had a happy affiliation for several years. When they moved location, the new chart had an intercepted Sun, which coincidentally was within minutes of being conjunct her own Sun, which was not intercepted in her own chart but got dragged into the intercepted position of the organization's chart. She felt uncomfortable in the new surroundings and was continually confronted by one situation after another which she felt was completely uncalled for. She rarely goes to meetings any more and when she does she tries very hard to keep a low profile. As one witty friend said to her, "every time you go there you seem to have a bulls-eye pinned to your back."

A Political Event

Figure 75, is for a political event (see chart on following page). In a Canadian national election on May 22, 1979, the Liberal Government of Pierre Elliott Trudeau lost its majority after 11 years in power. Joe Clark became prime minister with a minority Conservative government. The seal of office was handed over on June 4, 1979, at high noon.

The Clark Government was dissolved on December 14, after only seven months in power following a non-confidence vote. This government was operating from a slim majority, and when the prime minister called for a crucial vote in the House of Commons, several of his key members were out of the country and he lost the vote. The government was dissolved and a new election was called for early in the new year putting Pierre Elliott Trudeau and his Liberal Government back in power. The Clark regime was a bumbling folly right from the beginning. While in office, he received the unfortunate nickname of "Joe Who?"

The tenth house is the government in power and the Sun represents the head of that government.

The inauguration chart had an intercepted Gemini Sun, square the Nodes and Saturn, as well as a Gemini Mercury intercepted, which is co-ruler of the tenth and ruler of the Ascendant. Clark's natal Sun was coincidentally at 13 Gemini 26.

The intercepted Sun in the tenth represents the government in power. The fourth house is the opposition party.

In Conclusion

I trust that in some way I have provided additional understanding into the much misunderstood concept of interceptions. As mentioned in Chapter One, we may not all agree on the type of house cusp structure we use, but we must at least consider that the way the earth rotates, both around its own axis and around the sun, must surely have some effect on the way life unfolds on this wonderful planet. Any geometric division, be it time or space, will produce unequal divisions. Our open-mindedness is one of the characteristics that brought us into astrology in the first place.

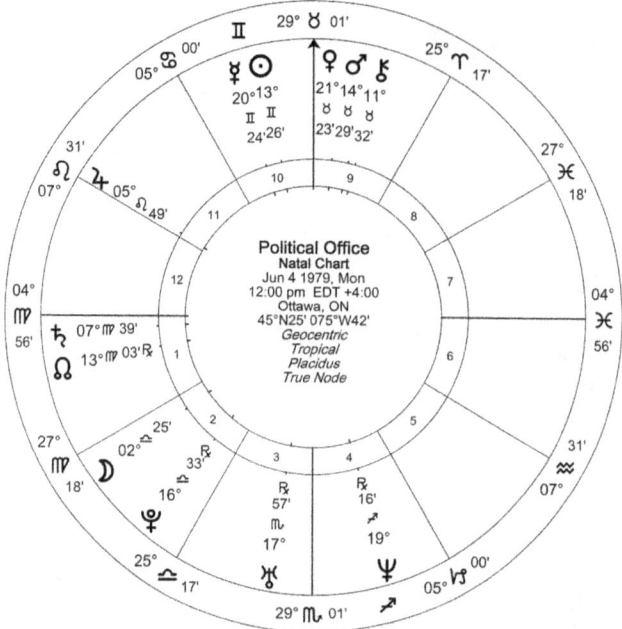

Figure 75

As one journey ends . . .
So another one begins . . .

Bibliography

Wickenburg, Joanne, *Intercepted Signs*, Seattle, WA: Search, 1978.

George, Llewellyn, *A to Z Horoscope Maker and Delineator*, St. Paul, MN: Llewellyn Publications, 29th Edition, 1972.

Tyl, Noel, *Teaching and Study Guide to the Principles and Practice of Astrology*, 1st Edition, St. Paul, MN: Llewellyn Publications, 1976.

Holden, Ralph William, *The Elements of House Division*, Romford, Essex: L.N. Fowler & Co. Ltd., 1977.

Ebertin, Reinhold, *The Combination of Stellar Influences*, Wurttemburg, Germany: Ebertin-Veerlag, 1972.

Rudyar, Dane, *Astrological Houses, The Spectrum of Individual Experience*, Garden City, New York: Doubleday & Company, Inc., 1972.

Tierney, Bill, *Perceptions in Astrology*, Lynchburg, VA: Mercury Hour, 1980.

Robertson, Marc, *Transits of Saturn*, American Federation of Astrologers, Tempe AZ.

Boehrer, Kt., *Declination: The Other Dimension*, El Paso, TX: Fortunata Press, 1994.

Rodden, Lois M., *The American Book of Charts*, San Diego, CA: Astra Computing Services, 1980.

Rodden, Lois M., *Profiles of Women*, Tempe, AZ: American Federation of Astrologers, Inc., 1979.

Rodden, Lois M., *Astro-Data IV*, Tempe, AZ: American Federation of Astrologers, 1990.

DeVore, Nicholas, *Encyclopedia of Astrology*, Philosophical Library, New York: Published by Bonanza Books, 1947.

Funk & Wagnalls Standard Reference Encyclopedia, New York: Funk & Wagnalls, Inc, 1963. (including various Yearbooks).

McEvers, Joan, and March, Marion. *The Only Way to Learn Astrology, Volume I*, San Diego, CA: Astro-Analytics Publications, 1976.

Bosworth, Patricia, *Montgomery Clift: A Biography*, New York: Hartcourt, Brace & Jovanovich, 1978.

Planets, The Astrological Tools, Edited by McEvers, Joan, Article by Sullivan Erin, Llewellyn's New World Astrology Series, St. Paul, MN: Llewellyn Publications, 1989.

Zinker, Joseph, PhD., *Creative Process in Gestalt Therapy*, New York: Brunner/Maze, Publishers, 1977.

Oken, Alan, *Complete Astrology*, New York: Bantam Books Inc., 1980.

Perry, Glenn, Ph.D., *Essays on Psychological Astrology, Theory and Practice*, San Rafael, CA: The Association for Astrological Psychology, 1998.

Goldstein-Jacobson, Ivy M., *Simplified Horary Astrology*, Pasadena, CA: Pasadena Lithographers, 1970.

Jones, Marc Edmund, *Horary Astrology*, London: Shambhala, Berkeley and London, 197 5.

Robson, Vivian, *Electional Astrology*, New York: Samuel Weiser, 1972.

Website: http://www.biography.com

www.ingramcontent.com/pod-product-compliance
Lightning Source LLC
Chambersburg PA
CBHW080224170426
43192CB00015B/2747